Sterling Ruby

Sterling Ruby

EDITED BY ALEX GARTENFELD AND EVA RESPINI

Institute of Contemporary Art/Boston
Institute of Contemporary Art, Miami

DelMonico Books • Prestel
Munich London New York

Contents

Directors' Foreword

The Institute of Contemporary Art/Boston and the Institute of Contemporary Art, Miami are pleased to bring this long-awaited survey exhibition of Los Angeles-based artist Sterling Ruby to our audiences. Both institutions are dedicated to creating necessary scholarship on the artistic expressions of our time. We are inspired that this presentation of Ruby's work might increase understanding of the artist while encouraging exchange and interrogation by our audiences.

Sterling Ruby includes works from the artist's milestone series as well as unseen early and recent works, spanning almost twenty years of intensive production. Expanding on the exhibition, this catalogue illustrates related works and seminal installations in order to provide a resource that might deepen the understanding of Ruby's diverse works across media. Both exhibition and publication investigate the artist's ongoing exploration of historical forms and sites of labor, from sewing, ceramics, fashion, and painting, to factories, and more. Central to his work is the consistent inquiry into the role of the artist—as an outsider, as a historical figure, and as an agent of the images that inform American life and identity.

The exhibition has been conceived by Alex Gartenfeld, Artistic Director, ICA Miami, and Eva Respini, Barbara Lee Chief Curator, ICA/Boston. Jeffrey De Blois, Assistant Curator and Publications Manager at ICA/Boston and Tyler Britt, Director at Sterling Ruby Studio, have been instrumental to the organization of this exhibition and to our understanding of Ruby's work. Amanda Morgan, Curatorial Assistant, Exhibitions and Publications, at ICA Miami, provided invaluable support and research. We are grateful to Isabelle Graw for her interview with the artist, relating his work incisively to the postwar history of painting as well as the commercial enterprise of fashion production.

This exhibition would not be possible without the generous loans from the Broad Art Foundation, Los Angeles, La Colección Jumex, Mexico City, and Whitney Museum of American Art, New York and many private collections throughout the United States (for a full list of exhibition lenders, see page 186).

Major support for *Sterling Ruby* is provided by Sprüth Magers, Gagosian, and Xavier Hufkens. Exhibitions at ICA Miami are generously supported by the Knight Contemporary Art Fund at The Miami Foundation. Major support at ICA Miami is provided by Carlo Bronzini Vender, Andre Sakhai, and Inigo Philbrick. Additional support at ICA Miami is provided by Michelle Simkins and Jason Rubell. Additional support for the Boston presentation is generously provided by Stephanie Formica Connaughton and John Connaughton, Jean-François and Nathalie Ducrest, Bridgitt and Bruce Evans, James and Audrey Foster, Ted Pappendick and Erica Gervais Pappendick, David and Leslie Puth, and Charlotte and Herbert S. Wagner III. Through the enthusiastic and unwavering leadership of each of our boards of trustees, ICA/Boston and ICA Miami are able to continuously present rigorous, groundbreaking programming.

Our final thanks go to Sterling Ruby, for sharing his work with our audiences and for all his myriad contributions and commitment to the art of our time.

Alex Gartenfeld
Artistic Director, Institute of Contemporary Art, Miami

Jill Medvedow
Ellen Matilda Poss Director, the Institute of Contemporary Art/Boston

EVA RESPINI

Illicit Mergers

STERLING RUBY'S STUDIO, known by the initialism SRS, occupies a vast complex of buildings in the industrial city of Vernon, California, about a twenty-minute drive from downtown Los Angeles. The studio adopts a Bauhaus logic, in that every medium has its own dedicated space, all materials within his output are considered equal, and creativity is applied to every format, from painting and metalwork to ceramics and textiles. The complex houses a painting studio flooded with natural light, a building for kilns and experiments in clay, an outdoor area for welding, a pavilion with racks of clothing, an office space with an extensive library and archive, and a cavernous viewing and working area for large sculptures. At the center of the complex is the fabric studio, visible from several areas and used as a pass-through to access other parts of the facility. This is where Ruby's work in textiles, and what he calls soft sculptures, comes to life. Yards of dyed and bleached fabric are organized in large heaps, paintings made from sewn and pieced fabric scraps (QUILTS or FLAGS) hang on the walls. Ruby uses historical and contemporary quilts as both inspiration and material, and his collection of vintage American quilts here covers the floor [fig. 1].

During a studio visit with the author in 2018, Ruby used the phrase "illicit mergers" to describe the collaging, or weaving, of different fabrics and materials in the textile studio.[1] It captures the kind of collage that is his consistent working method,[2] not least as concerns the relationships between various strands of his own practice: surpluses from soft sculptures feature in paintings, cardboard on the studio floor becomes the support for collages, metal scraps are welded into large-scale mobiles, bleached textiles are sewn into clothing, and failed experiments in the kiln are subsumed into larger ceramic works. A work such as *QUILT (4858)* (2014) [p. 135], for example, is collaged and sewn together using a variety of fabric scraps from the artist's soft sculptures.

"My intention is to use many media as a kind of schizophrenic labor strategy," Ruby remarks. "Works may not look the same formally, they might not even be within the same medium, but there is a lineage that links everything that I do."[3] This self-referential system, the cannibalization of his own materials and art into new works, results in a cross-pollination that is the hallmark of Ruby's singular aesthetic language. His reuse and layering can feel (and look) messy, frenetic even, in ways that are further heightened through his maximalist installations.[4]

Illicit mergers can be seen in the work's transdisciplinarity and Ruby's resistance to received forms or confining ways of thinking about art, including craft. The phrase suggests a transgressive and, at times, contradictory approach to making art. On the one hand, Ruby embraces humble materials, but the work is monumental. It maintains both a DIY aesthetic and a high level of finish. Ruby has attained commercial success, yet a subversive strain runs through all his endeavors. The works are hard *and* soft. Ruby is punk *and* high fashion. These uneasy unions underscore that *illicit mergers* describes not simply a working methodology, but, rather, the ethos that fundamentally informs who Ruby is as an artist.

Writers have acknowledged that Ruby's work is difficult to explain beyond its formal qualities,[5] and because his production is prolific, an exhaustive account of his output is almost impossible. In this sense, *illicit mergers* also characterizes the striking diversity of Ruby's formal, material, and conceptual concerns. Yet throughout his oeuvre, the artist uses illicit mergers to excavate America's history and cultural legacies, specifically through traditions of American craft, from the Amish quilting culture from his native Pennsylvania to the countercultural ceramic practices in his adopted California.[6] Ruby's work traffics in America's icons, such as the Stars and Stripes, gun culture, graffiti and skate culture, supermax penitentiaries, and the assembly line. It is a reflection on the dark forces at play in America today—violence, war, urban decay, and the legacy of a collapsed auto industry and depleted rust belt. Ruby's apocalyptic tendency, the sense that we are living in an ending, has only become more apt as a response to the state of America today. His illicit mergers viscerally capture the restless, divided, and uneasy times in which we live.

The social and historical functions of Ruby's chosen materials—predominantly textiles, clay, and metal—are crucial to the meaning of his work. The artist's reconsideration of material histories through the lens of a collage proposes a new way to understand the craft traditions he excavates. It is worth underscoring here that *craft* continues to be a loaded term, despite the art market's recent embrace of ceramics and fiber arts, including Ruby's sought-after ceramics and soft sculptures. Before this turn, handmade processes and craft-based practices were considered second-class citizens within the hierarchies of modernism, and within the medium-specific organization of the museum they were understood as decorative objects and associated with women's work.[7] Several recent exhibitions have sought to explore art known as craft, folk art, applied art, or fiber art through a more complex lens, among them *Outliers and American Vanguard Art* (2018) at the National Gallery of Art in Washington, DC; *Dirt on Delight: Impulses That Form Clay* (2009)—which featured Ruby's work—at the ICA Philadelphia, and, at the ICA/Boston, *Fiber: Sculpture 1960–present* (2014–15) and *Leap Before You Look: Black Mountain College 1933–1959* (2015–16). Among the leading scholars advocating for a more nuanced understanding of craft in art discourse is Jenni Sorkin (a contributor to the catalogues for several of these exhibitions), who outright repudiates the outmoded binary of high and low art: "distinctions between craft/applied art and the so-called fine arts have always been patently false. Artists themselves do not create hierarchies of materials: they work with what is at hand, in hand, by hand, cognizant of the critical

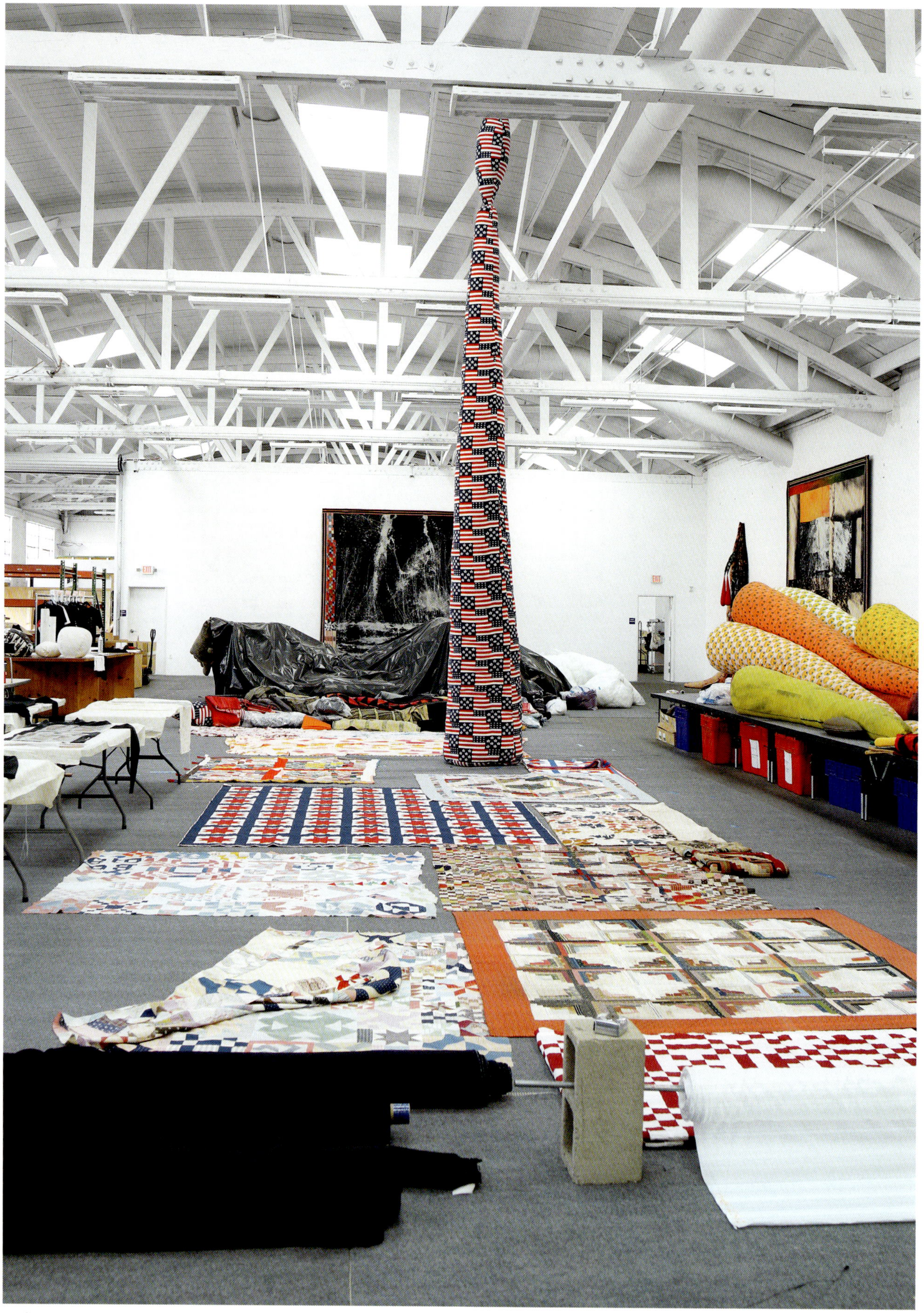

Fig. 1 **Textile production, Sterling Ruby Studio, Vernon, California**

intimacies required by materially driven abstraction."[8] But the problematic associations around craft persist.[9] Although Sorkin and other writers, historians, and curators have pointed out that this hierarchical dichotomy is out-of-date, Ruby nevertheless plays on the residual energies of the historical fictions of high art and low craft. And these residual energies haunt the artist's work, further deepening its complexities and contradictions.

The politics of craft are central to Ruby's art, who takes up the traditions of Amish quilt-making and postwar California experiments in clay precisely for their affiliation with utility, gender, and handiwork, and because of their perceived outsider status in the realm of the so-called fine arts. Sewing, making clothes, quilt-making, and metal and woodworking were an essential part of Ruby's identity as a teen rebel, skater, punk, and protoartist, and the complexities of the histories of hand-based traditions became all the more fertile as his artistic practice matured. Despite Ruby's prolific production and the size of the studio—and although skilled assistants work on his art—virtually everything in the studio passes through the artist's hand. His studio does not embrace atomized labor in the age of FedEx and Amazon, but, rather, harks back to American craft traditions, which are not seen through the lens of nostalgia, but, rather, are complicated through the political and socioeconomic situation of America today. The monumental scale of his sculptures (many of them graffitied or spray painted) (see *ZEN RIPPER*, 2008) [pp. 90–91] conjure the scale and monumentality of institutional and penitentiary architecture. These forms, merged with squatter aesthetics, forms that look like ruins, and graffiti-laden works, point to failed political states and political dystopia. The inherent violence implicit in such illicit mergers point to his complicated relationship to America and the histories of violence and nihilism that he excavates.

Born on a United States Army base in West Germany, Ruby grew up on a farm in rural, working-class Pennsylvania, deep in Amish country, where his chores included chopping wood and tending the wood-burning stove that heated the house. His Dutch mother collected West German pottery and dishware, both his mother and grandmother were seamstresses, and Ruby began sewing at the age of thirteen. He admired the well-constructed skate ramps made by Amish friends[10] and recalls his discovery of Amish quilting at a friend's home: "The quilt was vibrant; its colors seemed to glow, and the geometry, although slightly off, seemed to exude a spiritual aura. I remember thinking how out of place this quilt felt in relationship to my friend's family who primarily dressed in drab or black colors. Amish quilts were originally intended as a dowry, given by the wife to the husband to be placed on the bed upon marriage. Part ritual, part aesthetic, part utilitarian, part therapy, the quilt would be made by a group of women including the bride-to-be as a communal and family oriented rite of passage, those quilts stuck with me for years. . . . The quilts are my own version of utilitarian frugality, similar to Japanese boro textiles and quilts from Gee's Bend, Alabama. I am seeking to create a transformation via craft at the convergence of the functional and visual object."[11] Indeed, the communal aspect of quilt-making is evident at Ruby's studio, where several studio assistants are often at work on a piece, and the studio as a whole functions as a tight-knit community.

Ruby attended an agricultural high school where classes on woodworking and sewing were a part of the curriculum. He rebelled against the school's strict binary gender norms by making clothes, and fabric and collage works, on his sewing machine. He maintained an outsider status in several ways and embraced sexuality and sex as expressive tools that have through lines in his work to this day: "I got into so many fights in high school because people thought I was one thing or another. I had sex with men. I had sex with women and started to identify with the idea that I could be something else, I could be both. Of course, at that point, I had no knowledge of queer theory."[12] The hand-based processes and crafts he was already practicing as standing for otherness and its associations with traditional binary gender roles became intrinsic to the gender politics of Ruby's work, especially after he learned about, and embraced, feminism and queer theory. This can be seen in his choice of materials that have gendered histories, such as textiles and ceramics, long associated with domestic, and therefore female, makers. It should be mentioned that Ruby's aesthetic is sometimes described, and dismissed, by critics as "masculine" in its monumentality and brashness.[13] These contradictions are themselves, however, part of the complex gender politics embedded in Ruby's work, contributing to the ethos of *illicit mergers*.

After high school, Ruby attended a four-year art foundation program in Lancaster, Pennsylvania, where art was seen as means to jobs such as illustration for wildlife publications, and contemporary art and theory were non-existent in the curriculum. But in 1999, he enrolled at the School of the Art Institute of Chicago and worked at the Video Data Bank, an important collection of video art. There, he studied the work of many key moving-image practitioners, from the early collage experiments of Stan Brakhage to the work of Joan Jonas and Adrian Piper, all artists who would influence his ideas of the political body. At that time, video was his primary medium, but in Chicago he also discovered clay. He enrolled in a community art center's clay class and he was intrigued by the medium's "outsider" status (a term that can be characterized in many ways). Clay's pliability allowed Ruby to render different kinds of sculptural forms and its immediacy and proximity to the hand was appealing.

Ruby's early ceramics, such as *Blue Angel* (2007) [pp. 68–69], seem intentionally clumsy and are extremely tactile as they carry the imprint of his fingers and hands. The ceramics' crevices and dips are molded and penetrated, finished with shiny, drippy, and bright glazes, but still retain their raw, handmade,

Fig. 2

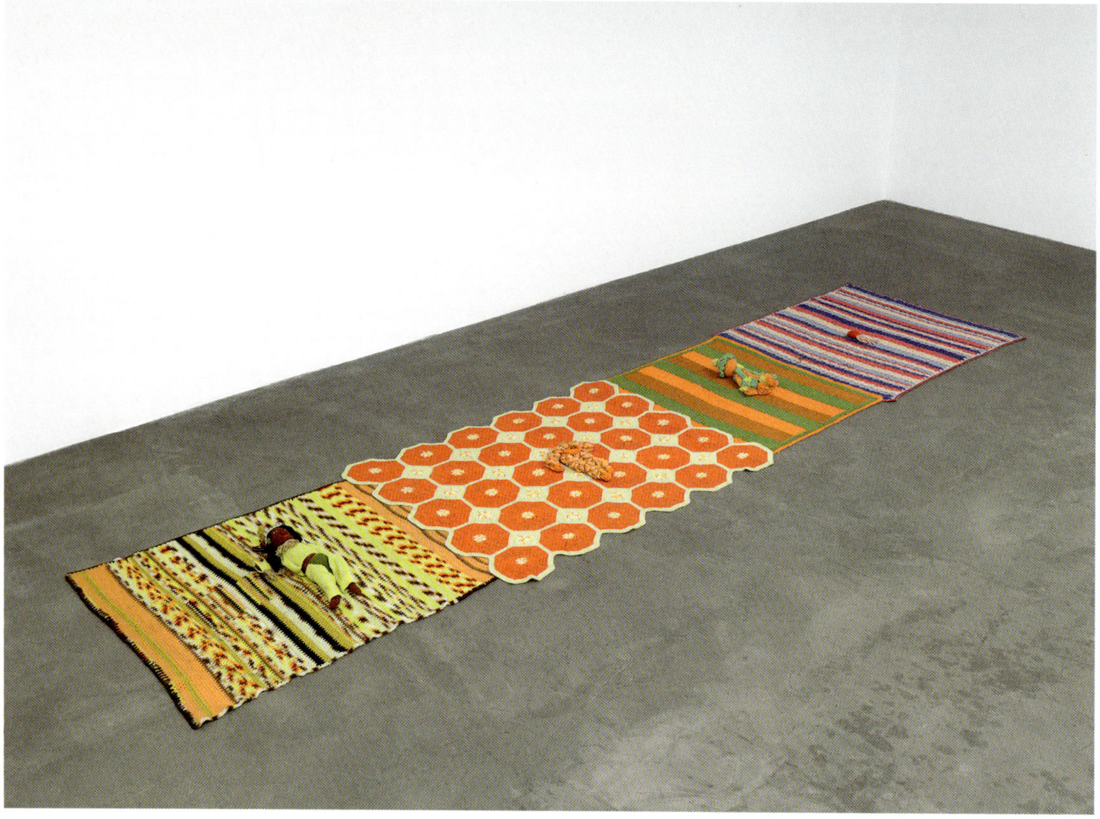

Fig. 3

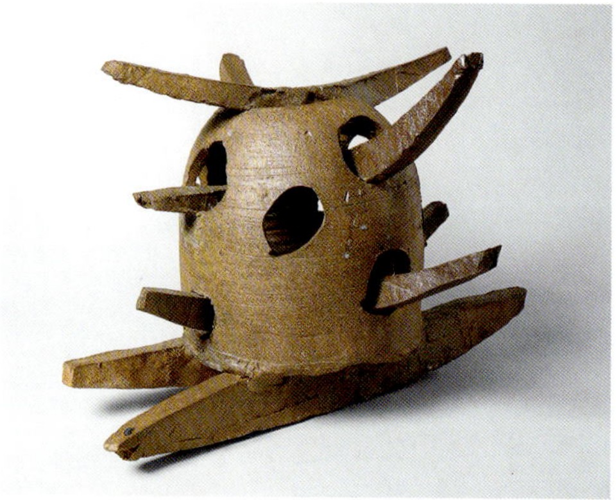

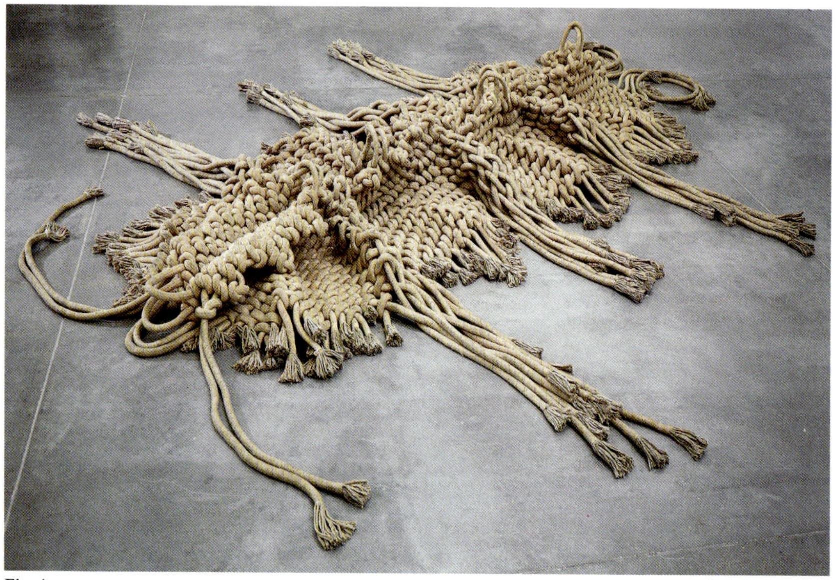

Fig. 4

Fig. 5

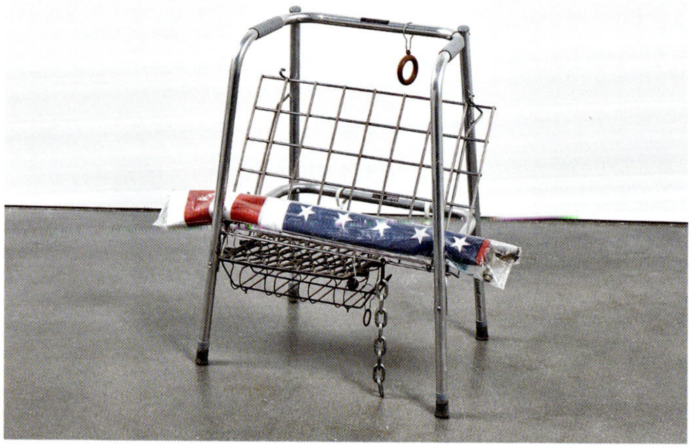

Fig. 2 Mike Kelley, *Untitled*, 1990
Found afghans and stuffed dolls. 6 × 245 × 52 inches (15.2 × 622.3 × 132.1 cm). Gift of the Louis and Bessie Adler Foundation and purchase, The Museum of Modern Art, New York

Fig. 3 Peter Voulkos, *Rocking Pot*, 1956
Stoneware with colemanite wash. 13 5/8 × 21 × 17 1/2 inches (34.6 × 53.3 × 44.5 cm). Gift of the James Renwick Alliance and various donors and museum purchase, Smithsonian American Art Museum

Fig. 4 Françoise Grossen, *Inchworm*, 1971
Industrial cotton piping cord. Approximately 24 × 240 × 156 inches (61 × 610 × 396 cm). Gift of the artist, in honor of Jenelle Porter, The Institute of Contemporary Art/Boston

Fig. 5 Cady Noland, *Objectification Process*, 1989
Metal, plastic, and fabric. 31 1/8 × 40 1/2 × 17 3/4 inches (79.1 × 102.9 × 45.1 cm). Promised gift of Barbara Lee, The Barbara Lee Collection of Art by Women, The Institute of Contemporary Art/Boston

and erotic forms. Ceramics became a vehicle for Ruby to explore ideas about the body and sexuality. "I was interested in the fact that my fellow classmates [in clay classes] were not artists," recalls Ruby. "I became fascinated with the fact that very different people were making the same type of biomorphic and anthropomorphic work. A lot was sexual, with holes, extensions and everything overly glazed. Clay does give people an innate and unfettered sensibility. I loved it."[14]

The history of ceramics is tied to utility, specifically the gendered realm of domesticity, and historical functional forms such as vessels, bowls, and pots are ever-present in Ruby's work. Although much has been done in recent years to change the perception of clay in the art world, Ruby picked a material that represented a certain freedom from canonized art history and a material that had everyday use value that he could mold. Ruby's early ceramics acknowledge the medium's utility—he made ASHTRAYS that were titled accordingly (see, for example, *ASHTRAY 141*, 2010) [p. 70]—and reference breadbaskets, perhaps in a nod to what might have appeared on Amish tables in rural Pennsylvania. He pushes ceramics to their technical limits (especially in his choice of glazes) and his ceramic vessels (see, for example, *Basin Theology/Redox*, 2013) [p. 83] have recently grown to monumental size, the largest over sixty inches in diameter. His Basin Theology pieces (which can also be seen as vessels or mortars and pestles) are containers for Ruby's previous failures. The remains of the mistakes and explosions of earlier clay works line the Basins and then go through a process of repeated glazing and firing. Essentially, the Basins become memorials for previous works, revealing a kind of paradox that is present in all his ceramics. In the case of the Basins, he takes a utilitarian form and makes it a receptacle not for liquid use, but for art, similar to the ASHTRAYS, which purport a function, but are not to be used, instead displayed on pedestals in a gallery.

In 2003 Ruby moved to California to attend graduate school at ArtCenter in Pasadena, where he studied with Mike Kelley and was also his teaching assistant. Kelley's interest in diverse materials (including fabric, textiles, and stuffed animals) [fig. 2] and his embrace of music, pop culture, American horror, and the abject body left its mark on Ruby's work. Other influential teachers included Diana Thater and Richard Hawkins. The ethos at the school was one of relentless experimentation across mediums. In this anything-goes context, clay continued to be a material of choice for Ruby. He took note of California clay artists such as Robert Arneson, Ron Nagle (whom Ruby admires enough to collect), Ken Price, and Peter Voulkos [fig. 3]. These men were seen as avant-garde experimenters making expressive art, and did not suffer the same fate as their female counterparts, whose work was deemed domestic or decorative.

Like ceramics, textiles and fabrics have similarly complex associations with ideas of labor, utility, and gender, and would likewise take a central role in Ruby's work. After graduating from ArtCenter, Ruby made *2 Stacks of Husbands* (2005) [p. 126], the first of his soft sculptures. This group of works are sewn textiles stuffed with fiberfill and feature a variety of different iconography—giant figures sporting yarn hair and interconnected limbs, gaping vampire mouths with fangs and blood (see *DOUBLE VAMPIRE 14*, 2013) [pp. 136–37], candles (see *DOUBLE CANDLE (6992)*, 2019) [p.129], and the so-called husbands, based on the gendered pillows that allow for ergonomic viewing of the twenty-four-hour news cycle while lying prone.

Ruby's soft figures are at once monumental in their scale and antimonumental in their flaccidness. In exhibitions, soft sculptures hang from the ceiling, on the walls, and are also piled on the floor, stuffed in corners and overflowing the confines of a white cube gallery, as if they don't belong. The soft sculptures recall the deflated sculptures of Claes Oldenburg, and also bear comparison with those of the (mostly female) pioneers working in fiber arts, from Sheila Hicks's sumptuous piles to Rosemarie Trockel's knitted wool paintings to Françoise Grossen's knotted rope sculptures that hang or lie prone on the floor [fig. 4]. The tactility of the soft sculptures also evokes the knots of Lynda Benglis, and Senga Nengudi's stretched pantyhose sculptures, both pointed feminist comments on the body. As often with his works, the uneasy combination of influences, from feminist artists, American craft traditions, to pop art, point to the multivalence of Ruby's illicit mergers, and to his capacity to intensify the latent energies in each by bringing them together.

Crucially, many of the soft sculptures traffic in American iconography and point to narratives of violence within American power structures. Are these large corpses covered in stars and stripes American soldiers (some piled high as to suggest a mass grave—see *FIGURES. PILE. (6991)* (2019) [pp. 138–39]—or the victims of ongoing conflicts in the Middle East and Afghanistan? In some of the quilts Ruby makes from the leftovers of soft sculptures, the fabric surpluses are sewn together to re-create the pattern of the American flag. These flag quilts are monumental in scale, some up to thirty feet long, reminiscent of the oversize flags that were omnipresent in the United States after 9/11. The use of the iconography of the American flag by artists from Jasper Johns to David Hammons looms large in Ruby's practice, as does the subversive work of Cady Noland, to whom he dedicated one of his sculptures, *Inscribed Plinth/LA Shotgun LX13/C. Noland Conjugal Visit* (2008). Like Noland's 1989 sculpture *Objectification Process*, which features a rolled-up flag on a walker, suggesting America's impotence [fig.5], Ruby wields the symbolism of American power with fierce criticality. His work draws out an overt violence, and underlying hostility toward America that feels especially potent in our moment.

Ruby's production of fabric and textiles has also directly addressed and adorned the body. In 2008, he designed a basic uniform of shirt and pants to be worn in the studio. This "work wear" uniform was made from leftovers of soft sculptures,

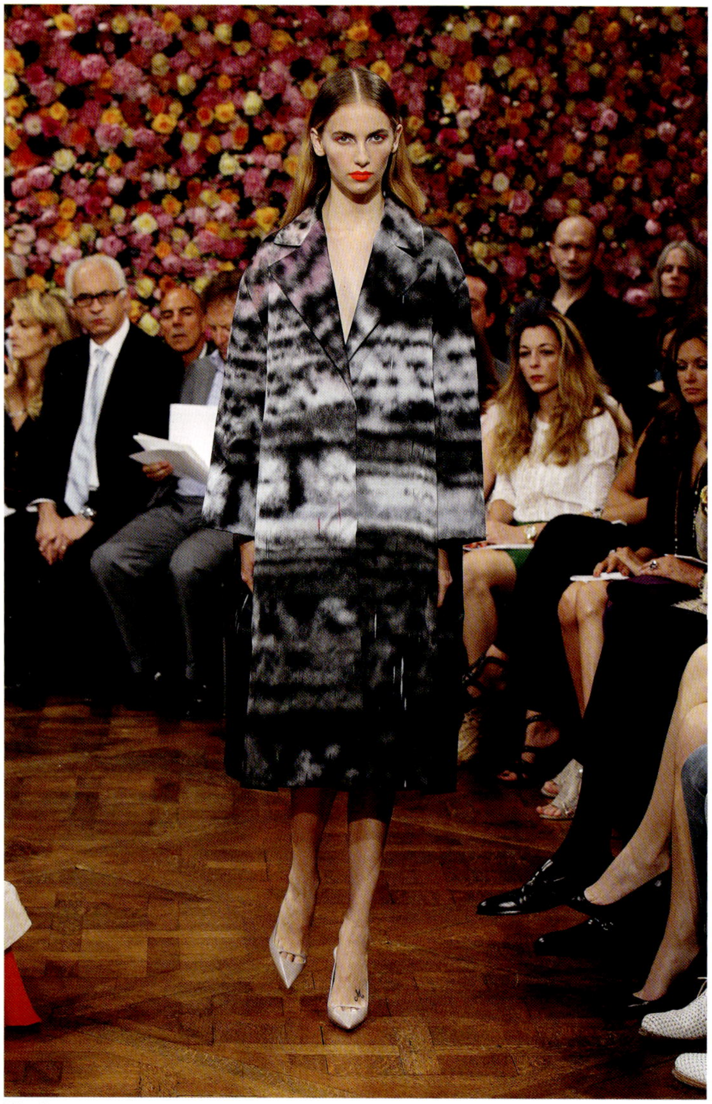

Fig. 6

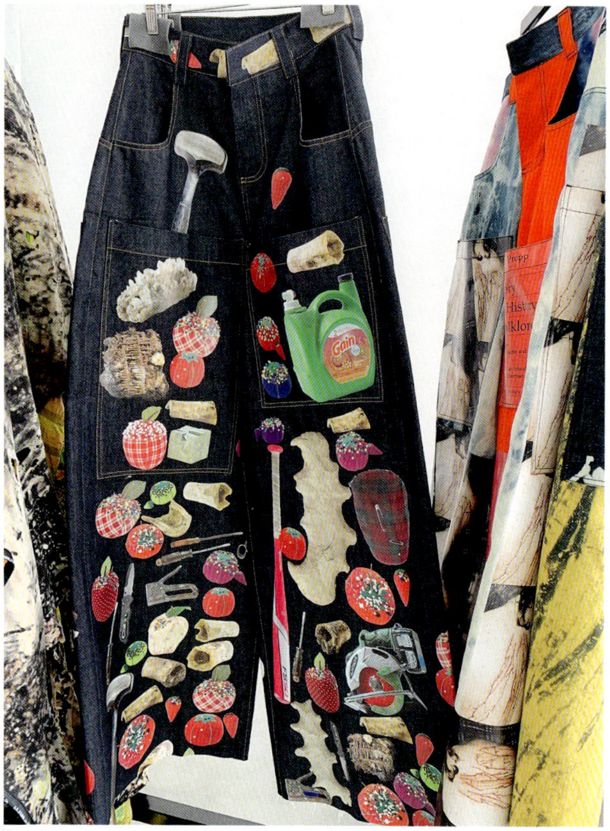

Fig. 7

Fig. 8

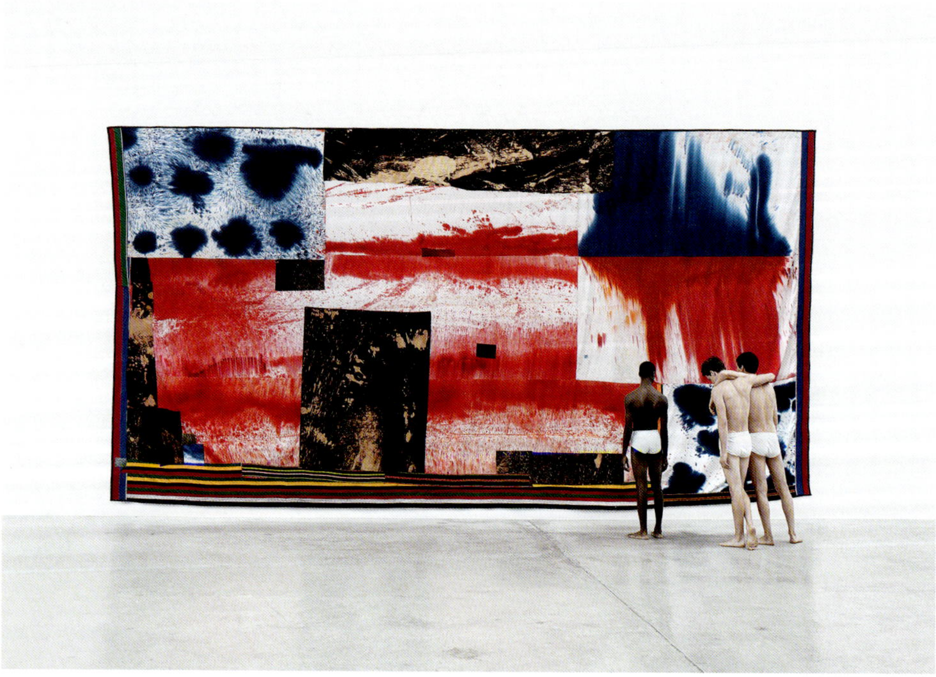

Fig. 6 Christian Dior Autumn/Winter Haute Couture Collection, 2012–13, Paris

Fig. 7 ED. 50 STUDIO TOOLS, Women's Patch Raver Pants, 2019

Fig. 8 Advertisement for Calvin Klein: Classic Cotton Briefs (Calvin Klein Underwear Est. 1981) featuring Ruby's *FLAG (4791)*, 2014

QUILTS, and FLAGS, and the uniforms became a type of "studio camouflage,"[15] symbolizing an extension of his painting and sculpture to the body. Ruby's experiments in clothing have outgrown the confines of the studio, too: first in a denim line the artist created in 2009 with the designer Raf Simons, whose 2012–13 Autumn/Winter Dior collection also featured fabrics created by Ruby [fig. 6]. In 2019, Ruby debuted S.R. STUDIO. LA. CA. at Pitti Uomo in Florence, Italy, [fig. 7] with the first delivery being available for sale through online retailer SSENSE. His clothing sports a label reading S.R. STUDIO. LA. CA.—a variant of the S.R. mark he scratches, welds, or tags onto his sculptures.

Ruby and Simons have collaborated frequently. Their first joint project was in 2008 for a store in Tokyo, and during Simons's tenure as chief creative officer at Calvin Klein—possibly the most iconic of all American fashion houses—Ruby held an official role that included designing store displays and showrooms. For the 2017 redesign of the company's New York showroom, Ruby created displays for bags and shoes from his signature formica, and covered the walls with fabrics dyed red, white, and blue. His artworks were also featured in the showroom, on the runways, and in Calvin Klein advertisements [fig. 8]. The depths of Ruby's influence penetrated pop culture at large, as Simons's collections for Calvin Klein squarely put Americana and craft traditions at the forefront of American style.[16] Producing clothing, display systems, and other such commercial pursuits is a natural outgrowth of Ruby's interest in material functionality, his earlier creative expressions on the sewing machine, and his initial art training. In many ways, through his work in fashion, Ruby bucks the limits set by the art world's system of artificial scarcity against that of fashion, where accessibility is also limited, but in a different way.

Illicit mergers also conjures a wealth of other associations, among them hostile takeovers, economic transactions, clandestine trysts, and the potency of the American economy. With its messy excavations and uneasy combinations of materials, forms, and ideas, Ruby's art offers a perfect analogy for our agitated times. America and its icons are currently undergoing a national reckoning, including America's "greatness," the heartland as symbol of American industry and power, and the pursuit of American-made above all else. Ruby's work embraces America's icons, from the Stars and Stripes to American craft culture, even as it delves into the dark forces at play in America today. It addresses a wide range of issues—from the political underbelly of the American landscape to material investigations of American craft traditions—and in the process, Ruby reexamines notions of beauty, value, and the history of sculpture itself. His oeuvre is, above all, an exploration of the social and psychological states of America, past and present. In our divisive era, and in our divided America, there is no more timely and resonant work than Sterling Ruby's *illicit mergers*.

1. Ruby has used the term "illicit merger" in several instances prior to 2018, including a 2012 interview with *032c* magazine. See "2 Traps Supermax," interview with Sterling Ruby by Steven Pulimood, 032c.com, January 3, 2012, https://032c.com/2traps-supermax/.
2. Two-dimensional collages (both analogue and digital) are a fertile part of Ruby's practice, and are represented in depth in this volume and the exhibition it accompanies. See Jeffrey De Blois's "Two-Dimensional Works" in this volume.
3. "Sterling Ruby: Sincerely Hostile," interview by João Ribas, *Flash Art*, March/April 2010, 81.
4. For more on the role of schizophrenia in Ruby's art, see Alex Gartenfeld's essay in this volume.
5. For example, critic Linda Yablonsky wrote in a 2007 review: "I don't get him—but I want to. His art is too weird, and too fierce, to dismiss." Linda Yablonsky, "Black in the Day," *Village Voice*, May 1, 2007, https://www.villagevoice.com/2007/05/01/black-in-the-day/.
6. For Ruby's own reflections on the topic of craft, see his conversation with Isabelle Graw in this volume.
7. Some examples of the rich body of literature on this subject include Rozsika Parker, *The Subversive Stitch: Embroidery and the Making of the Feminine* (London: I. B. Tauris, 1984); Glenn Adamson, *Thinking Through Craft* (London: Victoria and Albert Museum, 2007); Jenni Sorkin, *Live Form: Women, Ceramics, and Community* (Chicago: University of Chicago Press, 2016); Julia Bryan-Wilson, *Fray: Art and Textile Politics* (Chicago: University of Chicago Press, 2017); Tanya Harrod, ed., *Craft* (Cambridge, MA: MIT Press, 2018); and *The Journal of Modern Craft*, established in 2008 and published three times a year by Taylor and Francis.
8. Jenni Sorkin, "Affinities in Abstraction: Textiles, Otherness, and Painting in the 1970s" in *Outliers and American Vanguard Art* (Chicago: University of Chicago Press, 2018), 103.
9. One only needs to look at the history of exhibitions of quilts at the Whitney Museum of American Art, New York, to understand the thorny knot of issues at play. Although the 2002 exhibition *The Quilts of Gee's Bend* was overwhelmingly embraced by the art world, for some, the decontextualizing of the work made by black women in the rural American South echoed the tendency to set aside race, class, and politics to read quilts based only on their visual resemblance to abstract painting, as was done in the 1971 Whitney exhibition *Abstract Design in American Quilts*. For more, see Lynne Cooke, "Boundary Trouble: Navigating Margin and Mainstream" in *Outliers and American Vanguard Art* (Chicago: University of Chicago Press, 2018), 2–29.
10. Ross Simonini, "Craft," *Kaleidoscope*, Summer 2016, 213.
11. Sterling Ruby, *Stoves and Quilts* (Brussels: Pierre Marie Giraud), 5.
12. Franklin Sirmans, "Encounters with Sterling Ruby" in *Sterling Ruby* (New York: Phaidon, 2016), 54.
13. For example, critic Rachel Corbett noted in a 2012 review for Artnet: "His esthetic is masculine . . . " Rachel Corbett, "Sterling Ruby: The Principles of Eternity," Artnet.com, http://www.artnet.com/magazineus/features/corbett/sterling-ruby-9 23 11.asp.
14. Catherine Taft, "A Conversation with Sterling Ruby," in *Sterling Ruby* (Zurich: JRP Ringier, 2008), 105.
15. Sterling Ruby, "Work Wear," *Kaleidoscope*, Summer 2016, 198.
16. In 2018, Chloe Malle wrote in the *New York Times*: "For the formerly minimalist Calvin Klein, Raf Simons constructed a sinister barn set and sheer, breast-exposing, bib-front gingham dresses paired with knit balaclavas and metallic leather gloves. And as part of a series of advertisements hashtagged #myCalvins, Mr. Simons placed those most American of superstars, the Kardashian-Jenner sisters, in an abandoned horse barn with the reality pioneers swathed in red-and-white patchwork quilts." Chloe Malle, "Pioneer Women Are Roaming the City," *New York Times*, September 12, 2018, https://nyti.ms/2Mun9ag.

ALEX GARTENFELD

Hyperproductive: Subjectivity and Sterling Ruby

TWO SEEMINGLY IRRECONCILABLE FORCES animate Sterling Ruby's work. The first finds expression in the branded serialization that undergirds his prolific yield of artworks across a wide range of mediums. Ruby's immaculately conceived, carefully organized groupings of iconic bodies of work are frequently referred to by their materials—the ceramics, the soft sculptures, the urethanes—and function as autonomous lines of production that even correspond to designated spaces in his studio in Vernon, California [fig. 1]. As a site of production that surfaces in myriad ways in his work, Ruby's studio affords an extension of the mediated experiences the artist offers his audiences and testifies to the subjective construction of his inventive productivity. Standing in contrast with this serialization—and the coordination of labor it inevitably demands—is Ruby's consistent recourse to the personalized gesture as well as to American vernacular traditions and art-historical models within modern painting and sculpture. Ruby appropriates and caricatures the heroic gestures of action painting, graffiti, and other hallmarks of modern inspiration in order to historicize the artist's mark as a source of content in itself. Frequently taking the form of cartoons, these indexical and affective references focus on moments when positions promising psychological and political liberation reach inconclusive ends, which Ruby revisits in order to explore potential alternative outcomes.

Ruby has produced and exhibited works from his branded series since just after his first entry onto the popular consciousness at gallery shows in Los Angeles and New York in the mid-2000s. As well as those grouped according to their medium, some series take on almost self-evident titles that relate form to process: SP, for example, is a series of spray paintings on canvas (bulk 2007–2014); the drawings with nail polish that create drippy esoteric routes are titled Mapping (2006); and the freestanding, sometimes functional bronze or steel sculptures are known as STOVES (2012–ongoing). Ruby's efforts across mediums, which early on also more directly encompassed performance and video, date to the beginning of his studies at ArtCenter College of Design in Pasadena, California, in the early 2000s. Hindsight lets one see that the artist has tended to begin within a single idiom that increases in complexity through periodic updates, as if following the seasonal cycle of fashion or the iPhone. Ruby's soft sculptures, for example, have evolved from amorphous stackings of the androgynous furniture form of Husbands (2005–2013) to the anonymous grimacing forms of VAMPIRES (2010–ongoing) and DOUBLE VAMPIRES (2011–ongoing), to the FIGURES (2014–ongoing) and seemingly memorial CANDLES (2014–ongoing). His ceramics have grown from the small-scale ASHTRAYS (2008–ongoing)—of which there are now more than five hundred—through Baskets (2007–ongoing) to the monumental Basin Theology works (2010–ongoing) and Totems (2017–ongoing). The metal sculptures have grown from casts of toothy ceramic forms in multiple scales into the aforementioned STOVES and the gun barrel-like tabletop forms in the series MS (2010–2011). A similar pattern can be seen in Ruby's ever more ambitious work in the realm of fashion. His collaboration with Raf Simons, which began in 2008 with the design for the Raf Simons flagship boutique in Tokyo, was followed by a Raf Simons x Sterling Ruby Denim Capsule Collection for Spring/Summer 2010. Ruby's prints were featured in a collection at Dior when Simons was its creative director; and in 2014 Simons and Ruby presented the Raf Simons/Sterling Ruby Fall/Winter menswear collection. More recently, when Simons became chief creative officer at Calvin Klein in 2016, he asked Ruby to reimagine many of the brand's key visual motifs. Finally, in 2019, the artist launched his own line of wearable garments under the label S.R. STUDIO. LA. CA. Throughout, the motifs of his designs have continually overlapped with those in his paintings.

Antagonistic to the performance of corporate efficiency such endeavors might suggest is Ruby's recurrent deployment of imperfection, idiosyncrasy, and dropout gestures. The marginalized figure thematized in many of his early works were embodied by the artist himself as a kind of off-grid vagrant in the almost forty-minute-long video *Transient Trilogy* (2005–2009) [fig. 2]. The 2003 photograph *Transient Bed of John* [pp. 40–41] makes a metaphor of a found tableau of sandbags intended to contain a pool of tar, by virtue of being both a simple armature and a sanctified, improvised cushion. This image is an antecedent for many of the artist's sculptural forms. Its aesthetics and symbolism are, for example, apparent in the installation *Disintegrating Identities* (2003–2006) [fig. 3]—a hybrid, improvisatory living space or studio (equipped with bleach and fabric) that combined the artist's emerging interest in cushioned armatures with other motifs that would become prominent in his later work, notably foreshadowing the SP series in its use of crisscrossing sprayed paint. *Big Grid/DB Deth* (2008) [p. 97], meanwhile, anthropomorphizes the form with two eyelike portals, from which a graffitied teardrop seems to fall.

The balancing act between a productive position and the assertion of an individuated self plays out throughout Ruby's work, ultimately taking the form of an intensified version of capitalist hyperproductivity that amplifies subjectivity in order to consume it. Each of the pair of 2005 prints titled *Cry 2005* [p. 44] features a patchwork of imagery—one of an archaeological site and the other of spray-painted patterning—with the title scrawled over it as if with spray paint or a rudimentary paint app. The evocative word suggests a primal and uncontrolled mode of communication, while the mode of inscription relates to the artist's recurring and polymorphous use of the visual language of graffiti to describe both the artist's individualized authorship and an opposition to institutional forms—primarily symbolized in Ruby's work related to the prison system, which has been a touchstone for the artist at least since his 2005–2008 trio of exhibitions titled *SUPERMAX*.[1] One strand of works on this subject goes back to the 2004 collage *Prison* [p. 37], which features an image of a cell with its gridded bars in the foreground, with colored-pencil lines radiating jaggedly to the edge of the page. In subsequent, related works, including his large Grid collages of 2008–2010, Ruby has frequently contrasted personal, deliberately deliquescent lines with the more rigid geometries of social control.

Ruby has occasionally used the idea of schizophrenia to describe the range and volume of his production, and his handling of multiple modes and registers seemingly at odds with one another.[2] His embodiment of multiple roles—from manager of a

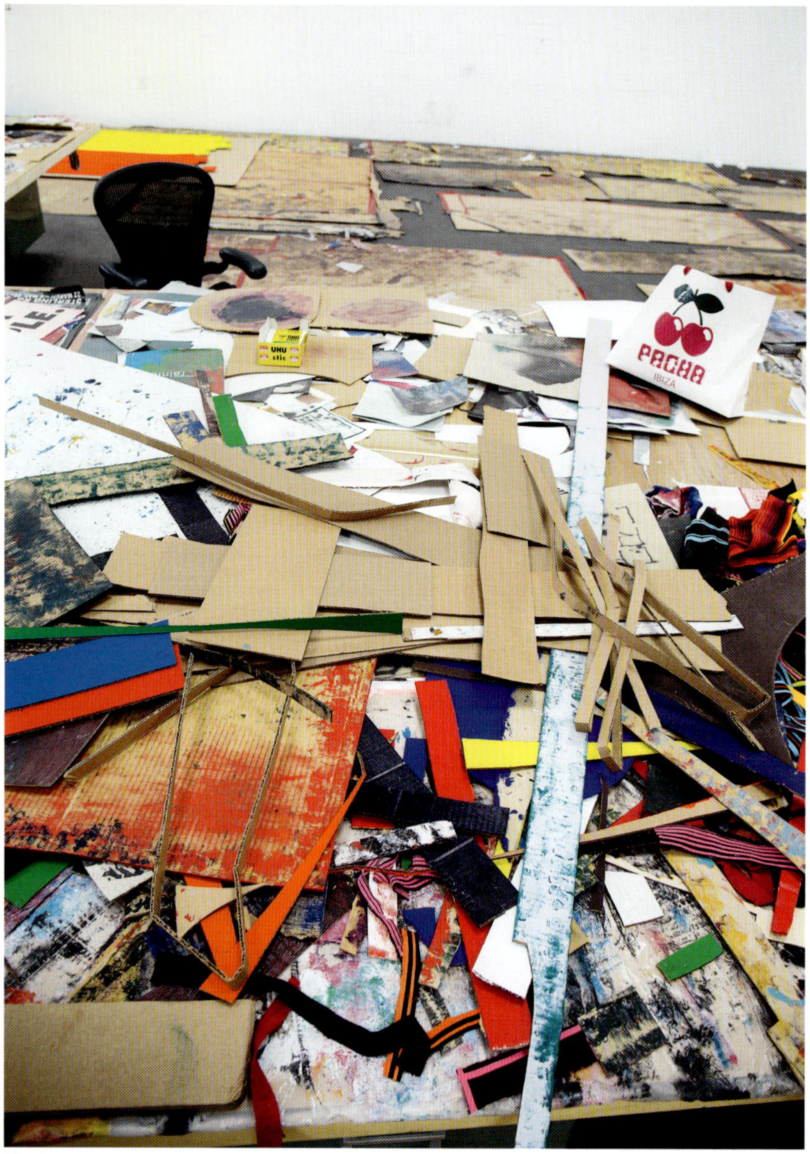

Fig. 1

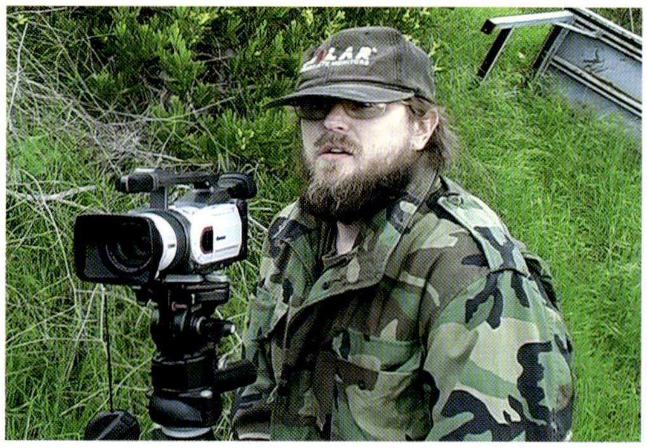

Fig. 2

Fig. 3

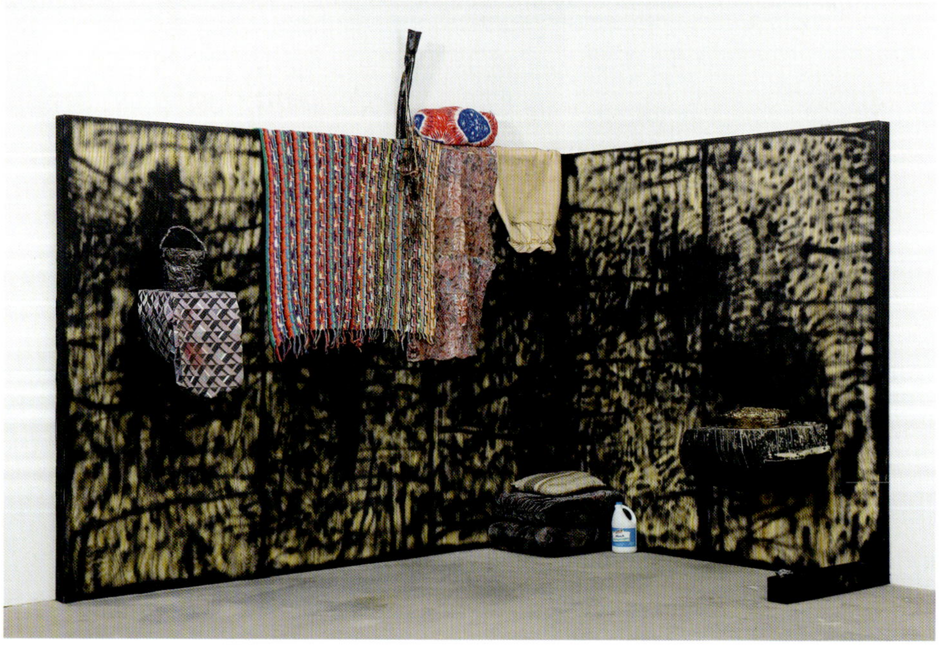

Fig. 1 **Collage production, Sterling Ruby Studio, Vernon, California**

Fig. 2 ***Transient Trilogy* (still), 2005–09**
Single channel video (color, sound; 37:22 minutes)

Fig. 3 ***Disintegrating Identities*, 2003–06**
Wood, tar, latex, synthetic hair, diamonds, ceramic, and bleach

highly mediated studio to head of a fashion business that operates across the realms of art and commerce—demonstrates an internalization of the obsolescence of a romantic understanding of the relationship of artists to their work within the regime of contemporary art. At the same time, the multiple conflicting modes of his production themselves complicate the notion of a fixed identity and unsettle the assumptions behind the idea of the artist as a vehicle of critique. In Gilles Deleuze and Félix Guattari's use of the term, schizophrenia (and the related concept of schizoanalysis) is operative to understanding (artistic) work. Where historically psychoanalysis had spoken of the sublimation of sexual desire to understand behavior among both individuals and societies, for Deleuze and Guattari the schizophrenic demonstrates that the libido is not repressed in order for society to exist, but rather constituent to it.[3] In subsequent texts, Guattari would further refine his understanding of the relationship of libido to subjective desire: "The dominant conception of social order implies a definition of desire (of collective formations of desire) that is fairly disastrous: as a flow that has to be disciplined, so that a law can be created to establish control over it."[4]

For an artist proposing manifold expressive modes, the performed condition of schizophrenia thus offers a way to come to terms with the inescapable drive to relinquish control over one's own identity by exploiting qualities such as scarcity, plenitude, novelty, and unceasing flexibility. Ruby's 2006 six-piece suite of collages *Physicalism/The Recombine*, named after a hypermaterialist mode of philosophy, combines pageant-ready bodies, shot in campy theatrical lighting, with images of decorative candles and wax. The juxtaposition is both striking in its equivalence of bodies and objects and continuous with Ruby's works of the period exploring the role of the body in extreme states. The 2009 video *The Masturbators* [fig. 4], in which male porn actors functionally masturbate to orgasm, merges performance and spectacle with a productivity that is sited within but nullifies desire.

At stake in the reception of Ruby's output is the nature of artistic work in a contemporary, largely post-Fordist ecology, and the question of whether it can be a force of resistance against capitalism's oppressive and unceasing demand for production and the accompanying conflation of work with identity. Under a regime that emphasizes immaterial labor and services, and above all time and flexibility, critics including Paolo Virno have identified today's workforce of data- and gig-driven professionals, typified by international artists, as a "new working class" that is responsible for generating the majority of what classical Marxist theory calls surplus value. The implications of Virno's turn to class are dual, suggesting both new modes of capitalist exploitation and an imagined potential to repossess the tools of alienation. In Ruby's works, too, this remains an operative tension, even as his work seems to play with the ability to master new modes of production seemingly immediately.

Significant in this regard is Mike Kelley, Ruby's mentor at ArtCenter, in particular for his idea that the working-class identity of an artist offered a basis from which to critique institutional and cultural hierarchies. Ruby grew up primarily in rural Pennsylvania before working construction jobs and attending an unaccredited art school. In various interviews, he has discussed the influence of his upbringing on his choice of references—the embarrassment he felt in arriving at graduate school with a broader knowledge of crafts than contemporary art, for instance.[5] Ruby overcame this inhibition as part of a broader embrace of self-taught artists and vernacular mediums such as ceramics and quilt-making. His inspiration from the quilts of Gee's Bend, Alabama, for example, is writ large in a number of the monumental, quilt-like works titled *QUILT* or *FLAG*.

Ruby's deployments of American symbols in these and other works is telling. In *FLAG (4784)* (2014), a small acrylic on paper, fingerprinted red forms have a childlike, laborious, and horror film-like quality. Ruby has also applied red, white, and blue to forms including abject honeycomb shapes, flaccid and architecturally parasitic spiderwebs, and fangs; quilted motifs referencing the American flag return in the body bag-like sculptures of *FIGURES. PILE. (6991)* (2019) [pp. 138–39]. Ruby's repeated invocations of the Stars and Stripes motif parallel the instrumentalization of the symbol itself in ways that are both theatrically affective (as when covering a stack of corpse-like bodies, for instance) and voided of meaning through repetition. From 9/11 through the 2008 financial crisis to the 2016 election, this century so far has demonstrated how right-wing nationalism and protectionism work in the service of capital, and at the same time how libidinal and suicidal the macrocultural impulses of America's ideology of individualism and self-reliance continue to be.

The American work ethic has also emerged as a trope for Ruby to reflect on the shifting role of labor in neoliberal capitalism. While some of the artist's heartland-style STOVES dutifully burn wood on occasion, others function simply by invoking a clichéd version of American industriousness. Ruby's frequent allusions to the American Puritan tradition, especially in view of his own incessant production, bring to mind Max Weber's early-twentieth-century treatise *The Protestant Ethic and the Spirit of Capitalism* (1905), in which the sociologist writes of the historical forces that have led to the marketization of society. The text focuses on the loss of value and authority when Catholicism was abandoned during the Reformation, but also on Protestant prohibitions of wastefulness that incentivized the accumulation of wealth for investment and attributed a moral value to labor that meant people dedicated themselves to their work even after their basic needs had been met.[6] Weber traces the historical origin of the forces that would enable the conflation of life and work under post-Fordism.

For his ceramics, Ruby doubles down on the Puritan ethos of not being wasteful with resources, while introducing significant irony and deviations. In the Basin Theology series, for example, roughly made ceramic bowls are filled with scraps of earlier clay forms that exploded in the kiln, often due to their deliberately improper preparation. In keeping with the religious dimension in the title of these works, the artist foregrounds the cult of productivity and efficiency, even as he undercuts it through the process of their production and their monumental scale. The profuse abundance of Ruby's serialized output is, moreover, often itself thematized in the way his exhibitions are installed. Take, for instance, the installation *SUPERMAX 2008*, on view that year at LA MOCA's Pacific Design Center [fig. 5]. Its name

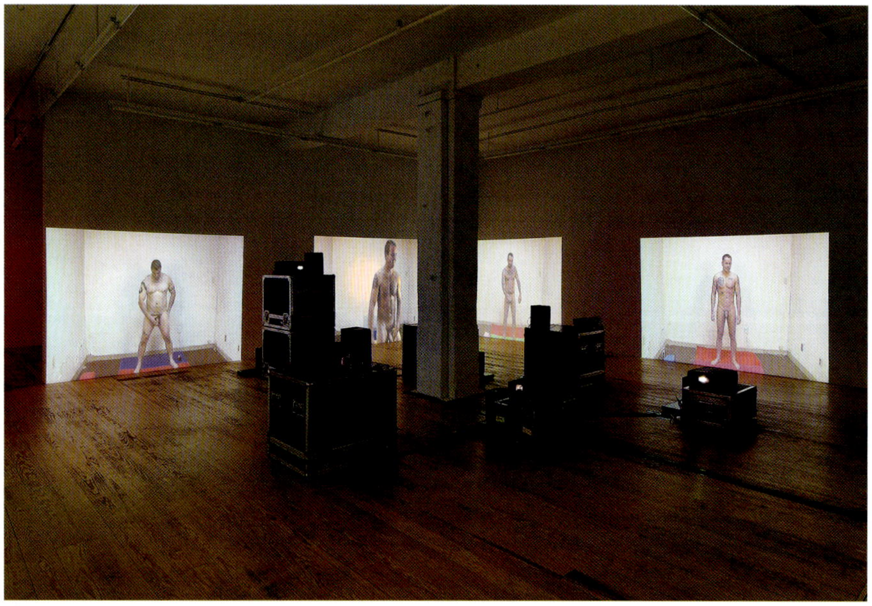

Fig. 4

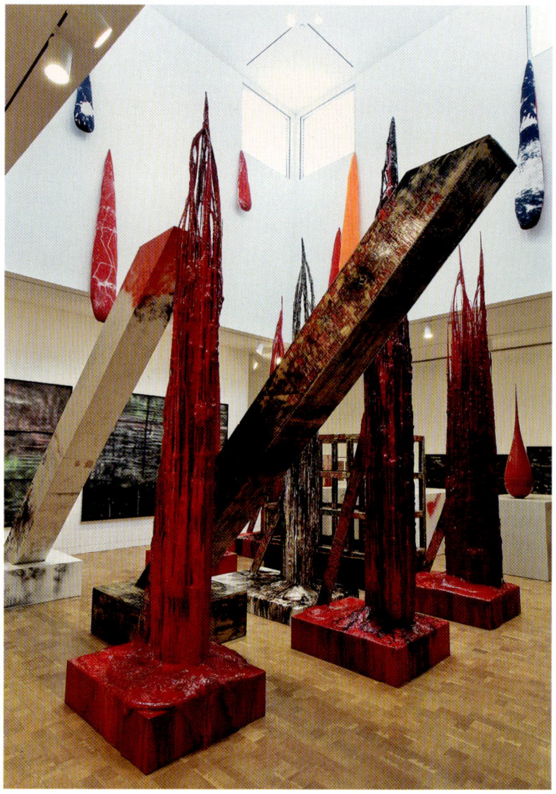

Fig. 5

Fig. 6

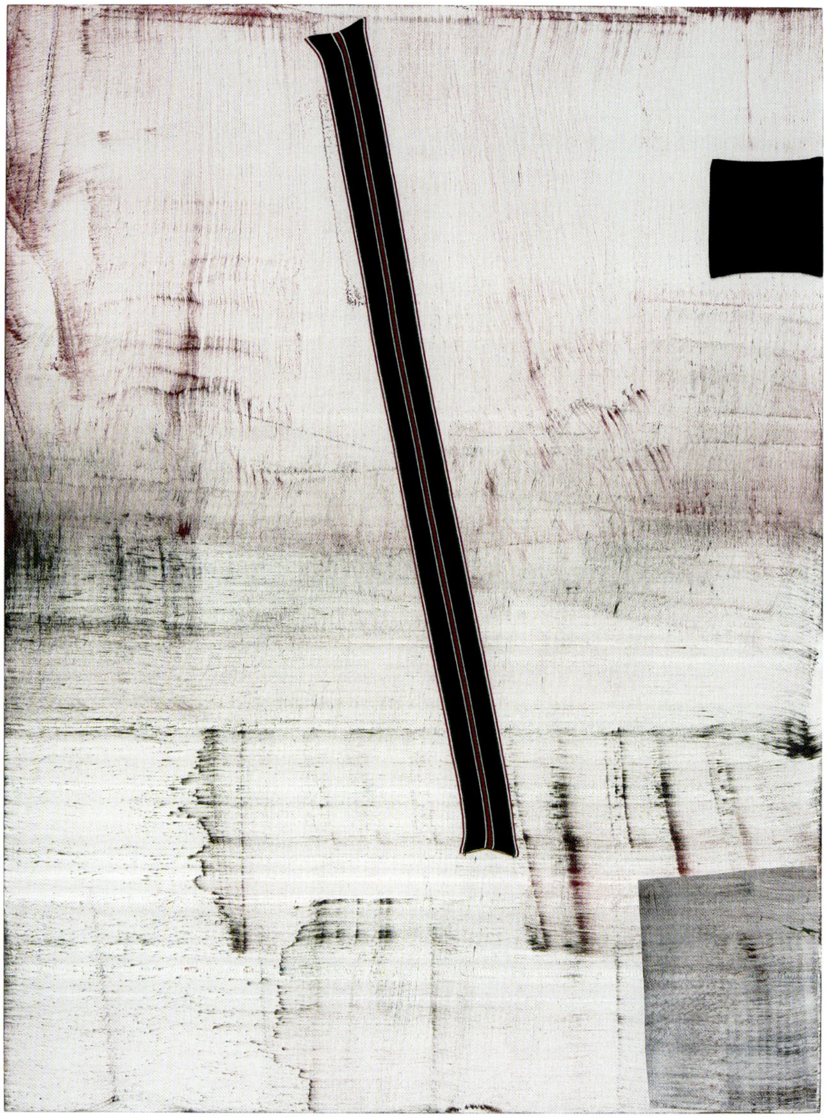

Fig. 4 **Installation view, *The Masturbators*, Foxy Production, New York, 2009**

Fig. 5 **Installation view, *SUPERMAX 2008*, Museum of Contemporary Art, Los Angeles, 2008**

Fig. 6 ***SUICIDE (LG)*, 2015 Acrylic, elastic, and treated fabric on canvas**

was a reference to super-maximum security prisons but also described the overly dense, stylized grouping of works. Ruby's approach to display frequently seems to follow Georges Bataille, for whom expenditure—a waste of value and material—defines the historical bourgeoisie and its economy, a condition it cloaks in miserliness (again, the values of Protestantism).[7] The critic Martin Herbert diagnoses a similar psychological tension in Ruby's work, noting that "heaving excessiveness is one of the registers [Ruby] invokes; disgust and self-disgust are others."[8]

Alongside this use of sheer volume to complicate the assumptions underlying artistic production, Ruby also explores the relationship between the artist and his output by manipulating the expression of time in his work. This is made apparent in various ways: the deployment of drips in paint or urethane that describe the flow of material; or the use of graffiti-like scrawlings on monumental surfaces that express the (simulated) toll of duration and the anticipation of an activated audience for the work. Equally compelling in this regard are the artist's cardboard collages, especially those in the series ECLPSE (2014–2015), whose impact is in their elegant assembly of found materials arranged on largely blank supports with an efficiency of means that suggests an expert leisureliness. In these configurations, mastery is expressed as an (impossible) control of time.

As Isabelle Graw suggests in her interview with the artist in this volume, Ruby has frequently used his studio as both a source of inspiration and an invocation of tradition. He is a paradigmatic case in point for the importance of Los Angeles in the mythology of the studio, in terms of both the city's relationship to cinema and celebrity, and its canon of artists. Yet Ruby may be alone in thematizing the studio as a hyperproductive space capable of creating multiple genres of experience and medium. Ruby's skillful expenditures (of materials, of labor, of time) also speaks to the artist's staging of his own relationship to the site of his work's production. The canonical reference for this aspect of Ruby's practice is Hans Namuth's famed portfolio on Jackson Pollock for *Life*, which marks the historical watershed when the artwork becomes truly and emblematically spectacular and commodified.

Ruby, like many artists of his generation, critically undermines the understanding of artistic autonomy that still accompanied the deployment of the unique gesture in abstract expressionism. The idea of abstract expressionism as the heroic unleashing of an individual's subconscious is inextricable from the American ideology of free expression, with all its attendant contradictions, both historically and in the present. (Consider, for example, Virno's description of the impact of capitalism on both labor and consumption as constituent elements of contemporary subjectivity: "Speaking of individuation implies that you consider the individual a result, not a starting point.")[9] In his multifaceted investigations of the limitations of the historical medium of painting, Ruby revisits period themes in all of their auratic manifestations. In his QUILTS, for example, Ruby reproduces Barnett Newman's zips as bands of brightly colored fabric. In this case, as elsewhere, the artist uses an outsized form of citation in order both to locate an aura and to displace it. By turning the haptic gestures of Pollock, and even their desublimation by Warhol, into a heavy and grotesque application of urethane for his Monument Stalagmites (2002–2013), Ruby restages the commodification of expenditure in the field of cultural production.

In SP, his large paintings made with spray paint, Ruby also enacts a complicated rehearsal of abstract expressionism. While their gradations of romantic color most obviously bring to mind the canvases of Rothko, and their evocations of a polluted horizon recall J. M. W. Turner's skyscapes, the only truly expressive marks on these paintings are almost incidental-looking yet in fact highly composed drips whose miniature relative scale and foregrounding creates a sense of pathos. Significantly, the drips appear frozen and dramatically staged, lending them a remarkable alienation from any particular maker or mode of making.

If such works already call into question the ideology of artistic production, Ruby's paintings have over the past few years increasingly synthesized abstract expressionist tropes with highly generalized geographic configurations. In his large-scale Yard paintings (2015–2016), the trappings of midcentury abstraction—the expressive gesture, a horizontal haptic picture plane, the motif of the studio floor—coalesce into generic, maplike configurations [fig. 6]. These siteless, endlessly allusive abstractions on canvas have titles that stress international zones of conflict, and strips of colored fabric here suggest both flags and some type of border. The works' extreme generality and their inclusion of detritus and working materials from the studio floor suggests that abstract expressionist gestures have been evacuated and commodified and may now communicate above all their own ability to generate value. By refusing the contradiction between prolific productivity and individualized resistance to it, Ruby's work captures the effects of the divergent pressures on human subjectivity in the first decades of the twenty-first century.

---

1. The artist's monumental geometric solids, such as *Big Grid/DB Deth* (2008), use the institutional material of formica to create analogies between modernist design and the institutional architecture of schools and prisons. In a 2010 show at Pace Gallery in New York, the artist turned a full-size bus into *BUS* (2010) equipping it with solitary confinement cages, speakers, subwoofers, chrome fixtures, and security doors. He showed this alongside a work that drew from the work of Bruce Nauman: a massive rectangular grid composed of customized rectangular blocks titled *PIG PEN* (2010). Most recently, aerial footage of California's thirty-five adult state prisons, presented as structures built into the landscape, was the primary component of *DAMNATION*, Ruby's 2019 exhibition at Sprüth Magers in Los Angeles.
2. "Sterling Ruby in conversation with Paul Schimmel," YouTube video, 1:04:02, posted by "HauserWirth," March 19, 2013, https://www.youtube.com/watch?v=aBfFf3C7IjQ.
3. See Gilles Deleuze and Félix Guattari, *Anti-Oedipus: Capitalism and Schizophrenia*, trans. Robert Hurley (New York: Viking, 1977).
4. Félix Guattari and Suely Rolnik, *Molecular Revolution in Brazil*, trans. Karel Clapshow and Brian Holmes (Los Angeles: Semiotext(e), 2007), 319.
5. See, for example, Ruby's conversation with Isabelle Graw in this volume.
6. See Max Weber, *The Protestant Ethic and the Spirit of Capitalism*, trans. Talcott Parsons (London: Routledge, 2005).
7. Georges Bataille, *Visions of Excess: Selected Writings, 1927–1939*, ed. Allan Stoekl, trans. Allan Stoekl, with Carl R. Lovitt and Donald M. Leslie (Minneapolis: University of Minnesota Press, 1985), 125.
8. Martin Herbert, "Sterling Ruby," *Frieze*, June 15, 2013, https://frieze.com/article/sterling-ruby.
9. "The Dismeasure of Art: An Interview with Paolo Virno," by Sonja Lavaert and Pascal Gielen, *Open*, no. 17 (November 2009): 77, https://onlineopen.org/the-dismeasure-of-art.

Ready to Wear: A Conversation between Sterling Ruby and Isabelle Graw

ISABELLE GRAW: Craft and manual labor are very important in your work, in contrast to the emphasis on deskilling so typical for one strain of modern art since Duchamp. The way you stage yourself as an artist is quite telling in this respect: you present yourself as an artist-worker who wears self-made uniforms that take up the patterns of your paintings and are sometimes covered with splashes of bleach—you seem to carry the traces of their craft-intensive making on your body. Why do you put so much weight on making and craft, considering that Art with a capital A has tried to distance itself from craft since the eighteenth century?

STERLING RUBY: First off, my background: my mother was European, from the Netherlands; and my father is from Baltimore. I grew up in an extremely rural setting in a Pennsylvania Dutch region with a strong Amish community. There was a huge emphasis on craft—and when I say craft I mean quilting, crocheting, woodworking. There was a very specific gender divide: men were woodworkers, women were quilters. I went to a high school where specific elements of craft and labor were part of the curriculum. Most of the guys in my high school were doing shop class, which involved making things in metal or wood. The only art class that they offered was calligraphy, which was taken by the girls. So it wasn't art-based: the creative endeavors that were outside the fundamentals of math, science, or history were geared to making things that had a kind of use value to them.

When I became a teenager, I wanted to have nothing to do with all of this. I resented having to live in this community; I found it hostile. I started doing mostly the kinds of crafts that were associated with the women of the community, and my grandmother and my mother were supportive of that. I don't know why, because it turned out to be a difficult thing for me in high school, but my mother gave me my first sewing machine when I was thirteen. As time went on, I started spending most of my time in Baltimore and in DC, seeing a lot of punk shows, bands from California and the East Coast. Most of what I was doing in terms of making things was either drawing album covers or sewing together scrappy uniforms for myself to wear. But I never necessarily thought of it as art, and I never thought of it as fashion.

After I graduated from high school, I got a job doing construction work. Most of the people—the male ones at least—that I graduated with either started to work on a farm or did construction. But after a while I felt beaten down and thought to myself, I can't do this for the rest of my life. I was miserable already and I couldn't imagine what it would be like in twenty years. My mother had a friend who was a wildlife illustrator. She introduced me to him, and he got me into art school. It was a nonaccredited art school, which means that it didn't have a degree associated with it, even though it was a four-year program. This school emphasized craft and technique as well: we did a lot of figure drawing, we drew the nude figure for eight hours a day, we did perspective drawing and learned additive and deductive sculpture. So I spent four years studying art in a very traditional way. It wasn't a contemporary art program, and the only textbook we read was *Gardner's Art through the Ages*. My first trip to MoMA [in 1995], I saw the Bruce Nauman survey and it shook me. It gave me a new appreciation for the curriculum I had just gone through, but also helped me realize that my education didn't include a lot of what other people were studying at the time.

GRAW: Your educational background felt useless at this point?

RUBY: Yes, and for a number of years, even to the point of my coming to LA, I felt embarrassed by it, and by the way I grew up. I felt embarrassed by the choice to go to this four-year school where we didn't learn any theory. We weren't reading French postmodernism, we were reading about the Renaissance and about mannerism, and so I switched direction and shunned all of that. But over time I realized that it was probably a great gift to experience the old ways of making art and the traditional aspects of making things. I realized that the new way of studying and making art—looking at a history specifically related to minimalism, performance art, or conceptual practices, and forgetting all the rest—maybe wasn't so right for me. I started to realize that I could be a more sincere artist by embracing some of those things that I had learned as a younger person.

GRAW: By emphasizing craft after having rejected it, did you want to distance yourself from the prevailing understanding of artists as intellectual, conceptually working quasi scientists engaged in so-called artistic research?

RUBY: I felt sad that so many artists of my generation were being taught that there was no way to move forward and that all things were dead. This was based on the idea that everything was a simulacrum, and under such circumstances there was no way to make a gesture that had meaning anymore. But if all things were a kind of precursor to a negation of making something that had any meaning, it just seemed like, why do it anymore?

GRAW: But then in LA, studying at ArtCenter College of Design, you came into contact with people who didn't have this approach—people like Emi Fontana and Mike Kelley, whose teaching assistant you were. I like this idea of you as combining some of their interests. [*Laughs*]

RUBY: I wouldn't put it like that, but they were very supportive of me. Mike and I constantly talked about craft and the fact that we were both brought up in very different times. His rejection of craft as something sincere aimed at using it in a conceptual way,

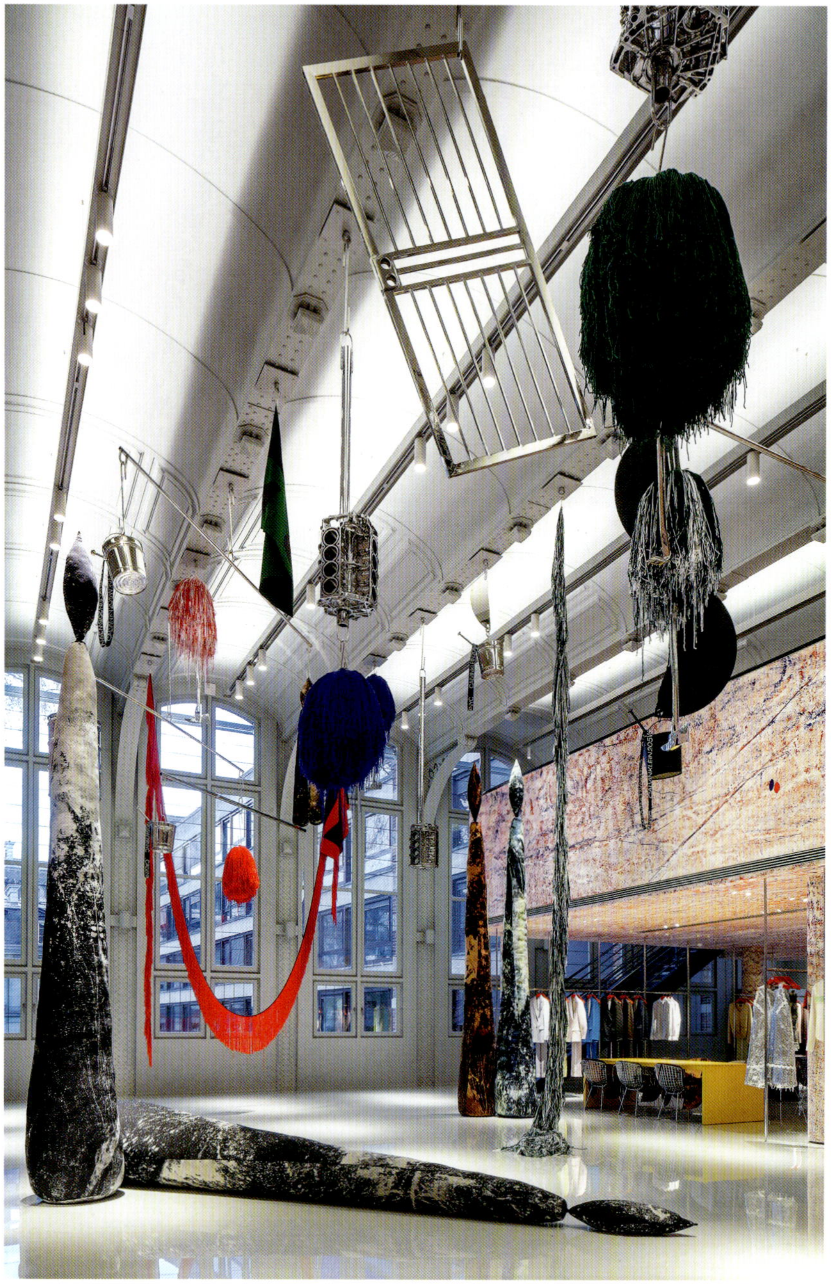

Fig. 1

Fig. 2

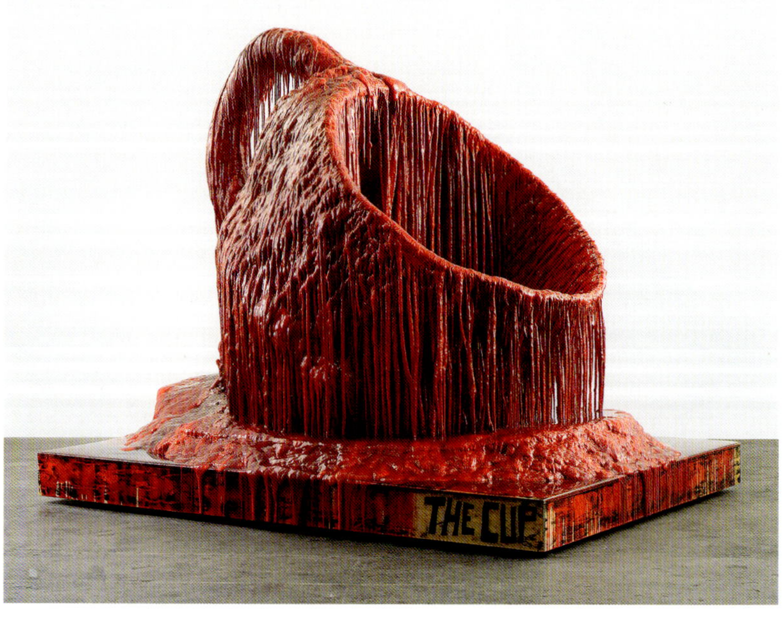

Fig. 1 **CALVIN KLEIN 205W39NYC brand headquarters, Paris, 2018**

Fig. 2 ***The Cup*, 2013**
Foam, urethane, wood, and spray paint

which was very new at the time for the artists of Mike's generation: the polarity between high and low was a big discussion at that time. But when Mike and I would talk about what it meant to have grown up with traditional ideas of labor and craft, he wanted to take people's preconceived notions and break them in an extremely aggressive way. This was interesting to me and I really respected Mike for it, particularly considering when he was doing it. But by the time I got there, it had already been done in the art world.

GRAW: Let me come back to these work uniforms that you make and wear. You said somewhere that you only wear clothes you have made. This reminds me of artists from the historical avant-garde—Rodchenko, for example—who also designed their own uniforms. But the nature of these uniforms was different: Rodchenko and others staged themselves as industrial wage laborers. When Moholy-Nagy was teaching at the Bauhaus he wore factory overalls every day. Your uniforms seem to have a different message, since they consist of textiles and patterns that we also find in your paintings. Do you want to underline the strong link between your life, your personhood, and your art by wearing your artwork like a second skin?

RUBY: Yes, that's a pretty good way of putting it. When I started to work with different textile mills and began researching rinses, enzyme washes, bleaches, and overdyes, I was making material for sculptures and for tapestries and paintings. I realized in this Bauhausian way that I could separate a certain amount of yardage and make something that I could wear, almost as if I was cannibalizing my own work. And I loved that: it was not only cannibalizing but also excavating it, in a sense. And then I started making garments from every project.

GRAW: One could also extrapolate your notion of painting from your clothes. Since your uniforms display textures and patterns from your paintings, painting is conceived in turn as a programmatically embodied craft—an activity that involves your body to such a degree that it actually leaves traces on it.

RUBY: I think you're absolutely right. After making paintings for a number of years I was starting to feel like they were being either hung in someone's home or on a museum wall, or put in storage. But I liked this idea that I could wear these things out in public. It became a behavioral scenario where I could reclaim the painting or give more exposure to it by putting it out there into the world in a way that is impossible for a painting on a stretcher. And then I started thinking: What would it be like if I made these things and people could wear them out in public? This would undo the hierarchy between a painting on a stretcher and a pair of pants. Paintings get cut up and reassembled, via a pattern, as a jacket or another item. I started to really enjoy the process. Collaging images on pants. The body became a canvas.

GRAW: This is interesting considering that the picture on canvas was invented around 1500 because of the increased mobility that it promised. Now, if a painting gets to be worn as pants, as in your work, it gains an even higher degree of mobility and becomes even more accessible. While its commodity value decreases due to the loss of uniqueness implied in the process, its mobility intensifies.

RUBY: Absolutely. It has a wider reach and it becomes more performative and conceptual: it can be folded, flipped, and moved in a way that a painting on a stretcher can't. My BC series began when I was thinking about quilts. I would use scraps, found clothing, and different textiles and would collage them onto canvas. The process was essentially the opposite of this painting-to-ready-to-wear process. The studio was reclaiming clothing and rags to make an artwork.

GRAW: Your work also constantly refers to the studio as its implicit horizon, and it is staged as central to your approach to artistic production. It gets thematized in your catalogues, for instance, which often show your studio as a place where a great number of material things get produced at the same time, things that get constantly reused and recycled. Their materiality and texture are emphasized. But next to this more traditional notion of the studio as workshop, your studio also seems to be organized and managed like a company. Alongside the traditional skills of making, there are new managerial and entrepreneurial skills embodied by the studio as well. It's a meeting place between old skills and a more recent process of reskilling that requires artists to have social and managerial skills.

RUBY: Faced with post-studio practices, I used to think that the idea of the studio was kind of passé: it didn't happen anymore. It meant letting someone else fabricate your work so that the artist's hand was not involved. The work was not supposed to have any dirty lineage connecting it to the artist who made it. I wanted to react to that. I started to think that if the studio couldn't be something that gave me comfort and autonomy, it wouldn't work. I felt very confident that the studio was the most important place. For me there is no hierarchy within the studio: we opted for an expansive scenario where everything is given the same value. But at some point, I also needed to start to work with people—mostly when it became necessary to lift a sculpture or when I needed someone who could weld. That said, I still make everything, I still have my hand in everything. But I also enjoy the kind of "creative director" scenario that has started to shape up within the studio.

GRAW: But isn't there a tension between what you just described as the studio's intimacy and your role as a manager who has to run the studio like a company? There is manual labor and the importance of your hand and touch, on the one hand, and on the other, there is an organization that runs according to more economic criteria of efficiency . . .

RUBY: I have more time to make work when someone else runs the "manager" part. We meet, but I don't spend my time on it.

GRAW: But what new freedoms and new constraints result from a studio that combines the specifics of manual artistic labor with a more entrepreneurial kind of organization?

RUBY: I feel like you want a different answer than I am giving you. For me, the studio is what it is. It is liberating to me, I have total freedom, but it is entrepreneurial at the same time. I work in my studio both as an individual and as a creative director. I have a staff and they help me make decisions regarding how to produce something, whether it be a sculpture or a pair of jeans. The staff assist me in making a schedule, they help decide what shows I do, what I sell, what galleries and curators I work with. In addition, and most importantly, the staff work with me to free up my time so that I can do and make whatever I want.

There is the privilege of having the physical space of the studio that I've been in for the past three years. It's big enough to encompass a lot of different rooms where I can do many different things. Some spaces can be extremely manic: they're dirty, utilitarian, and have a lot of ephemera and stuff in them. Other spaces can be clinical, clean, and open. Some spaces function as areas for research that allow me to contemplate how I can push a particular material, an anodizing process, a painting process, how to shape metal, how to weave a textile. The interplay of the studio allows for a kind of cross-pollination: a scrap from the sewing floor can wind up in a painting and the pattern that has come out of that might lead to research into a type of glaze for a ceramic. That same ceramic can be scanned and turned into a large outdoor work. The studio has allowed me to aggressively push for these kinds of cross-lineages.

GRAW: For me it is your YARD paintings in particular that seem to record studio activities in a quite literal indexical fashion, because they consist of a frottage-like representation of textures and objects from the studio floor. But from a devil's advocate point of view one could also argue that these works mystify or even fetishize artistic labor as being different from or freer than other types of labor. The ceramics are another example of this mystification or fetishization of artistic labor: they consist of leftovers from previous destroyed works. The Basin Theology works, for instance, could be seen as containing relics from your working process. In fact, all the Basin pieces look as if they were archeological relics that have survived a catastrophe. They have been in touch with your studio in a way that makes them quite similar to the YARD paintings. One could even go so far as to draw a connection to the Calvin Klein store that you designed in New York in 2017: it also looks like a work space.

RUBY: Yes, there is a recording or tracing element to the YARD paintings that in a sense makes it possible to take the studio out of the studio. They are remnants of it and they get sent out into the world, similar to what we were talking about with clothing and garments. There is also the notion of the yard, which can be traced back to say Nauman's *Mapping the Studio* video installations [2001–2002]. *Yard* is furthermore a clinical term for incarceration: you pace the yard when you have nowhere to go, to think about things. It's based on repetition, but there's also the notion of surveillance implied in it: we're all constantly looking at things from above, which is a kind of maniacal intensification of the way that we look at the territories of conflict from a distance. And I think you're right, those things wind up becoming sort of mythologized but they also seem to have, I would hope, some kind of sincerity. Even the Basin Theology pieces are themselves recycled and reincorporated into newer works. And I don't know how I could ever claim it didn't have a kind of devil's advocate component to it unless I only hoarded the work and never sent anything out. Because ultimately, as soon as the work leaves the studio, it becomes something in another system that I can't control, as much as I've tried—particularly if we're looking at the past ten to fifteen years of the art economy and the way that art is distributed and sold and viewed and exchanged. It has become so complex and so much of an industry and so much of a system in and of itself: I just can't keep thinking about those things.

GRAW: I would like to come back to the Calvin Klein store in New York. To me it signifies "work space" due to all the scaffolding, the mobile elements, the fabrics loosely hung over bars, which remind me of how Cady Noland hung stuff over bars in the eighties. All the stuffed textile objects are on pedestals that are similar to your earlier minimal objects. The one that's covered with the American flag fabric also has a quite central position in the store. Things lie around in a way that is quite similar to the photographs that I've seen of your studio. The space has a quasi-industrial atmosphere and is painted yellow, which is surprising considering the purist aesthetics formerly associated with Calvin Klein.

RUBY: I was brought into Calvin Klein to work with Raf Simons to give the company a different identity and to rebrand it. The New York flagship store was originally designed by John Pawson and it was kind of monochromatic: mostly grays and beige colors. Judd and Pawson were very good friends so there was a lot of very simple Judd furniture, while the palette was pure Pawson. I thought: Here's this very American company that's elevating itself to the high-fashion, couture level of European luxury-goods houses. And Calvin Klein's history is very clean, clinical, and often, in their ad campaigns, sexy. The idea of the store was that it would be temporary so that we would have a very quick turnaround with something that didn't need permitting or construction, something that signified a very quick change to the company. One of the things I thought right off the bat was: Let's add a lot of energy, let's add a lot of manic layering, and let's add color. I wanted to paint everything safety yellow, construction yellow, and I wanted to put scaffolding in there to signify what this new brand was going to be identified with, to create a collage that contained all the things that were to come for the company. My whole understanding of sewing and textiles when I was growing up was formed mostly through quilts and here I wanted to present them in the way I had experienced them on a farm after they had been washed and hung over quilt-drying racks. I liked that it was a different experience, that it freed up the hierarchies between the gallery and museum systems and the worlds of retail and fashion. People didn't perceive the store as they would perceive an exhibition of mine in a gallery. It was a different way to do things, and in a different setting.

GRAW: When I was looking at your FLAGS—*DEEP FLAG (6126)*, for example, which consist of bleached and dyed fabric—I was reminded of the nineties fashion trend of bleached jeans. In general, one could say that fashion is the subtext of your work.

RUBY: Yes, in a way. What appealed to me with those pieces was that bleaching was an industrial process that came out of the garment industry, not art. And I liked to push it into something larger than life, a painting or as a massive tapestry. But I also started to think about bleaching as a negation. It's not only about pulling color out of a garment, but also like a photographic process: we have to use a stop bath for instance, to stop the bleach from eating through the fabric. Technically I liked that there was a destructive aspect to it. But I couldn't have gotten there unless that genre of jeans had been created twenty or thirty years prior.

GRAW: What is it that attracts you to the visual language of fashion?

RUBY: I like taking something that exists and abstracting it into something new, and I do this in the studio with my own work. I enjoy the process of repurposing and reassociating, recannibalizing: to take something that has been dug up over time and give it a totally different assessment in a kind of archaeological way. I also like how fashion is associated with culture, and when you look back at the history of fashion, it's about gender, it's about performance, it's about sexuality. Fashion can be more democratic and direct. There's the performativity and public aspect of it, too. It's a tool wielded by bodies, to assimilate or to transgress.

GRAW: For me there is a tension in your work between the large, very craft-heavy steel sculptures—the STOVES for instance—and works such as the ceramic Basins, the textile paintings, the stuffed textile objects, the printed fabrics, which seem to occupy formerly female terrain. Of course, there is also a long history of women artists who have used aesthetics that were formerly associated with female amateurs and the sphere of reproduction, from Anni Albers and Louise Bourgeois to Rosemarie Trockel, Cosima von Bonin, and Lucy McKenzie. And there have been many male artists, say from Sigmar Polke to Mike Kelley, who claimed these aesthetics as well. You talked about crafts being gendered from an autobiographical perspective earlier, and I'd like to ask you about what it means to be a male artist occupying terrain that still has female connotations.

RUBY: I keep coming back to what I experienced before I knew art. My mother passed away a long time ago, and I never asked her why she gave me a sewing machine when I was going to a school that was so militant about gender. I would get into fights and get threatened and called things and there was such a confusion about what I was sexually or gender-wise because of it. I didn't realize that at the time that it must have seemed to these guys like I was fucking with them—guys who were so straight they wanted to kill anything that wasn't.

GRAW: So you were their target with your sewing machine.

RUBY: Yes, but whether or not I understood it like that at the time, I was empowered by it. Once I thought of myself as an artist, I felt that I personally embraced both female and male aspects in me and realized that what was being thrown at me when I was young was wrong. It never felt like I was repurposing or appropriating something.

GRAW: Let's talk about one sculpture more in detail, *The Cup*, from 2013 [fig. 2]. Due to the many dripped layers of red resin, this cup looks wet and liquid, almost like flesh that's alive. It evokes sexual associations in how it resembles a giant open vessel, perhaps female genitalia or a menstrual cup. Were you aiming for such connotations in this work?

RUBY: I think that it was a bit accidental. I was thinking more about the potential energy of this particular sculpture, whether it was pouring something out or scooping something up. I was also thinking about it in terms of America and older notions of the melting pot. It was meant to be an absolutely bloody, aggressive war cup, which was in a position of frozen stasis, unable to do one thing or the other for itself.

GRAW: This reading of it as allegorizing America is interesting considering that you have written its title on the plinth, where you can read THE CUP.

RUBY: [*Laughs*] So dumb, right?

GRAW: Yes, but it reminds me of artists like Picabia, who also wrote the titles onto his paintings—using a Dada strategy—which created this, as you say, stupid tautology effect. It is a way to suggest meaning while making fun of it and erasing it. Language often enters your work, but why did you write THE CUP on this plinth?

RUBY: When I was finishing up the work I kept telling myself *it's the cup, it's the cup*, and then—this piece took a while to make—we kept talking about it. We'd write it on the board, *it's the cup*. And I don't know, sometimes these things have to be so didactic that they weirdly become cryptic. And I wanted there to be no doubt in anybody's mind that it was THE cup.

GRAW: There's another detail in another body of work that also intrigued me. In your fabric paintings, such as the FLAGS, there are always stripes at the margins. I wondered why?

RUBY: For a while I was looking back at my earlier spray paintings which all have a frame painted on the edges of the synthetic canvas. It's a very hazy paint out, but I like it formally—when one of these paintings is hanging on the wall it has a very dark edge that gives it a kind of space and depth. This frame makes the painting appear as if it's recessed. When I'm working on collages and drawings, I always consider the frame, so this concept has always been on my mind. With the FLAGS, I started working with a mill in Minnesota that is mostly known for its sports jerseys: it is the biggest supplier of basketball and football sports jerseys and has the most vibrant colors we could find. I started thinking that not only did these textile pieces need a frame or a border, but also that the frame was a way to imbue them with a kind of politics. Flag production offers a conceptual way to lay out another history of textile production; it makes reference to other nationalities and other countries, other borders.

GRAW: That's interesting, because when I looked at these frames, as you call them, I thought that they created a picture-in-picture effect. They produce distance, as if what you see is put into quotation marks.

RUBY: That's right, that's also what I was thinking.

GRAW: So we agree here? [*Laughs*]

RUBY: We agree. Yeah, you got it.

Plates

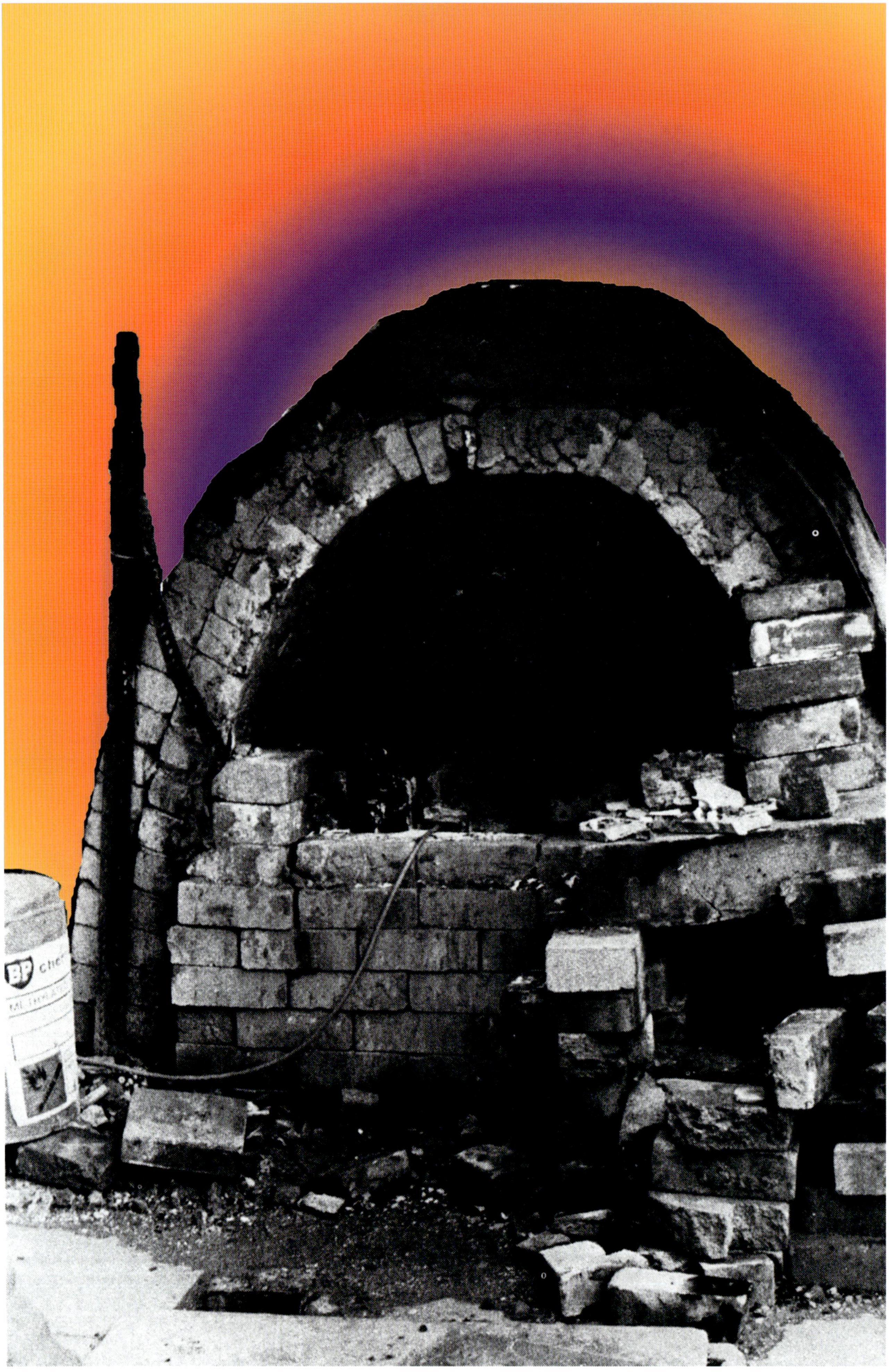
BP

Two-Dimensional Works

COLLAGE, as a formal and conceptual methodology, is the backbone of Sterling Ruby's multidisciplinary practice. It infuses all of his artistic output: from his early works on paper to his DRFTRS—collage-hybrids of "nomadic" images set against expressionistic landscapes—from his WIDW paintings, layered with cut cardboard and fabric swaths, to his bleached BC canvases, pasted over with colorful fabric. In his early collages, drawings, and prints, Ruby fleshed out the complex lexicon of forms and motifs that he returns to repeatedly through his work in all media. For example, the teardrops in *Crystal Cryer* (2001) portend the use of drops as a motif in Ruby's later works, just as *Kiln #1* (2005) emphasizes the centrality of the kiln. Ruby is a compulsive collector of images, objects, and materials, which he organized in the studio initially as series of archives conceived for research and development purposes. In 2009, he started converting these various archives into an image database housed on a once public website. It was through this process of digitization that the links between these materials crystallized for Ruby such that the archive became a work in itself—*Sterling Ruby: Desktop Vol. 1* (2011)[1]—and the studio as archive and site to be excavated came into sharper relief.

Ruby has described collage as an "illicit merger," and he often combines hand-drawn elements into his collages to build on the medium's transgressive potency. In *Prison* (2004), for example, Ruby extends the rigid geometries from an image of a locked jail cell in Day-Glo colored pencil lines that picture the cell within a weblike structure. The American prison-industrial complex and super-maximum security prisons in particular recur in Ruby's work, a theme he explores also in *CDC at PDC Study* (2008), where a centralized columnar shape made of cut octagonal images, including aerial views of prisons, is oriented on top of sullied paper the color of orange prison uniforms. Stills from American horror movies are a unique subset of images Ruby returns to often as well. A still from *Invasion of the Body Snatchers* (1978) is overlaid on a Pennsylvania Dutch quilt in *Quilt/Body Snatchers* (2004), while the ghoulish hands of the titular character of *Pumpkinhead* (1988) are juxtaposed again on orange paper with optically patterned spheres in Ruby's *Pumpkin Head* (2008). These images of the American prison system and horror movies are envisioned as part of a continuum in Ruby's incessant mapping of the dark terrain of the American subconscious.

Ruby's prints extend the logic of collage into the space of photography. In the claustrophobic *Cry 2005* (2005), a centralized image of a prospector's pickax—a tool of excavation that also points to the California gold rush—is crowded by densely kaleidoscopic images of a fractured domesticity, graffitied over with the word "CRY." Other works incorporate language in this spray-painted script, such as a group of works that reimagine the phrase "death cult" against different backgrounds. In *DEATH CULT (6150)* (2016), for example, Ruby revisits an earlier print, *Forest in Parts* (2005), a found picture of the forest cut up and reoriented so that a spider's web looms over the otherwise serene scene. In *DEATH CULT (6150)*, the saturated greens and browns of the original are flattened in black-and-white, and the text adds an intense layer that punctuates a sense of threat indicated by the spider's web. Ruby inscribes collage similarly in all of his work—whether he is reusing textile scraps, the cardboard from the floor of his painting studio, or old bleach bottles—as the studio superstructure itself spawns new, seemingly self-generated, self-referential works and series.

—J. D.

1. *Sterling Ruby: Desktop Vol. 1* was published to coincide with a solo exhibition.

Kiln #1, 2005
Lambda print

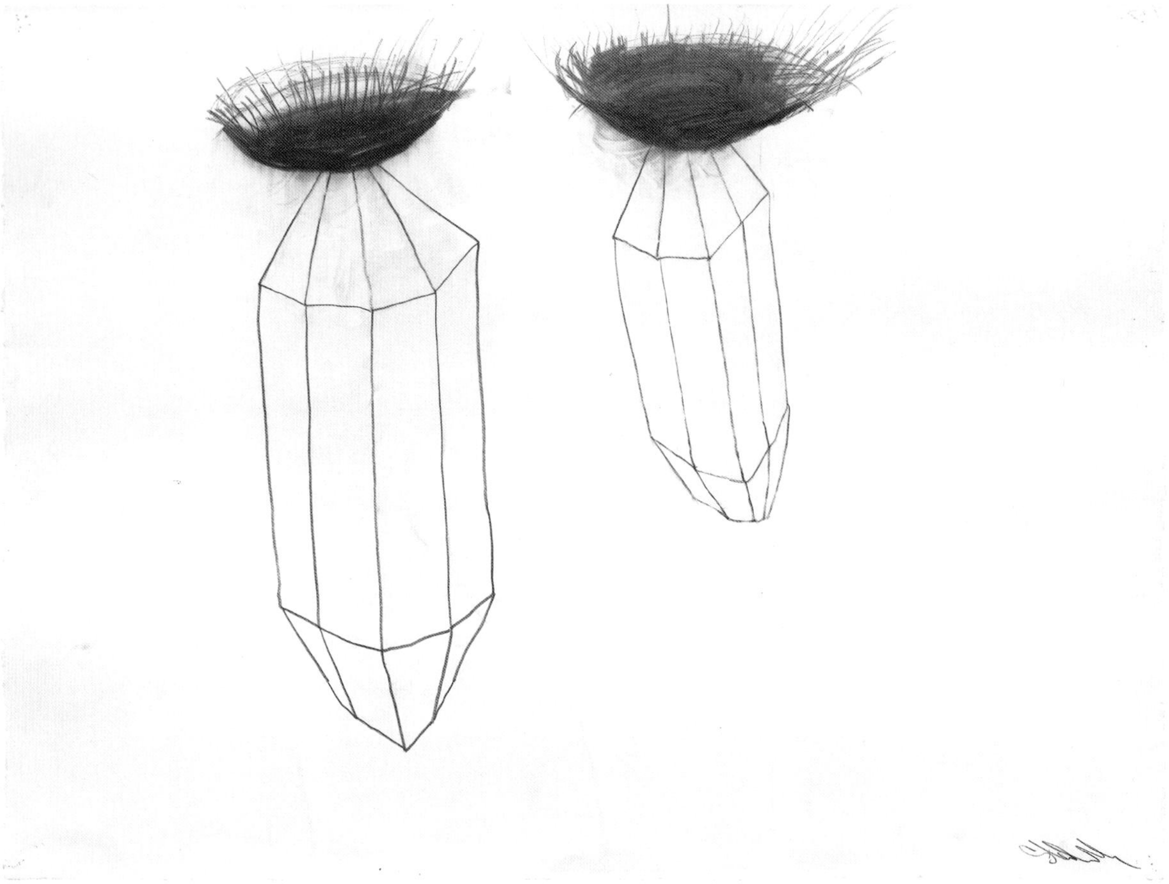

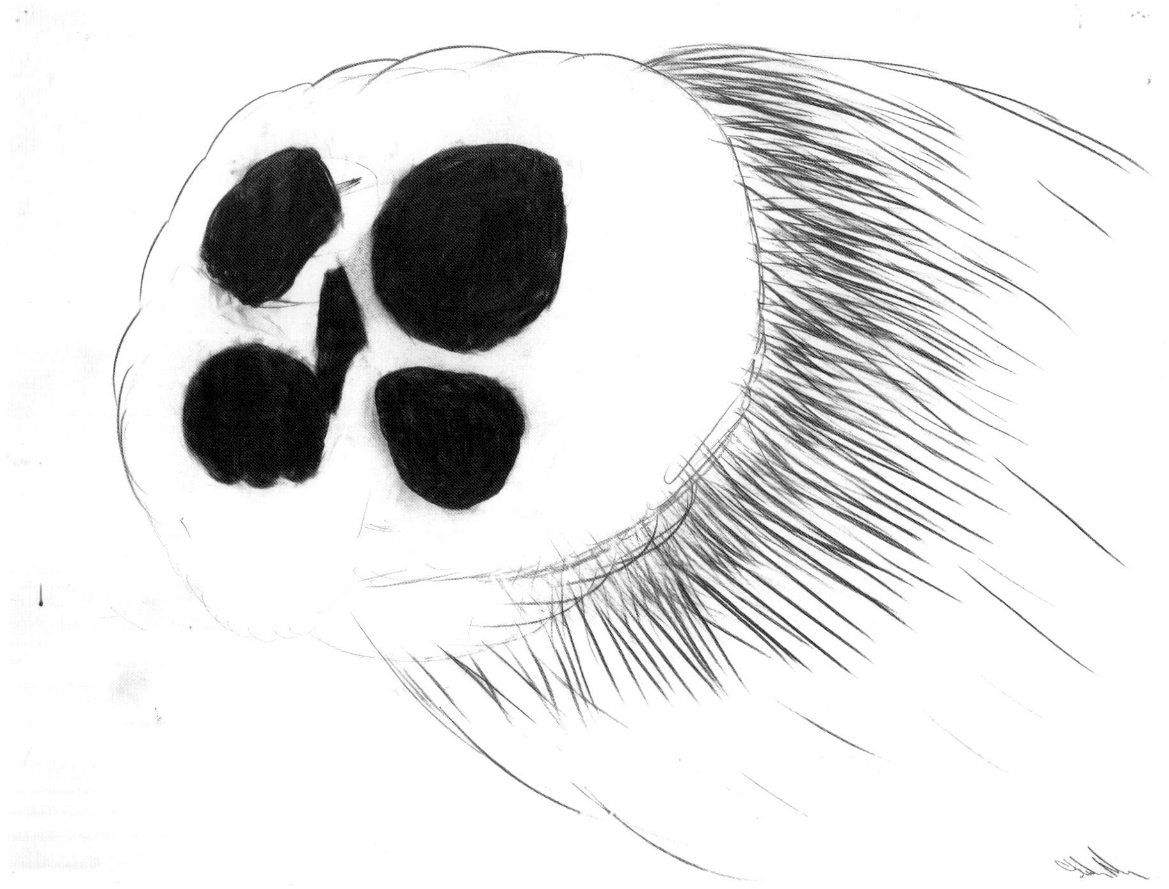

Top:
***Crystal Cryer*, 2001**
Pencil on paper

Bottom:
***Snowball*, 2001**
Pencil on paper

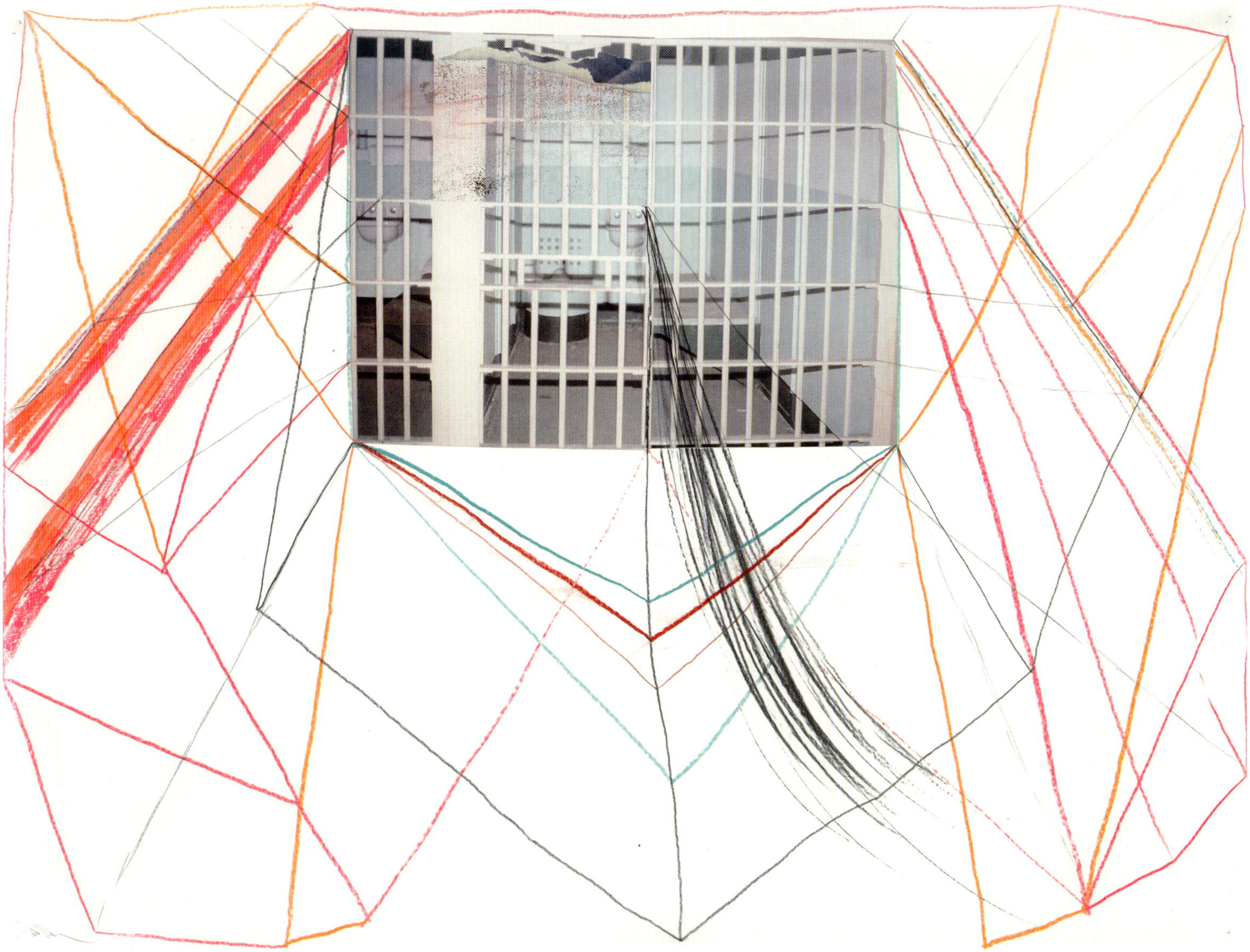

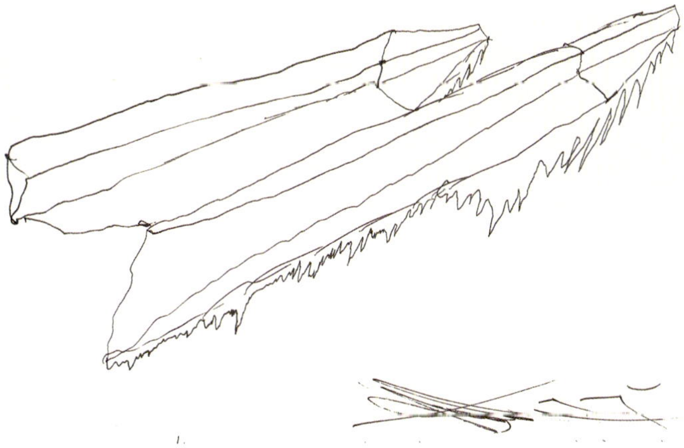

Top:
***Prison*, 2004**
Collage and colored pencil on paper

Bottom:
***DR (6503)*, 2017**
Pen on paper

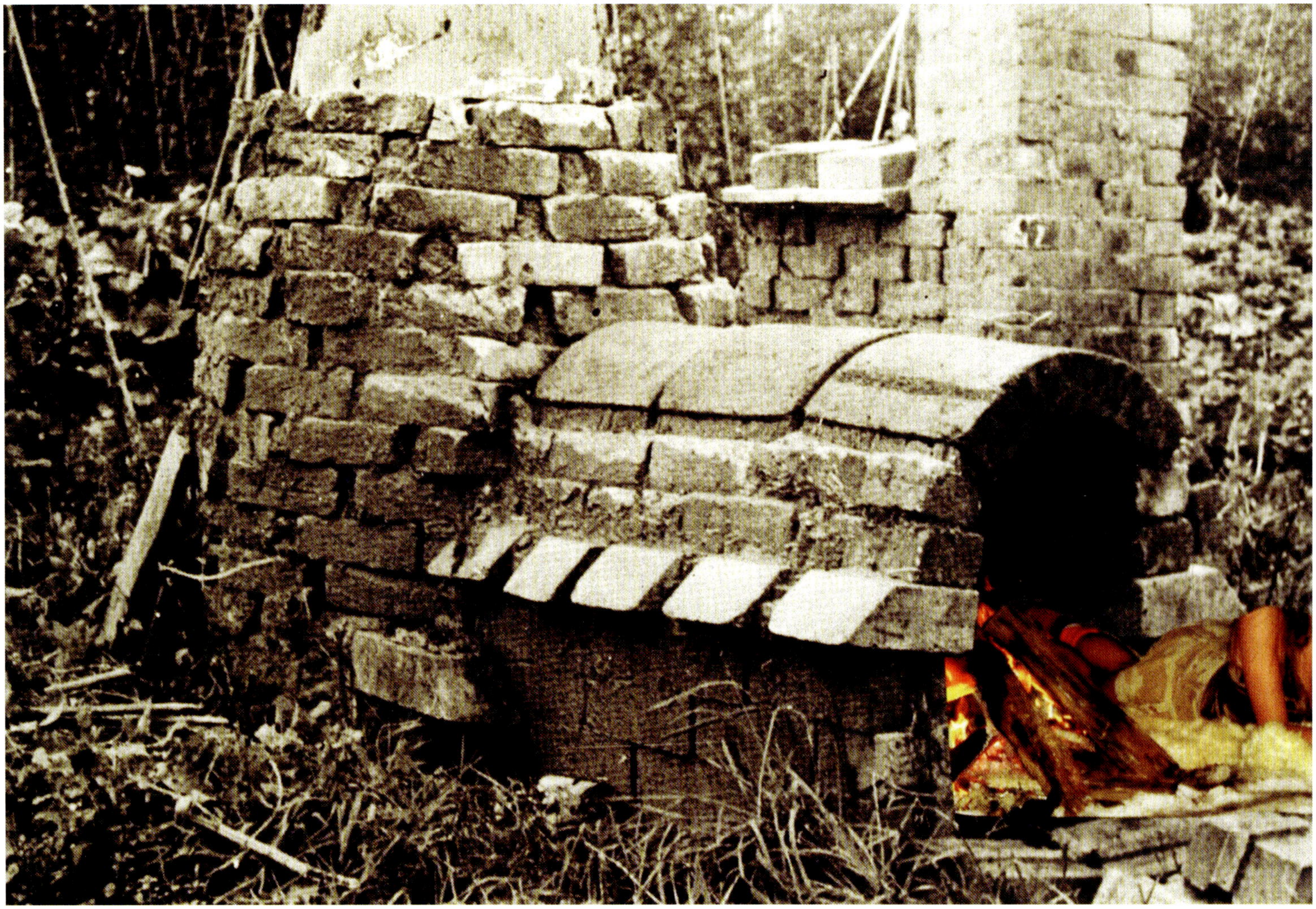

Girl in Kiln, 2004
Lambda print

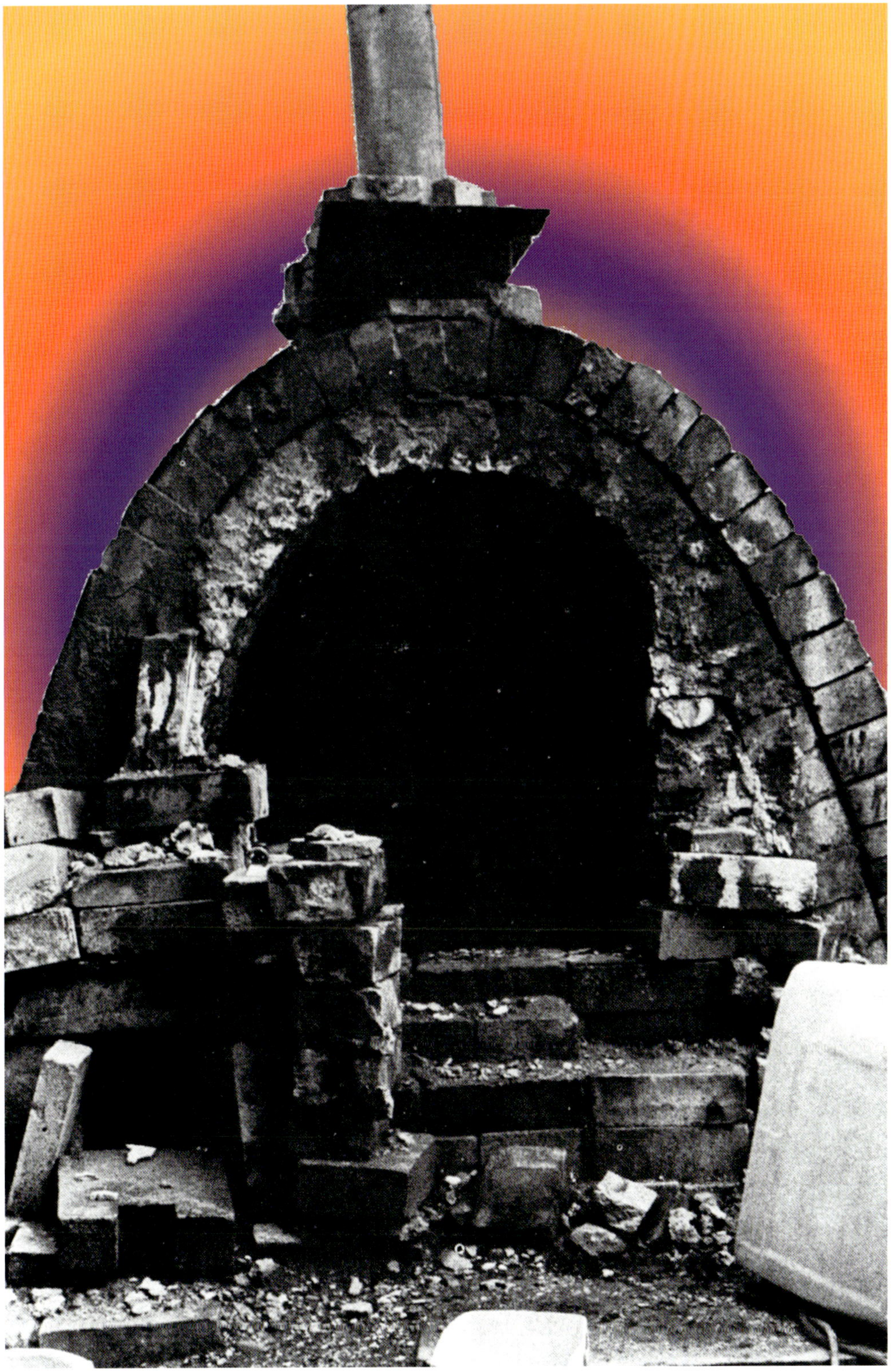

Kiln #2, **2005**
Lambda print

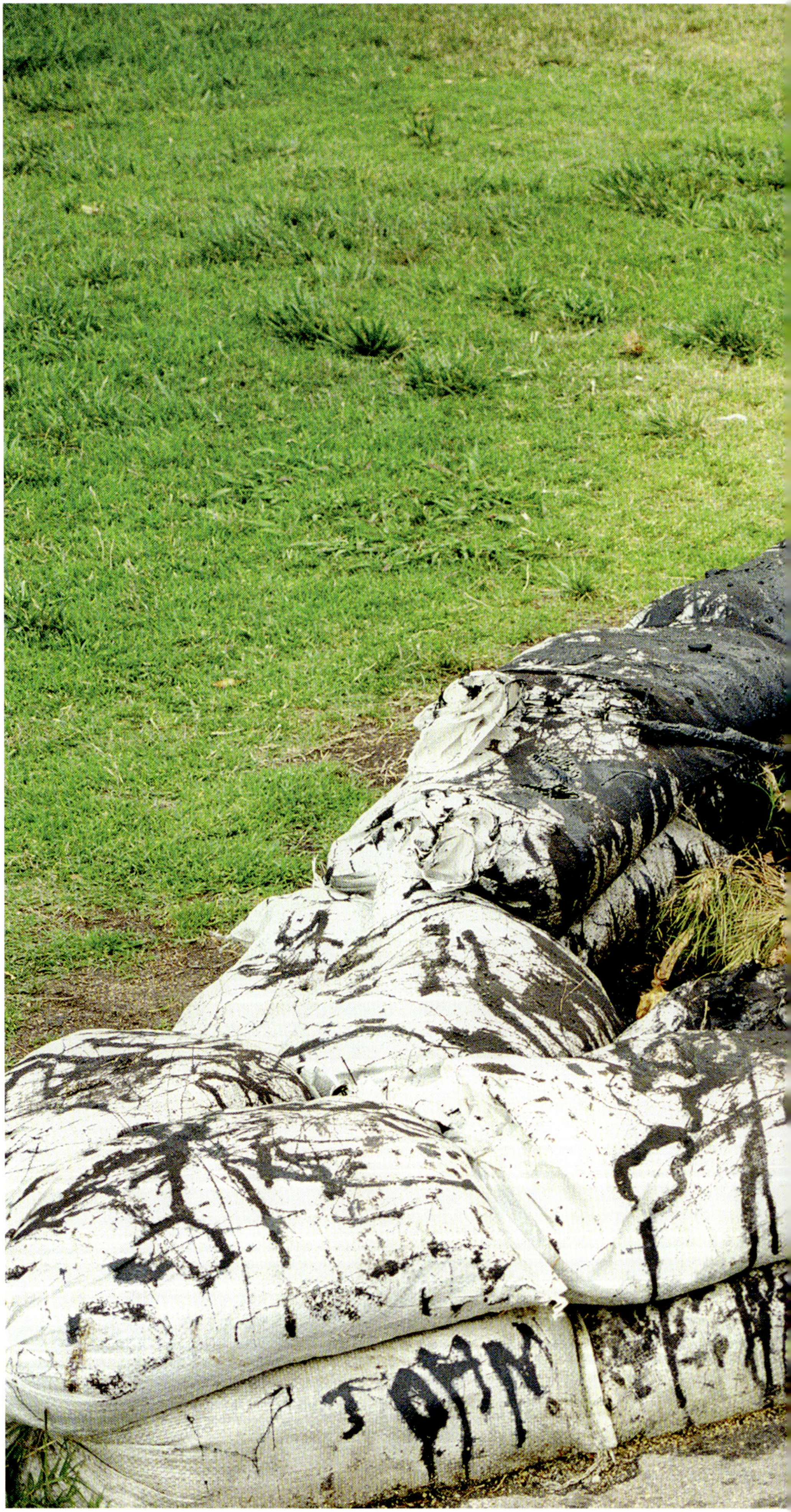

Transient Bed of John, 2003
Lambda print

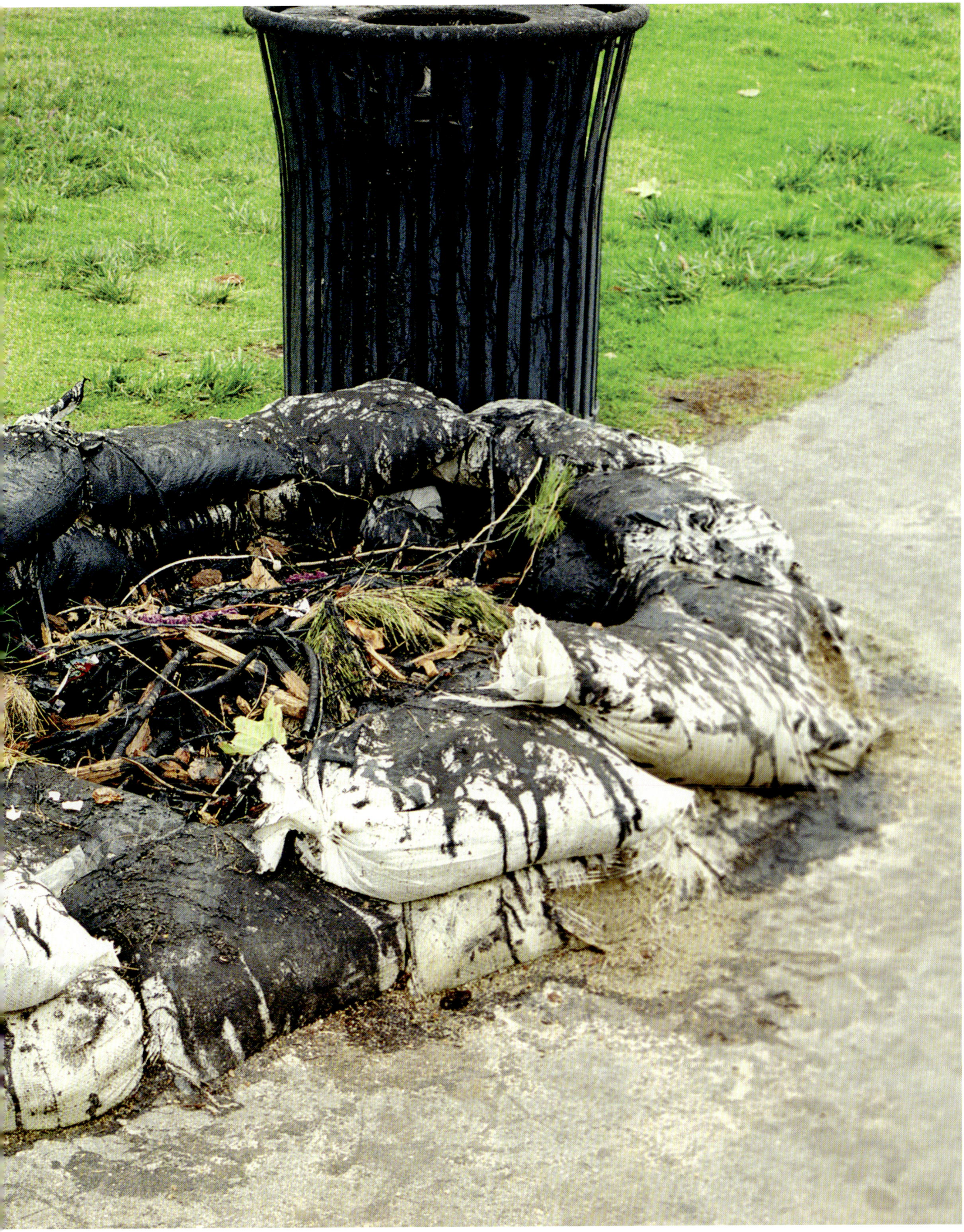

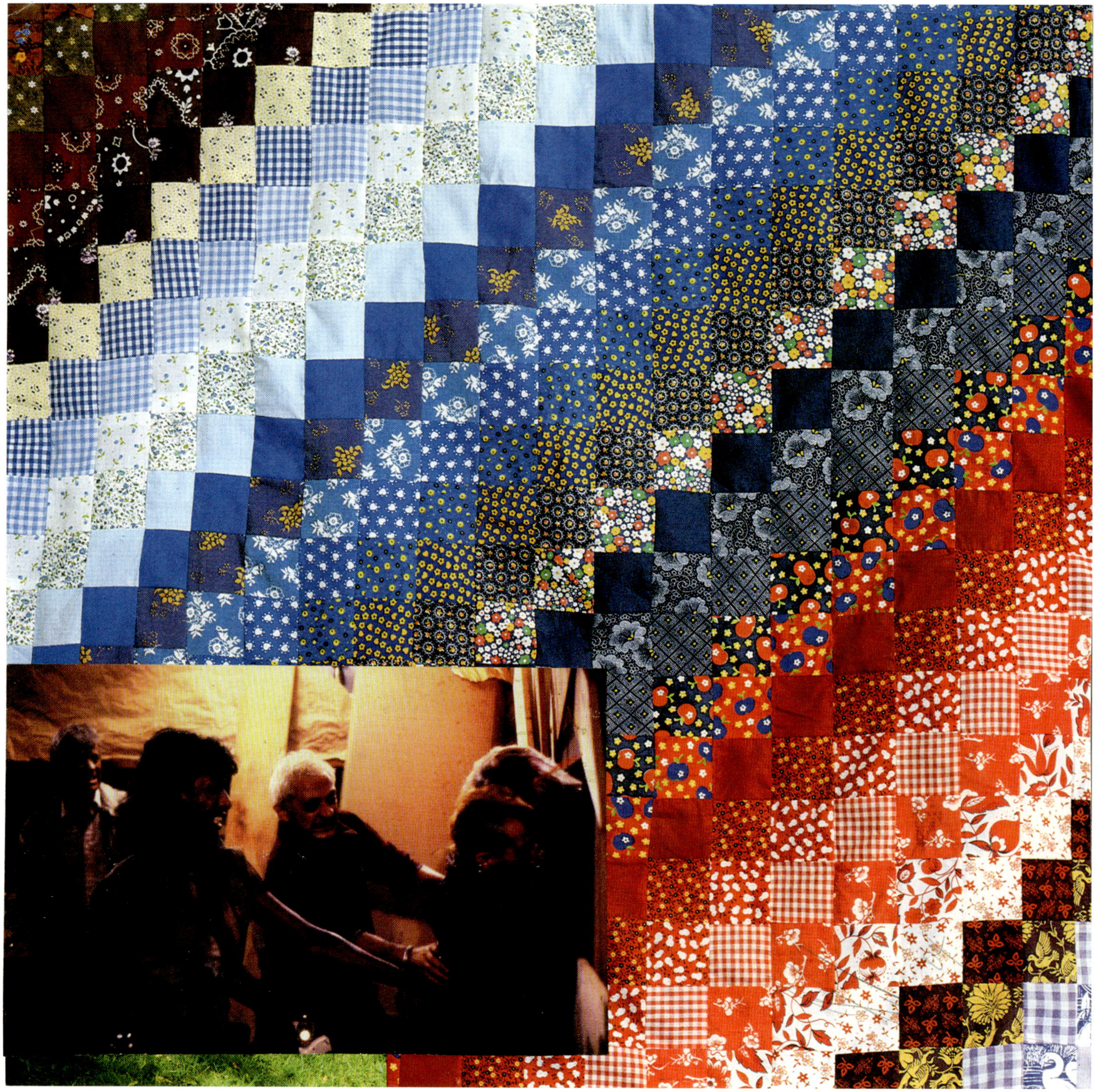

Quilt/Body Snatchers, 2004
Collage on paper

Opposite, top to bottom:

Nails, Mammary, Stalagmites, 2010
Collage on paper

DRFTRS (6007), 2016
Collage, paint, and glue on paper

STAR SKY, 2014
Collage, paint, and glue on paper

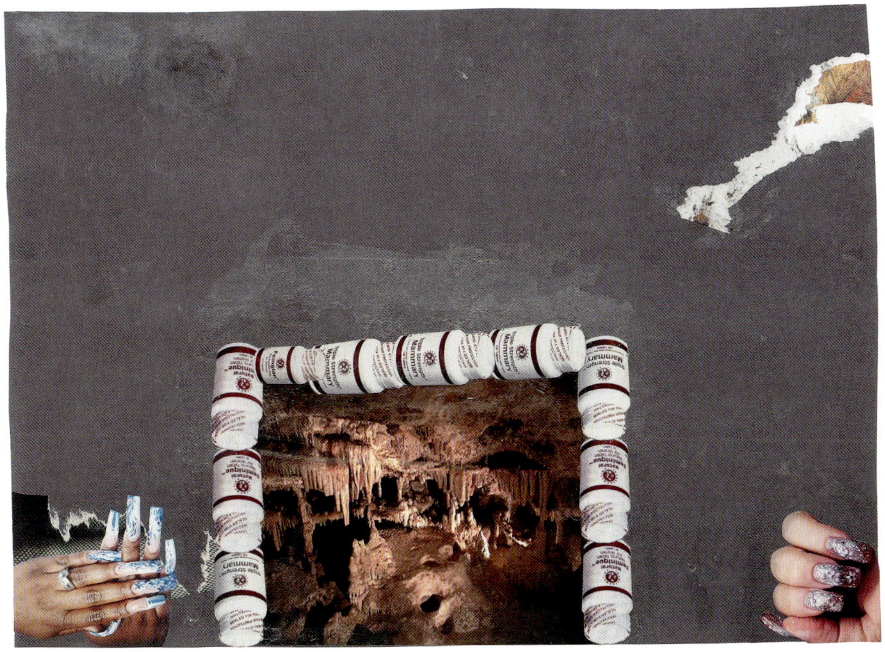

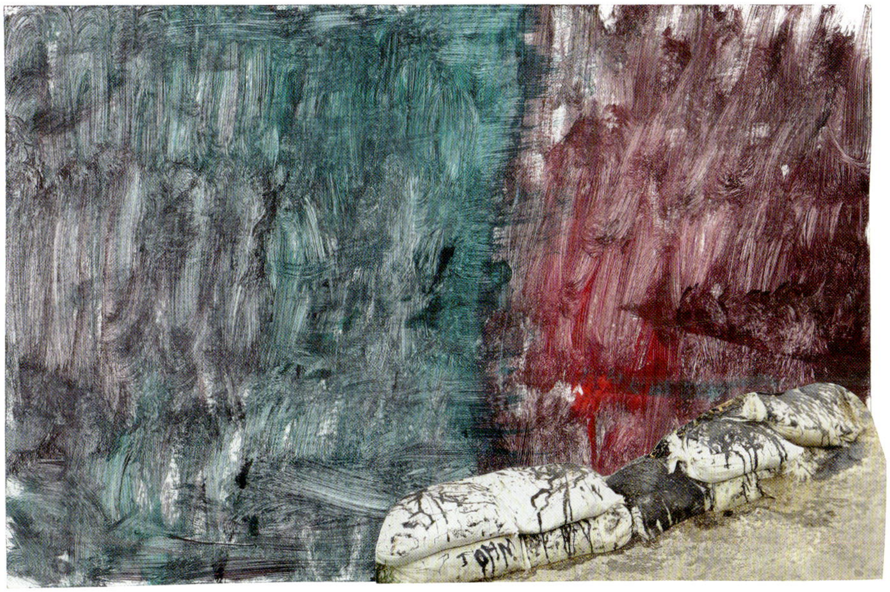

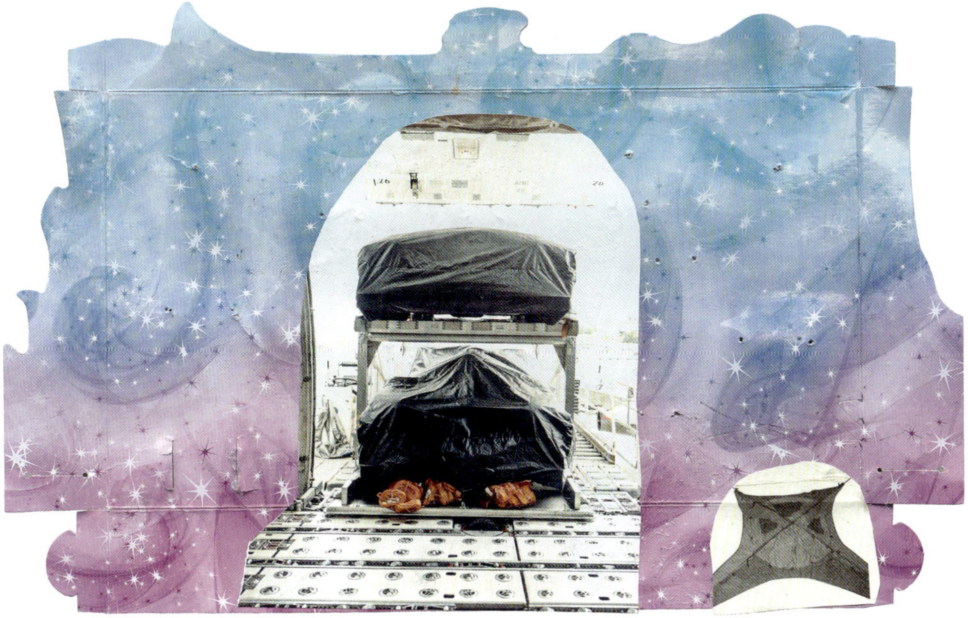

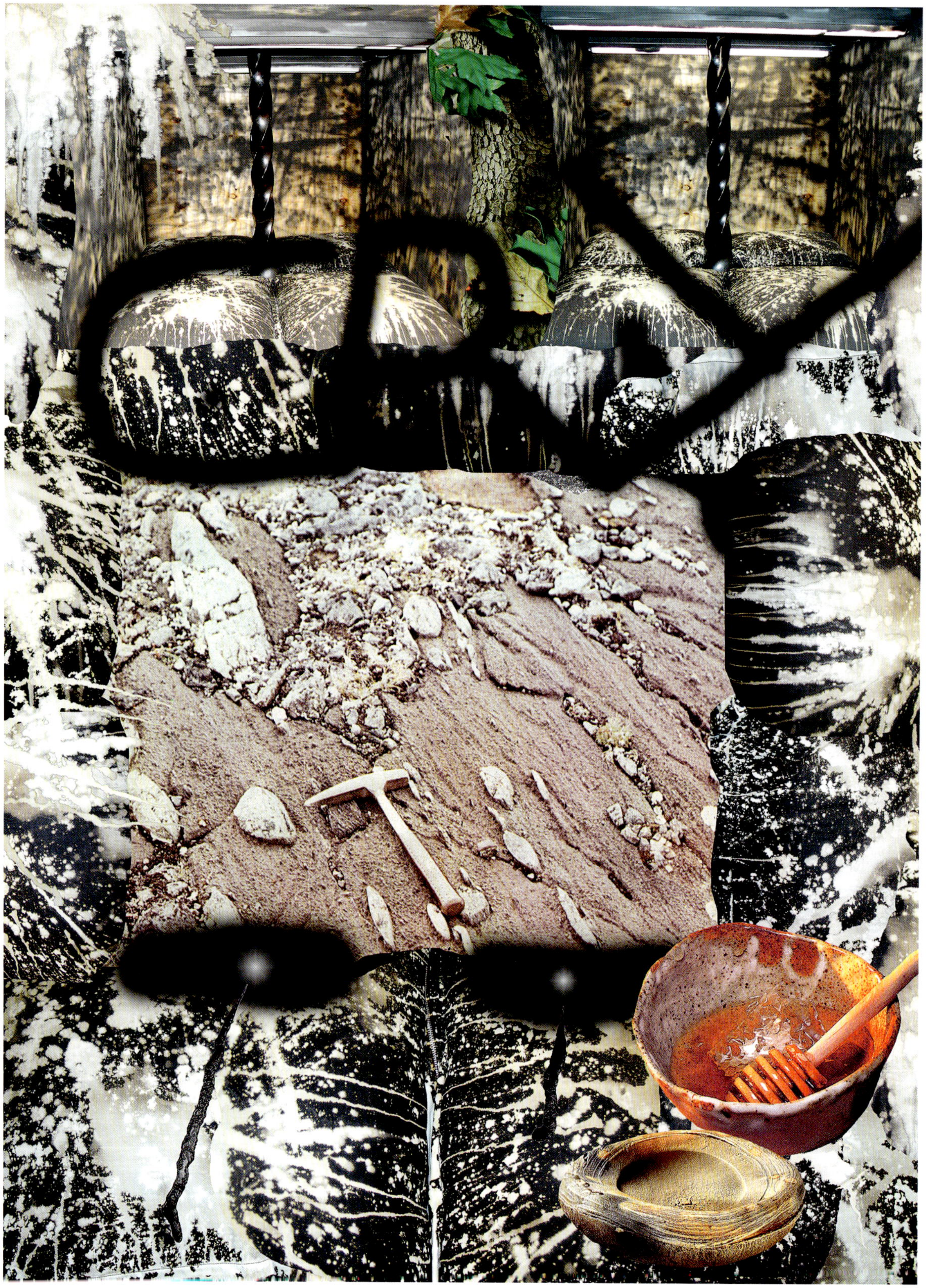

Cry 2005, 2005
Lambda print

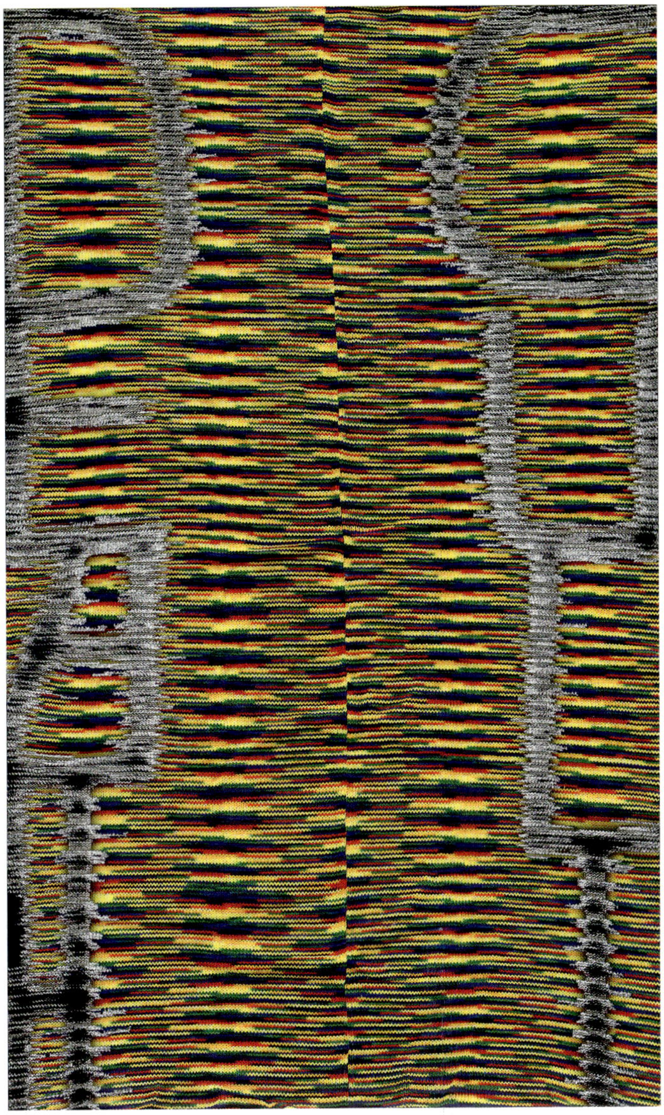

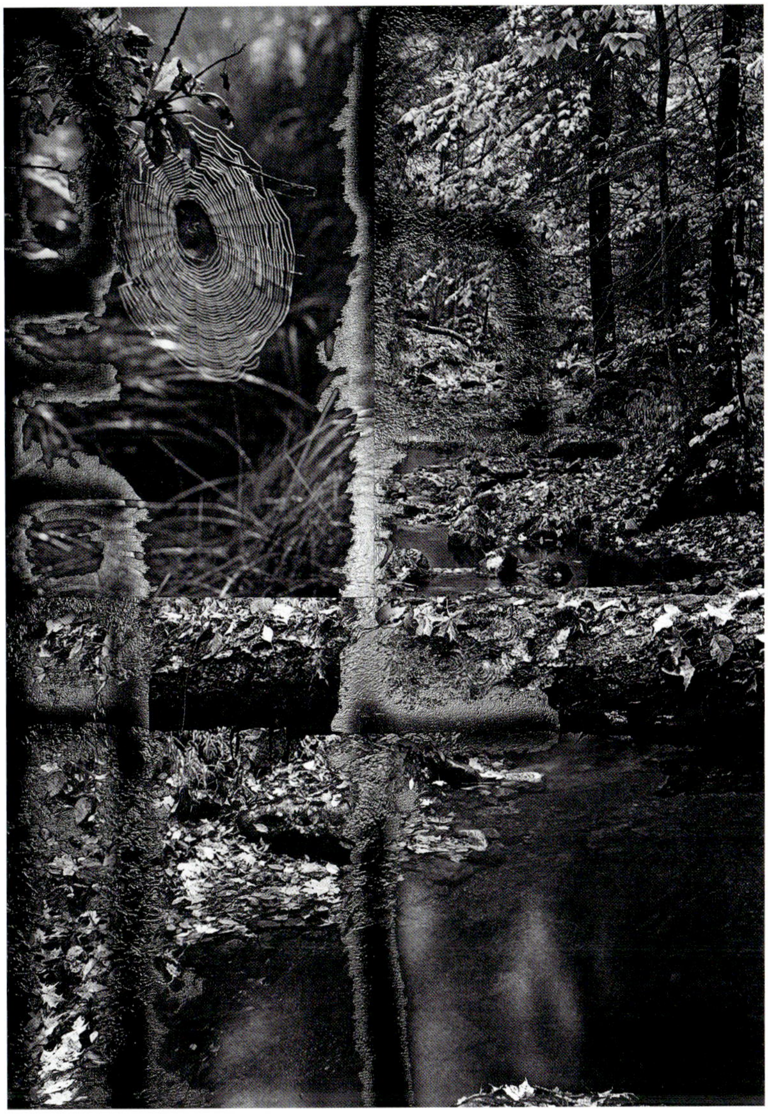

Left:
***DEATH CULT (6148)*, 2016**
Archival inkjet print

Right:
***DEATH CULT (6150)*, 2016**
Archival inkjet print

HRG Suite, 2006
Collage on paper

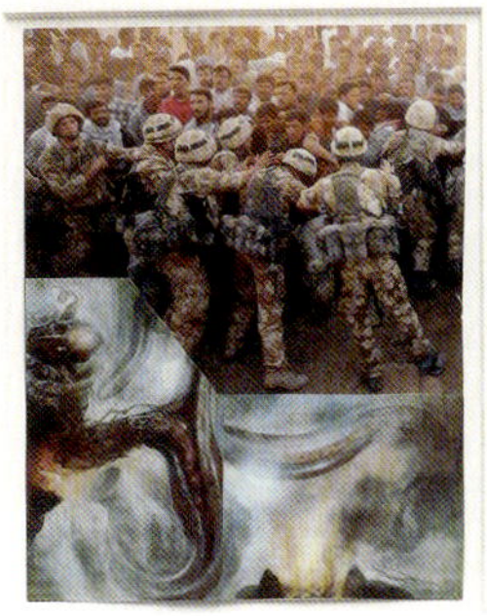
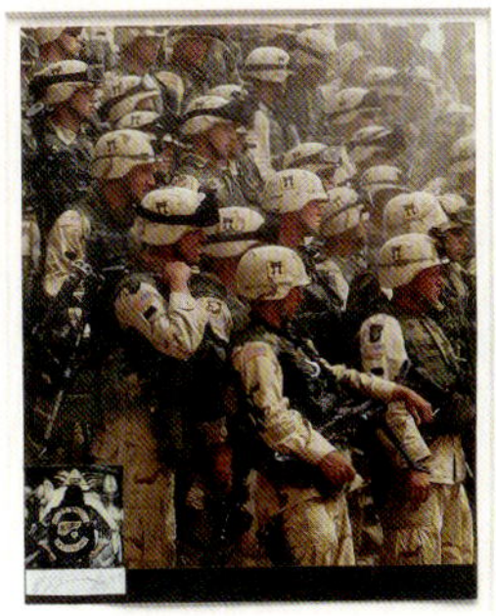
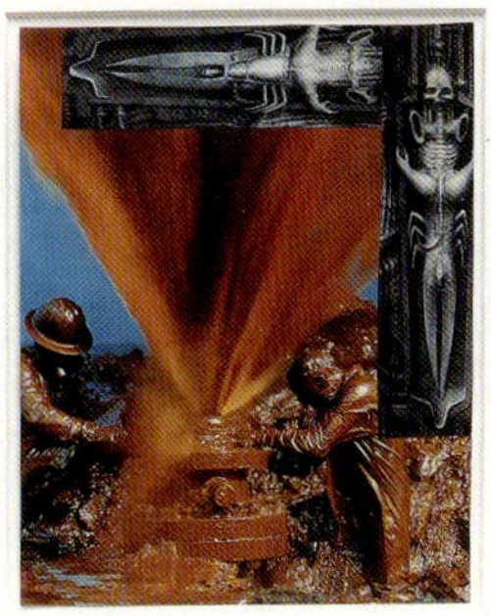
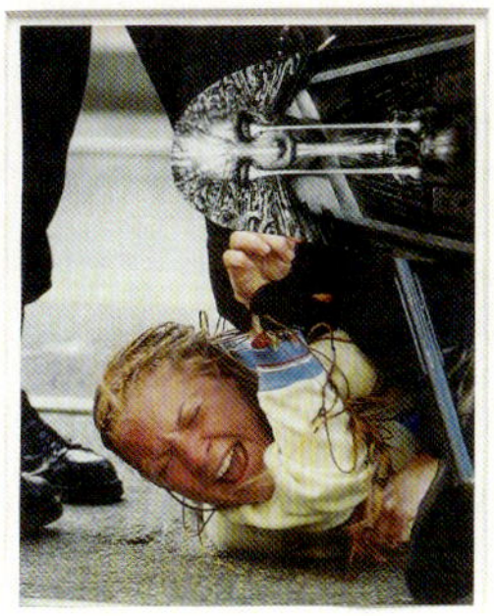
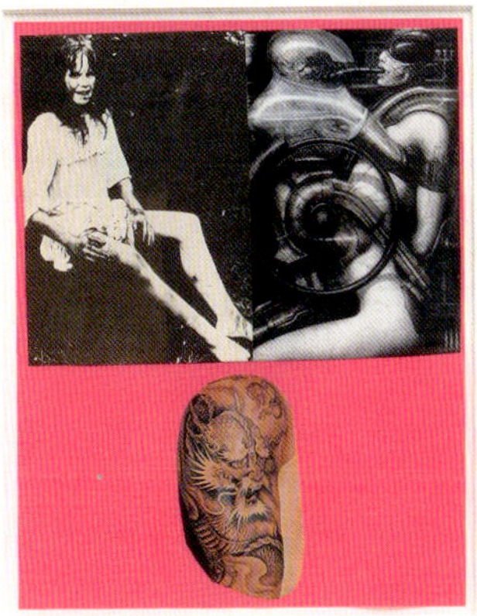
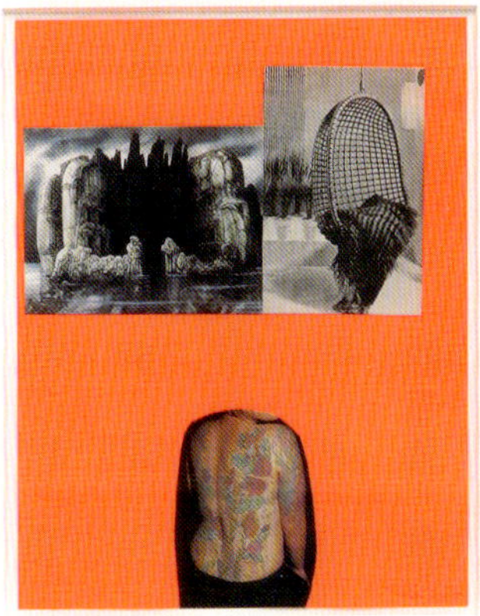
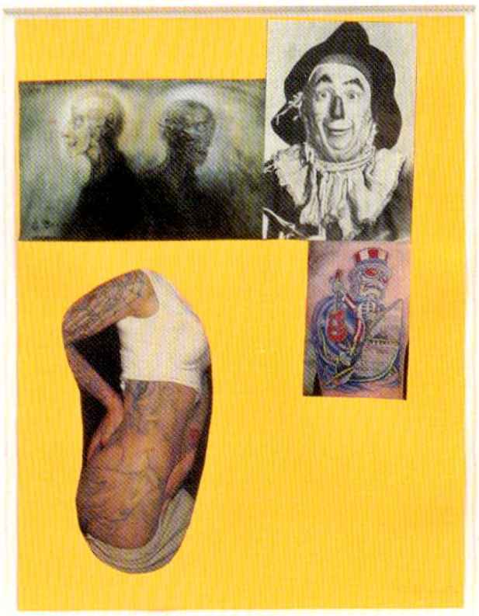
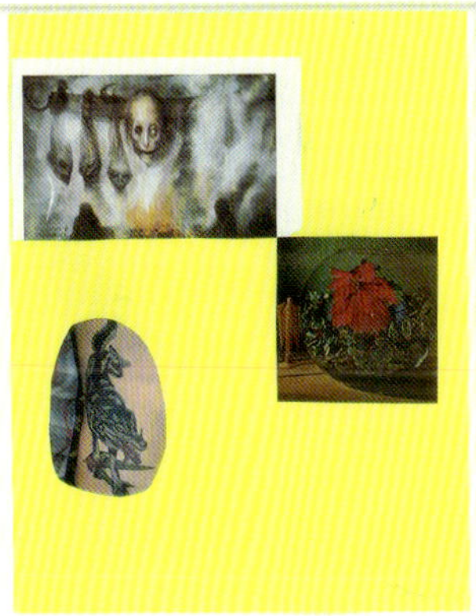
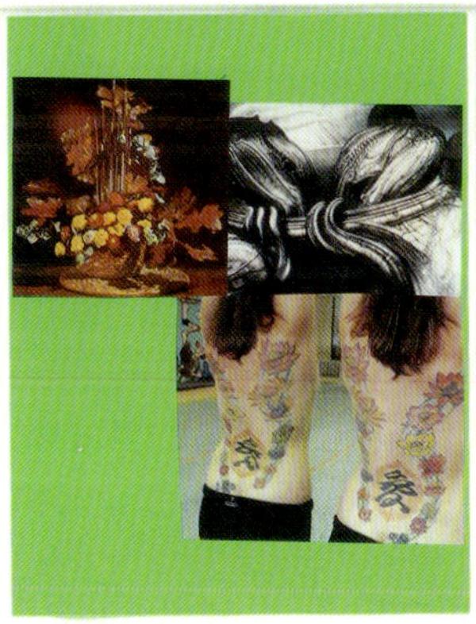

Pelican Bay Abstract, 2009
Collage and paint on paper

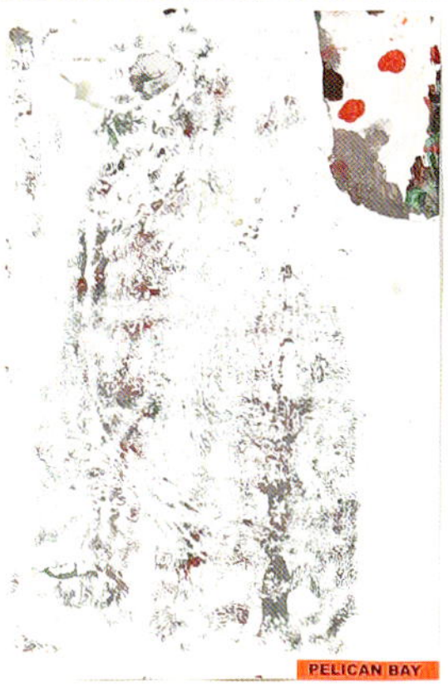
PELICAN BAY

PELICAN BAY

PELICAN BAY

PELICAN BAY

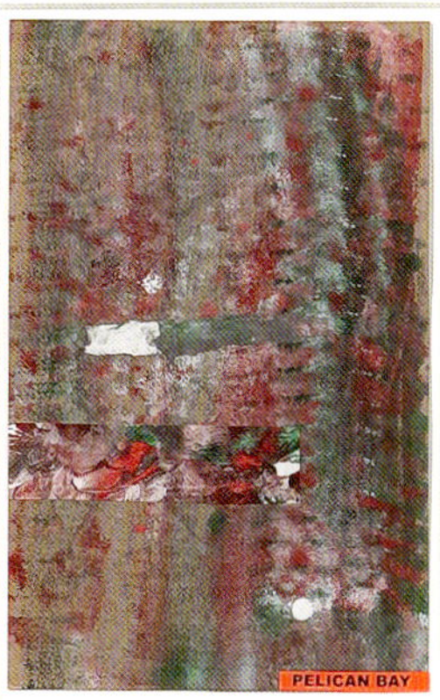
PELICAN BAY

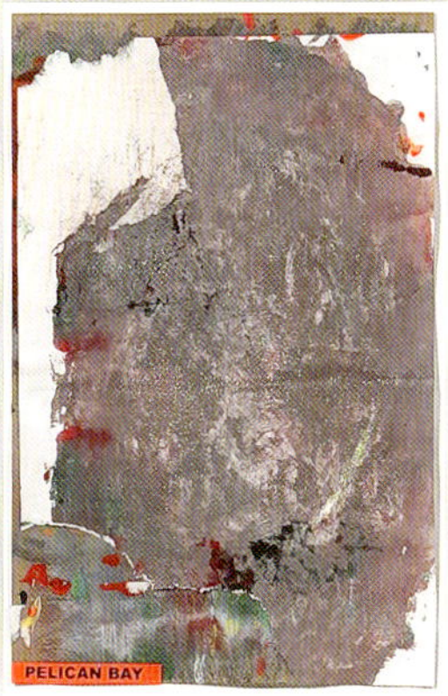
PELICAN BAY

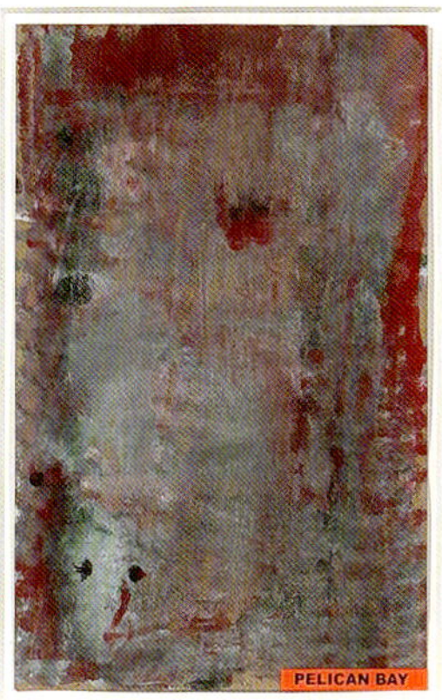
PELICAN BAY

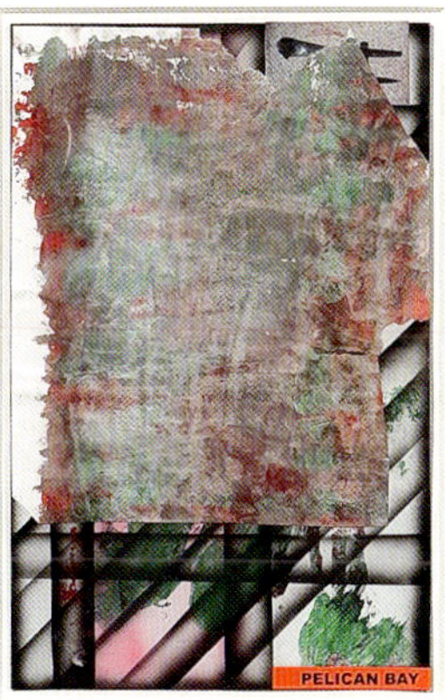
PELICAN BAY

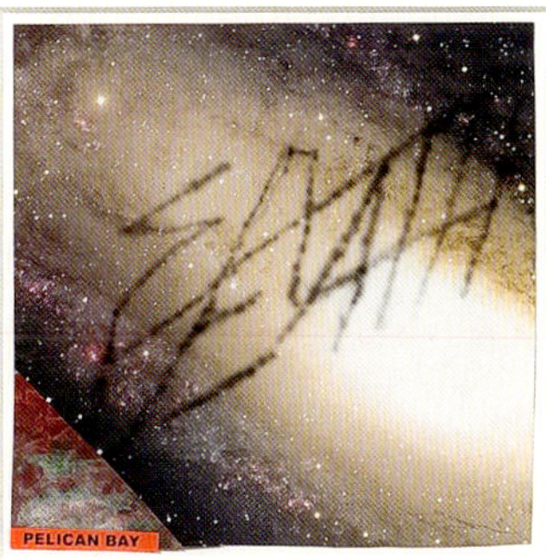
PELICAN BAY

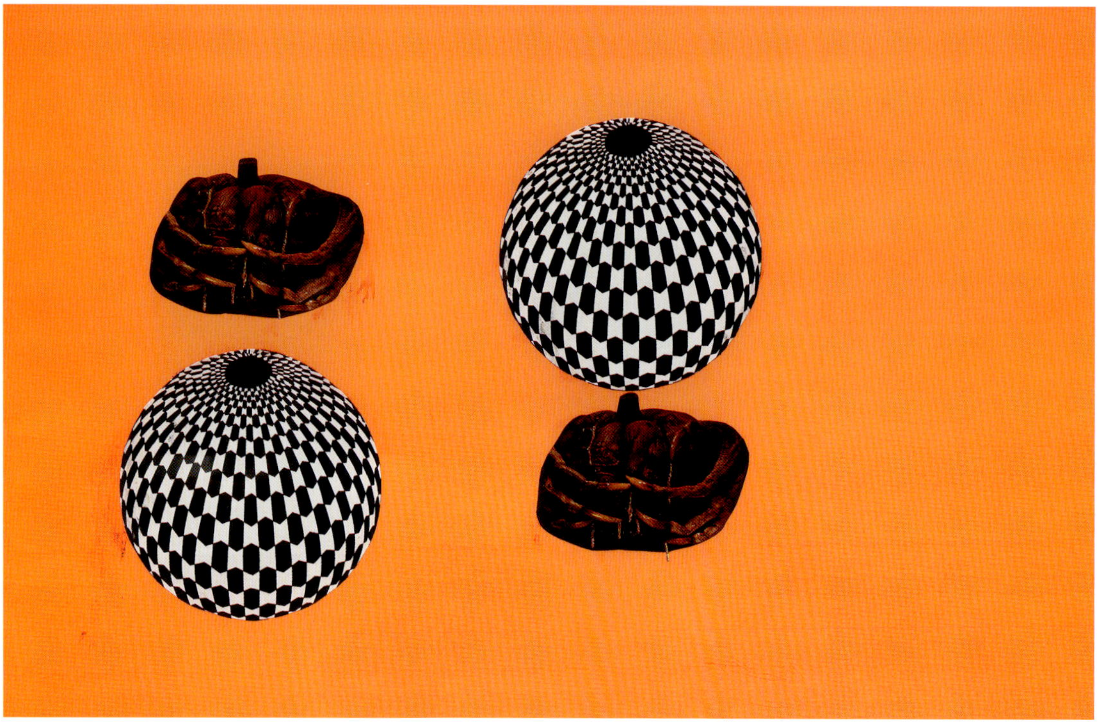

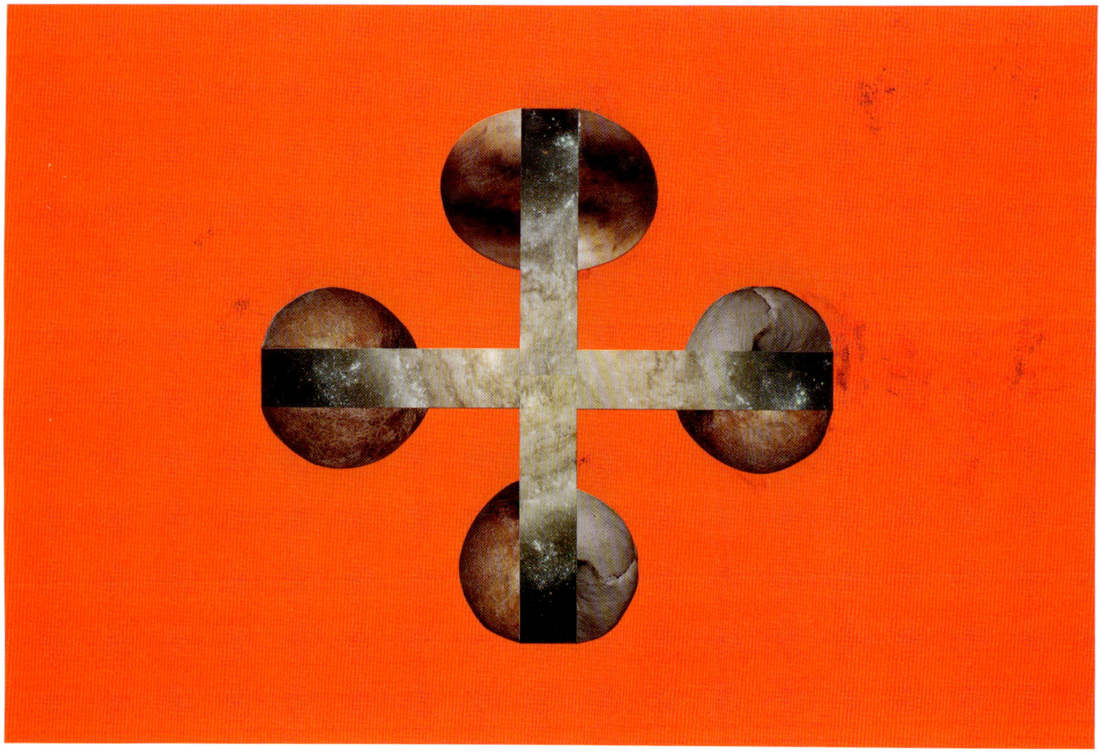

Top:
Pumpkin Head, 2008
Collage on paper

Bottom:
Head Trekkers 17, 2010
Collage on paper

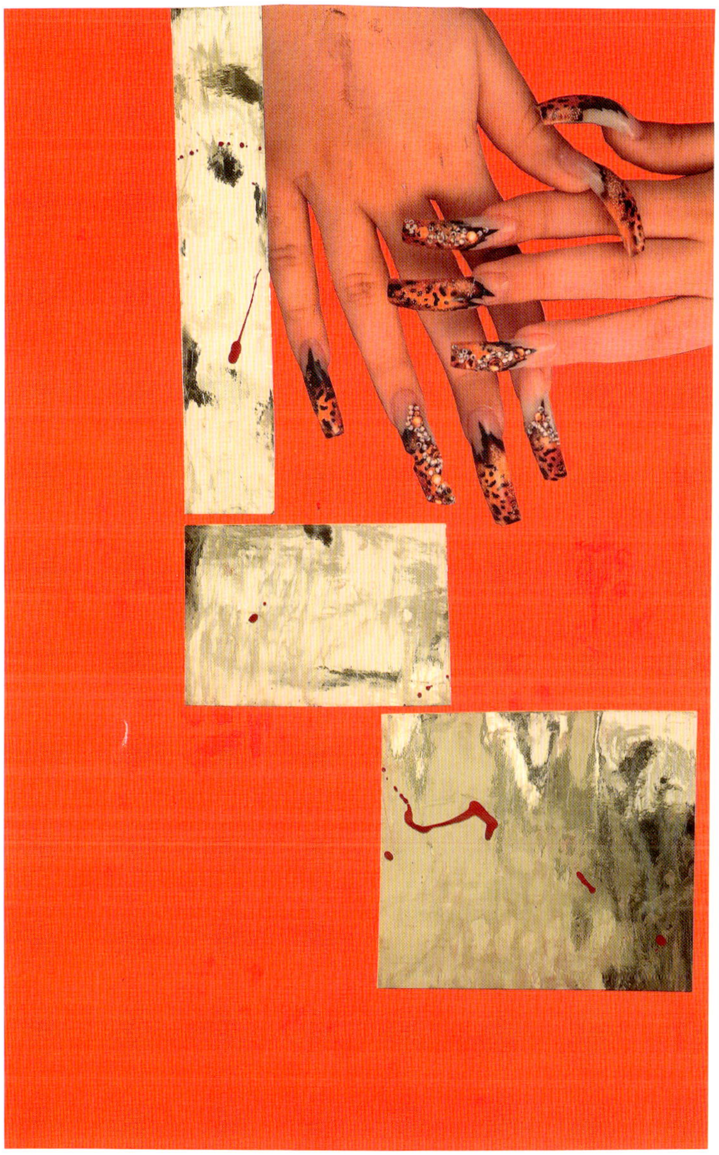

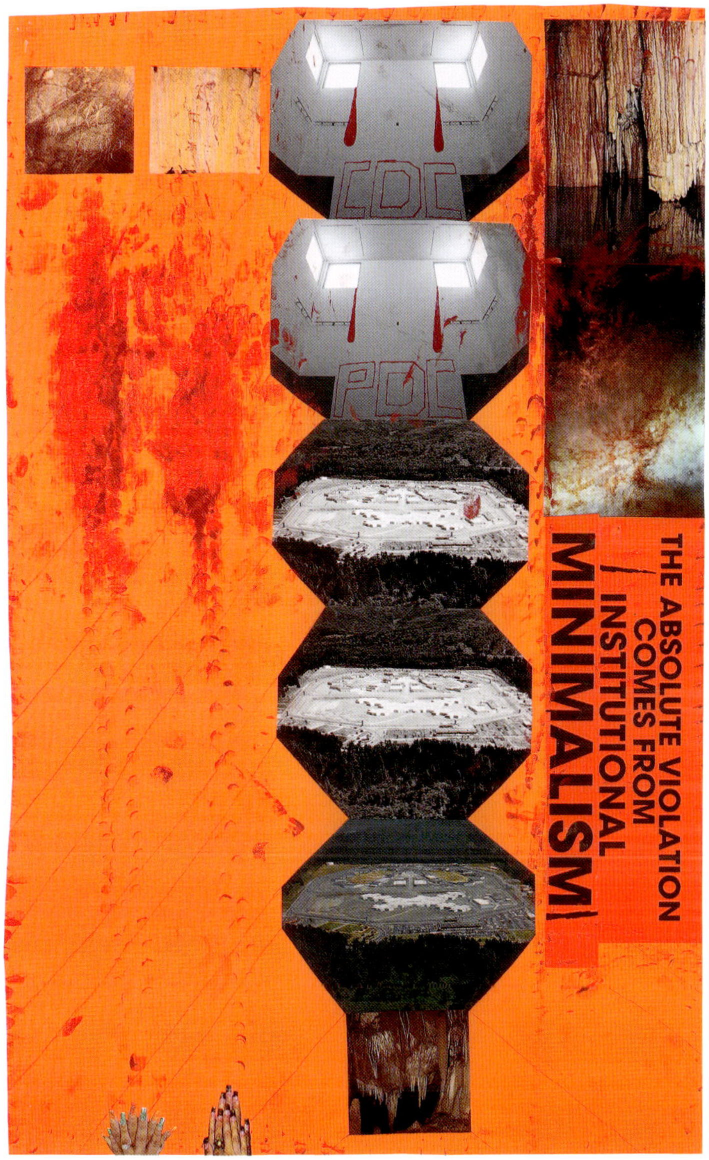

Left:
***Scratch/Chanel La Vernis*, 2008**
Collage, nail polish, and glue on paper

Right:
***CDC at PDC Study*, 2008**
Collage, paint, and colored pencil on paper

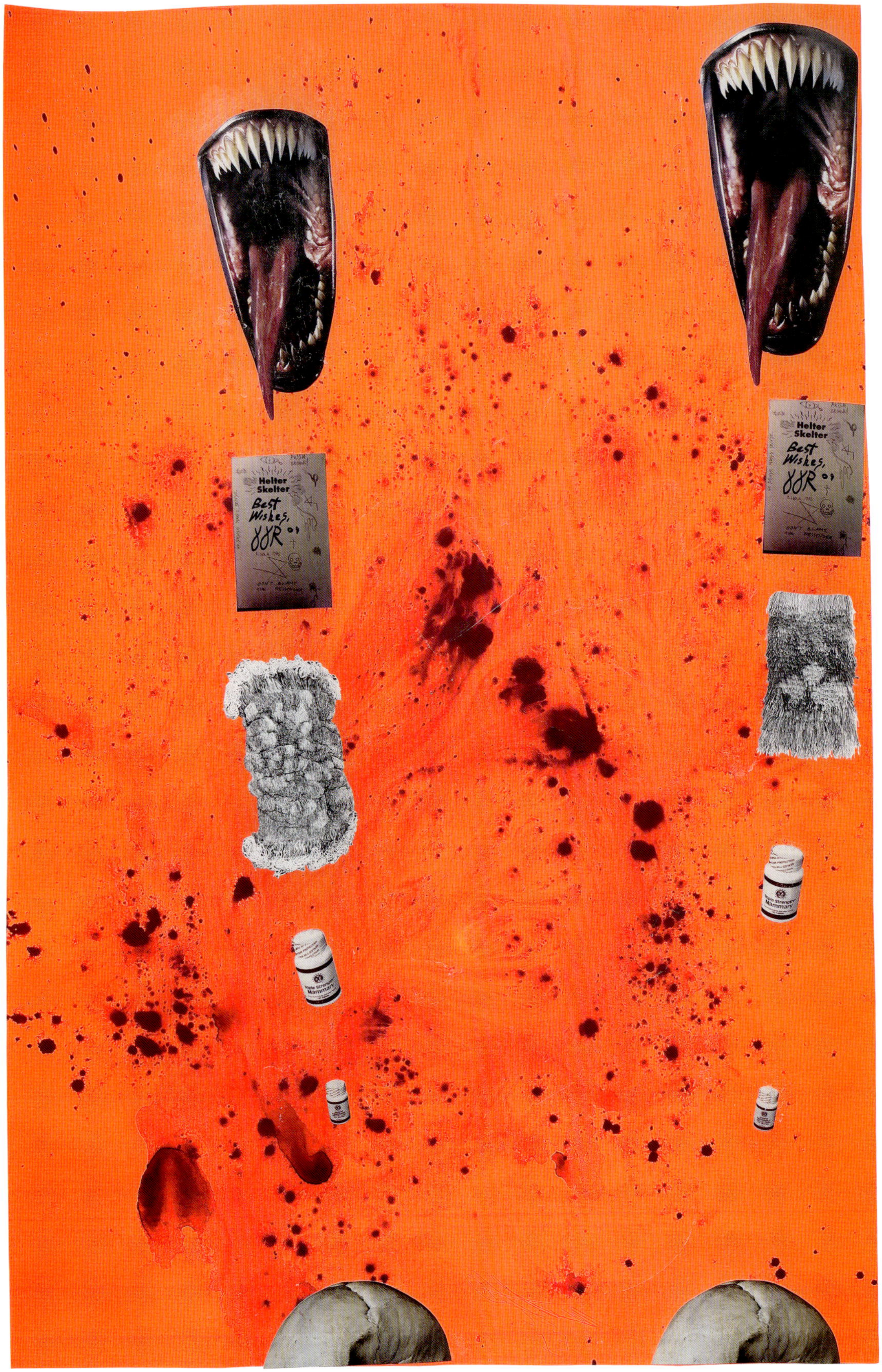

DRFTRS (4253), 2013
Collage, paint, and glue on paper

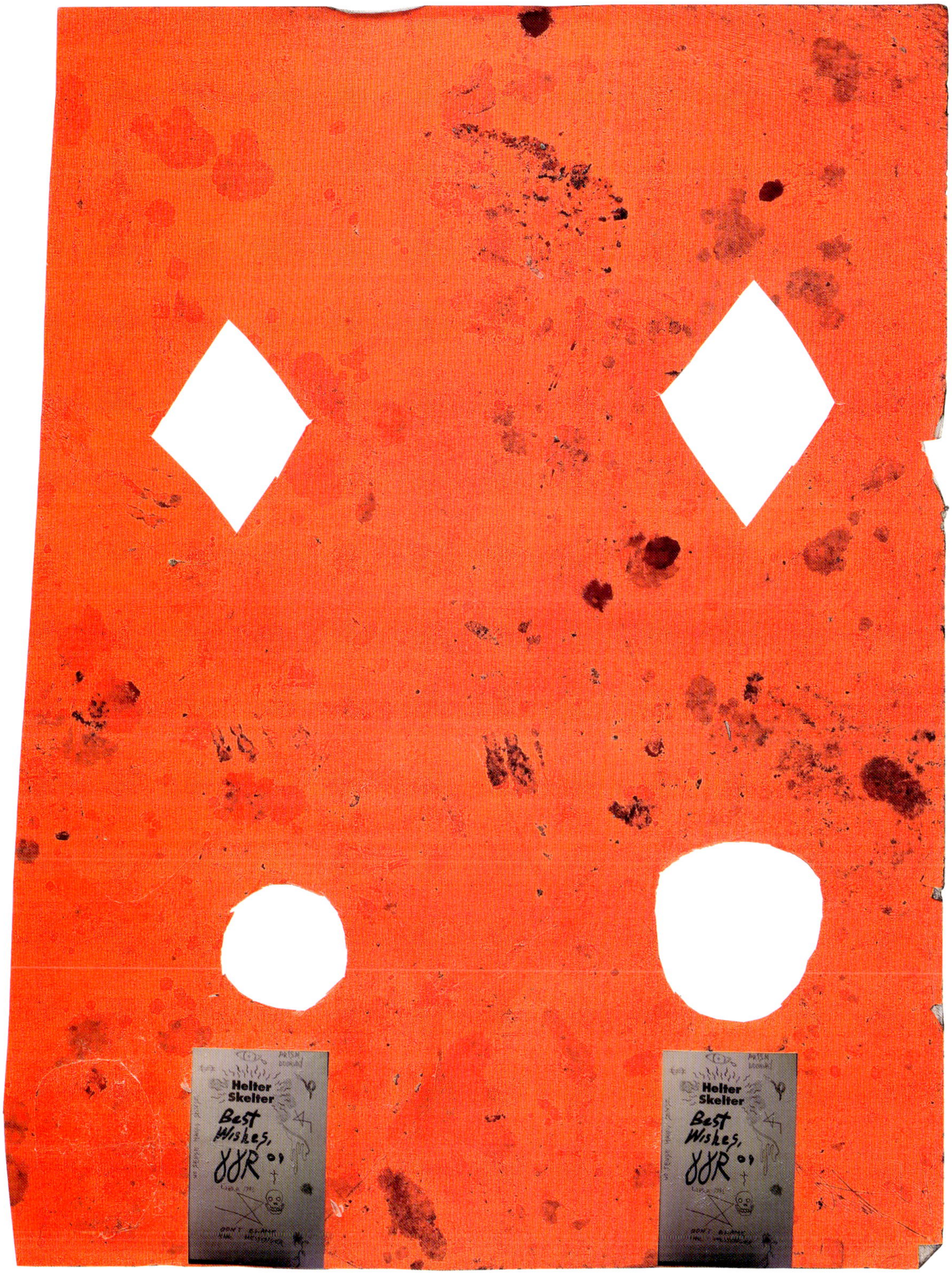

***DRFTRS (4257)*, 2013**
Collage, paint, and glue on paper

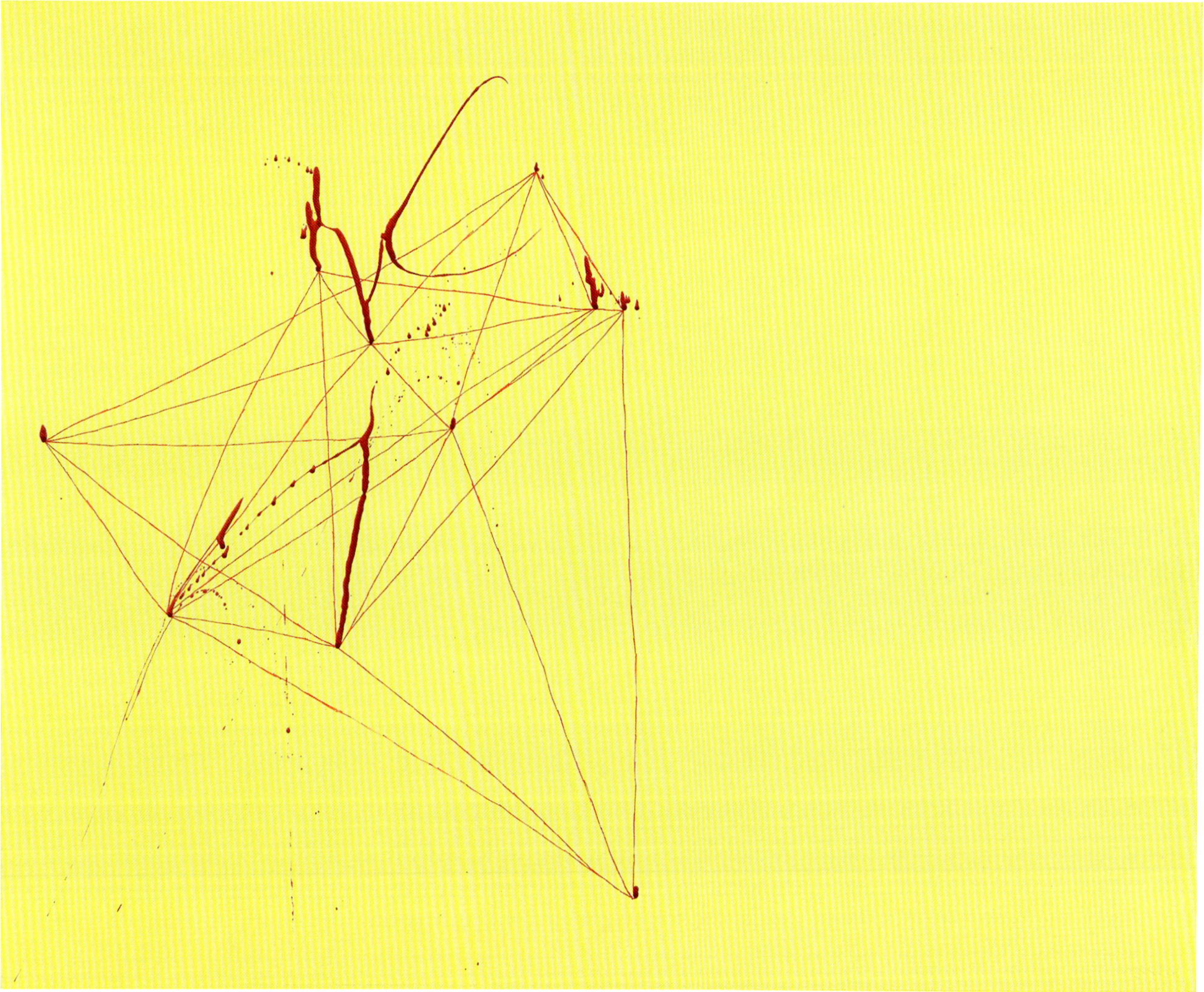

(Mapping) Jordache Nail Polish, 2005
Nail polish on paper

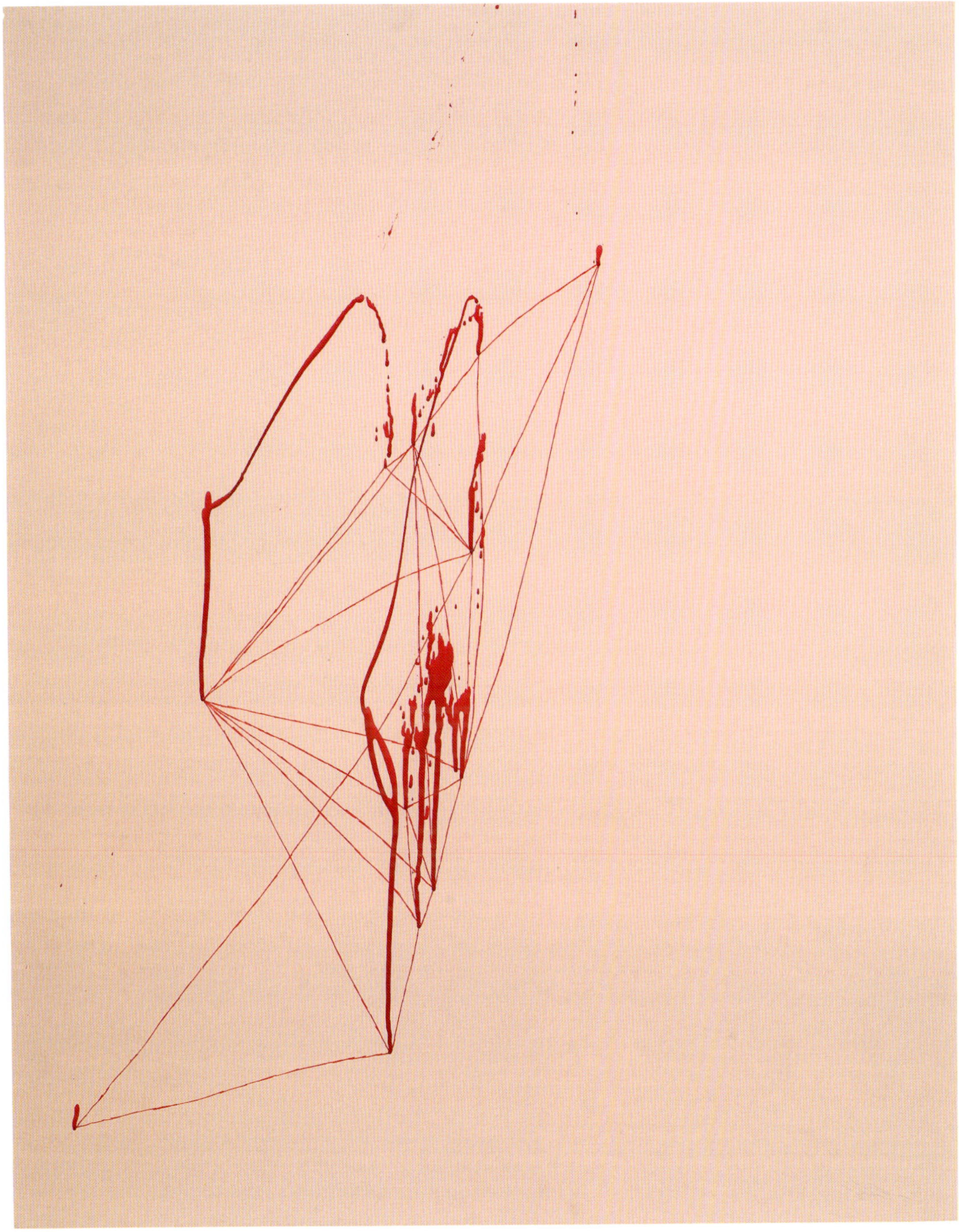

Mapping (Pink), 2005
Nail polish on paper

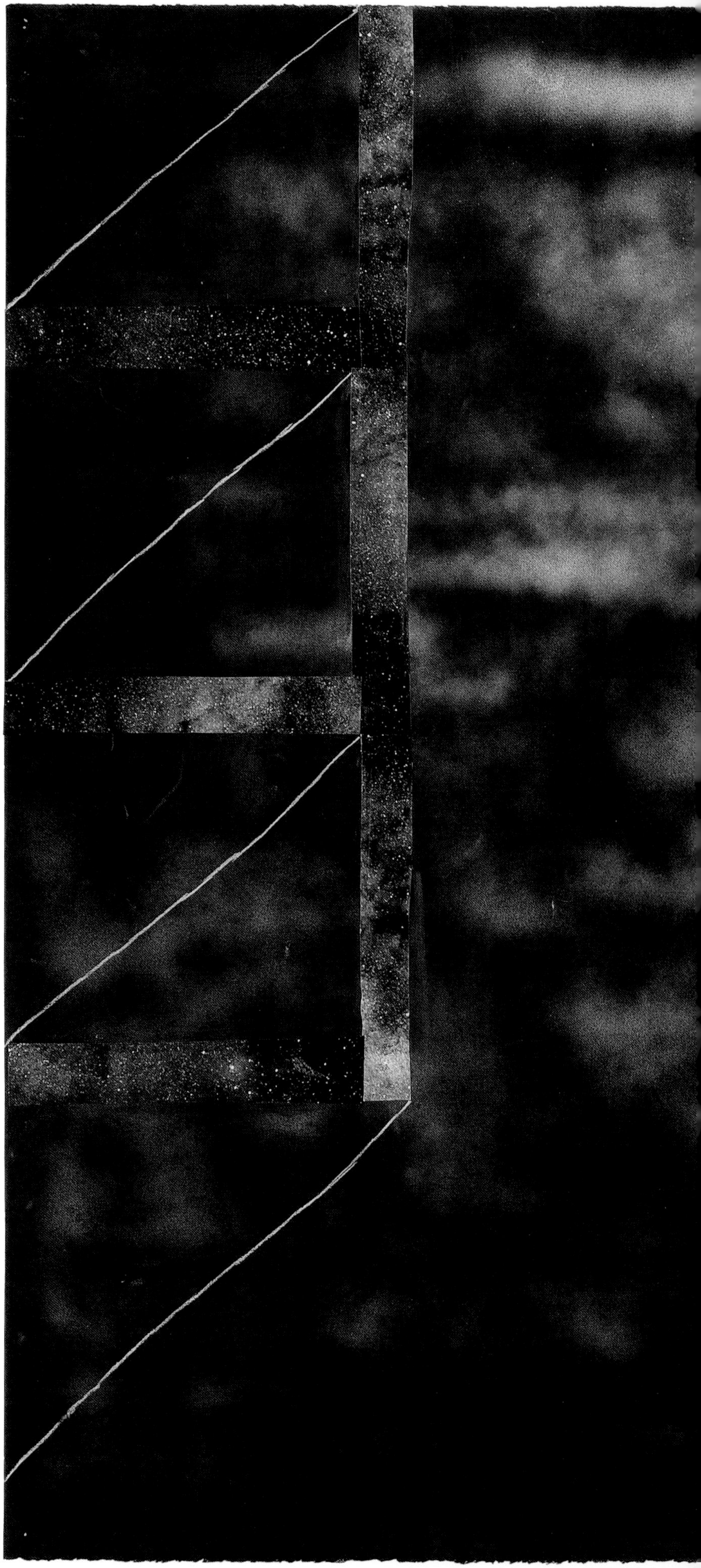

Block A, Tier 3 (Spatial), 2008
Collage, spray paint, and colored pencil on paper

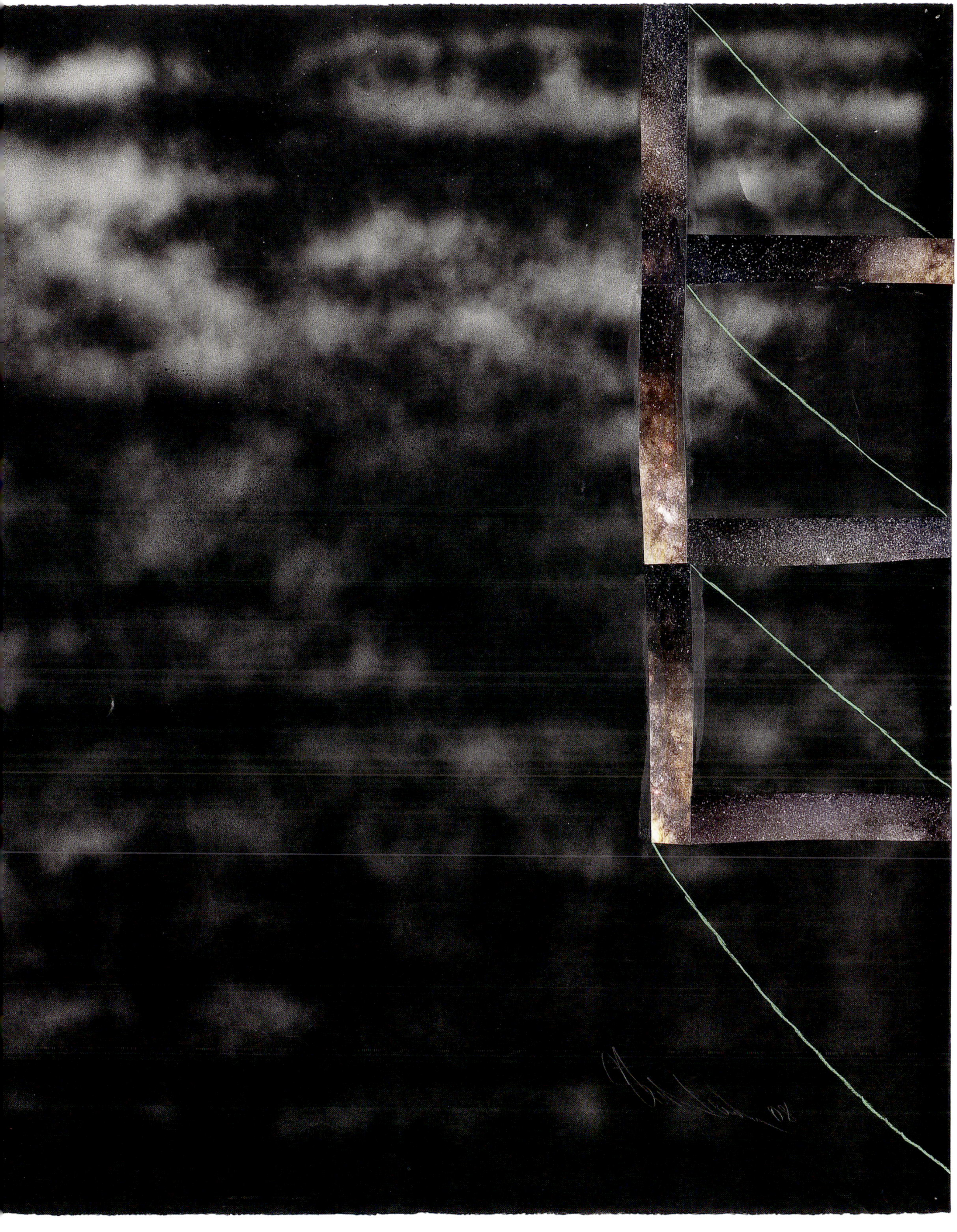

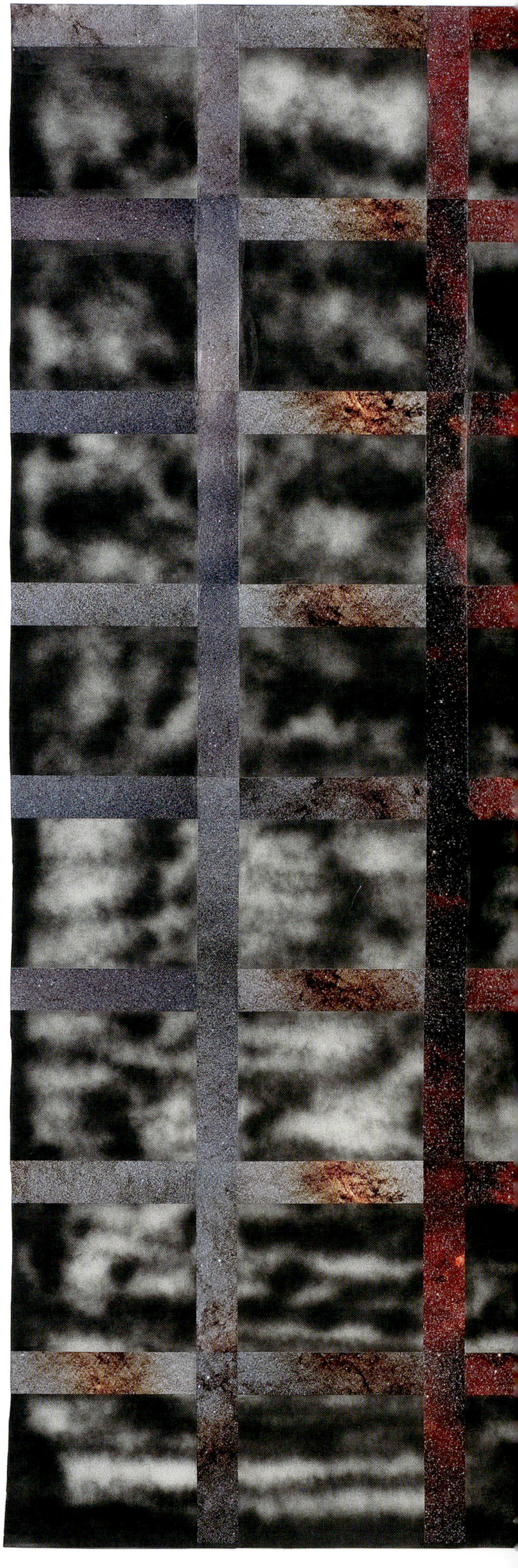

Head Trekkers + Gated Doors 2, 2010
Collage and spray paint on paper

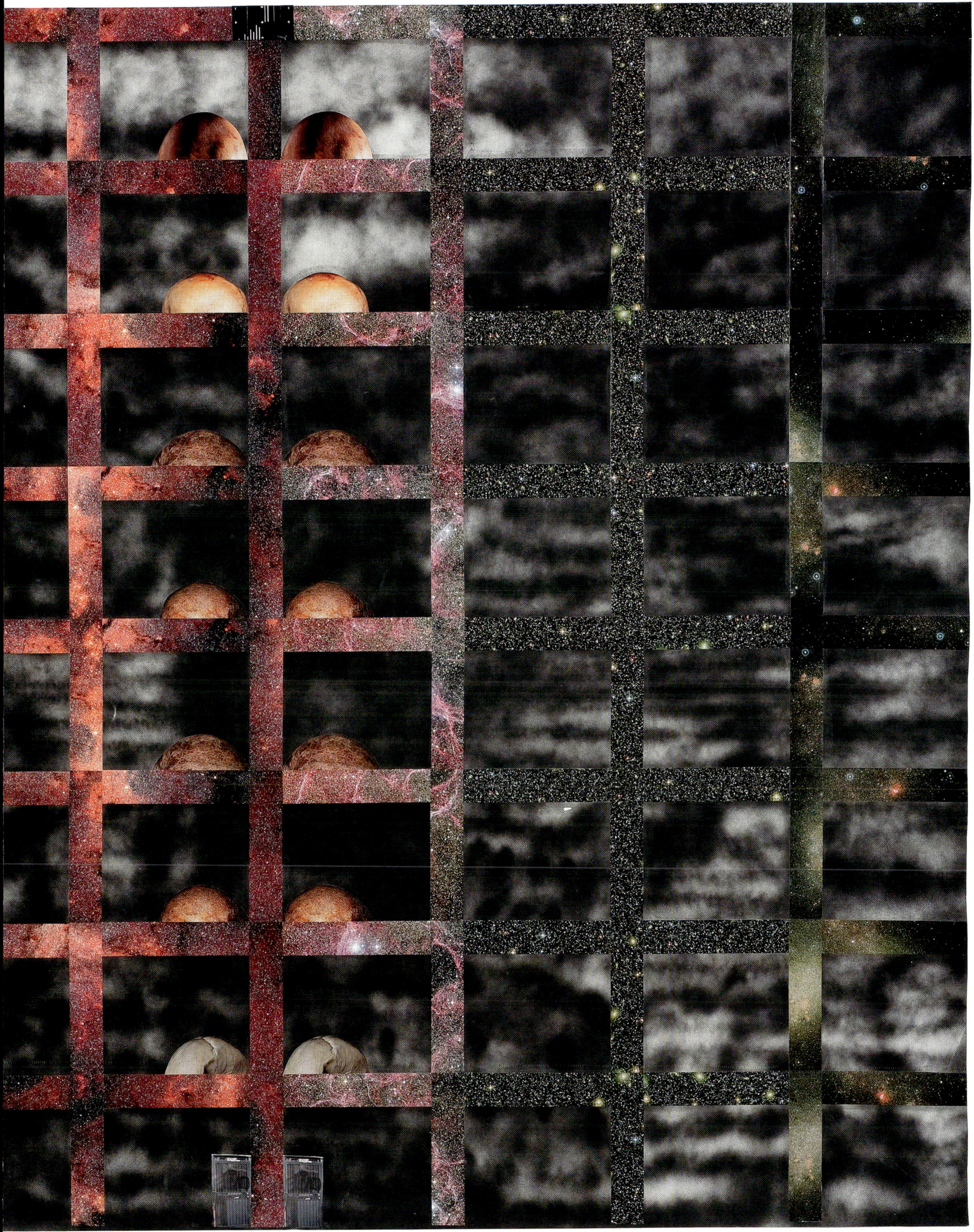

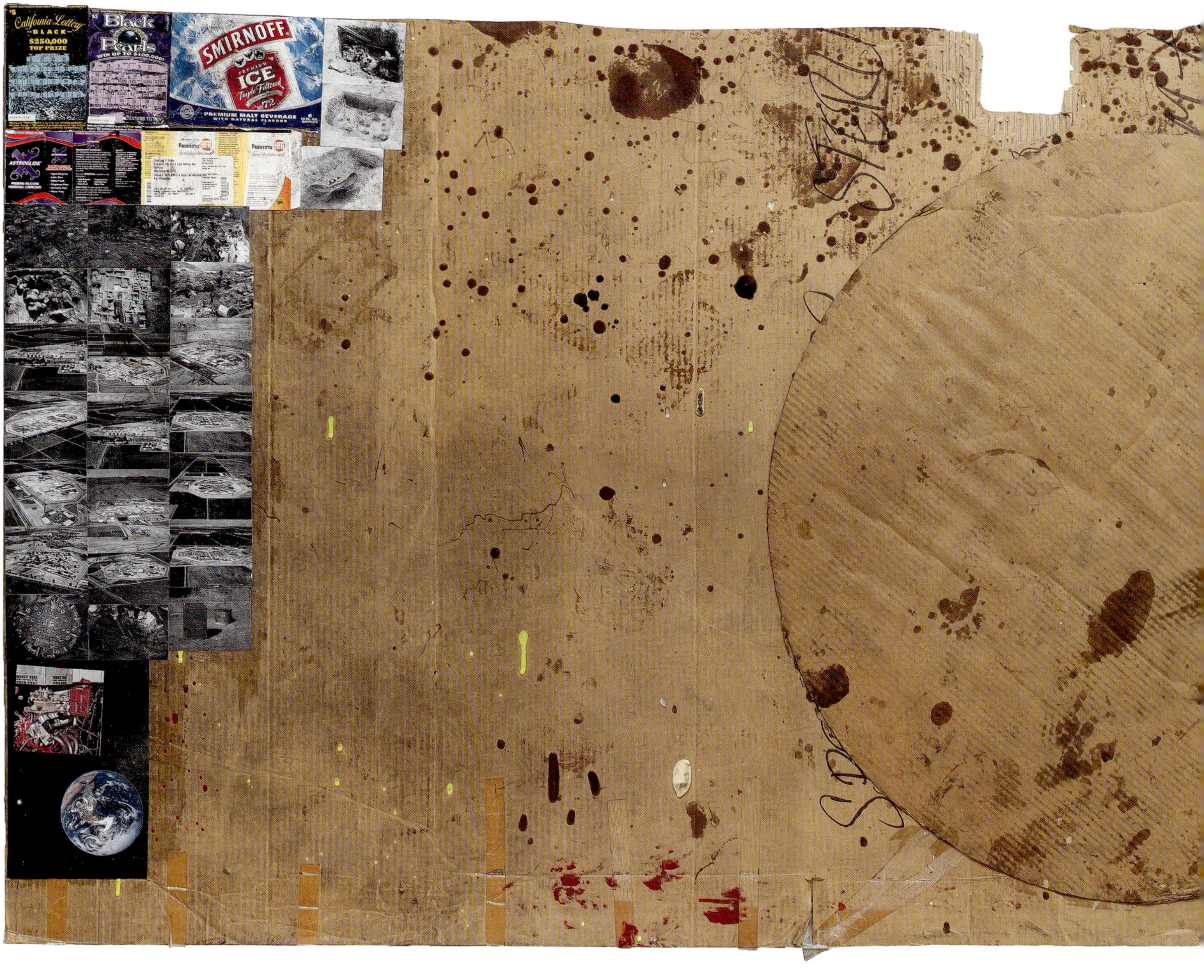

EXHM (4019), 2012
Collage and urethane on cardboard

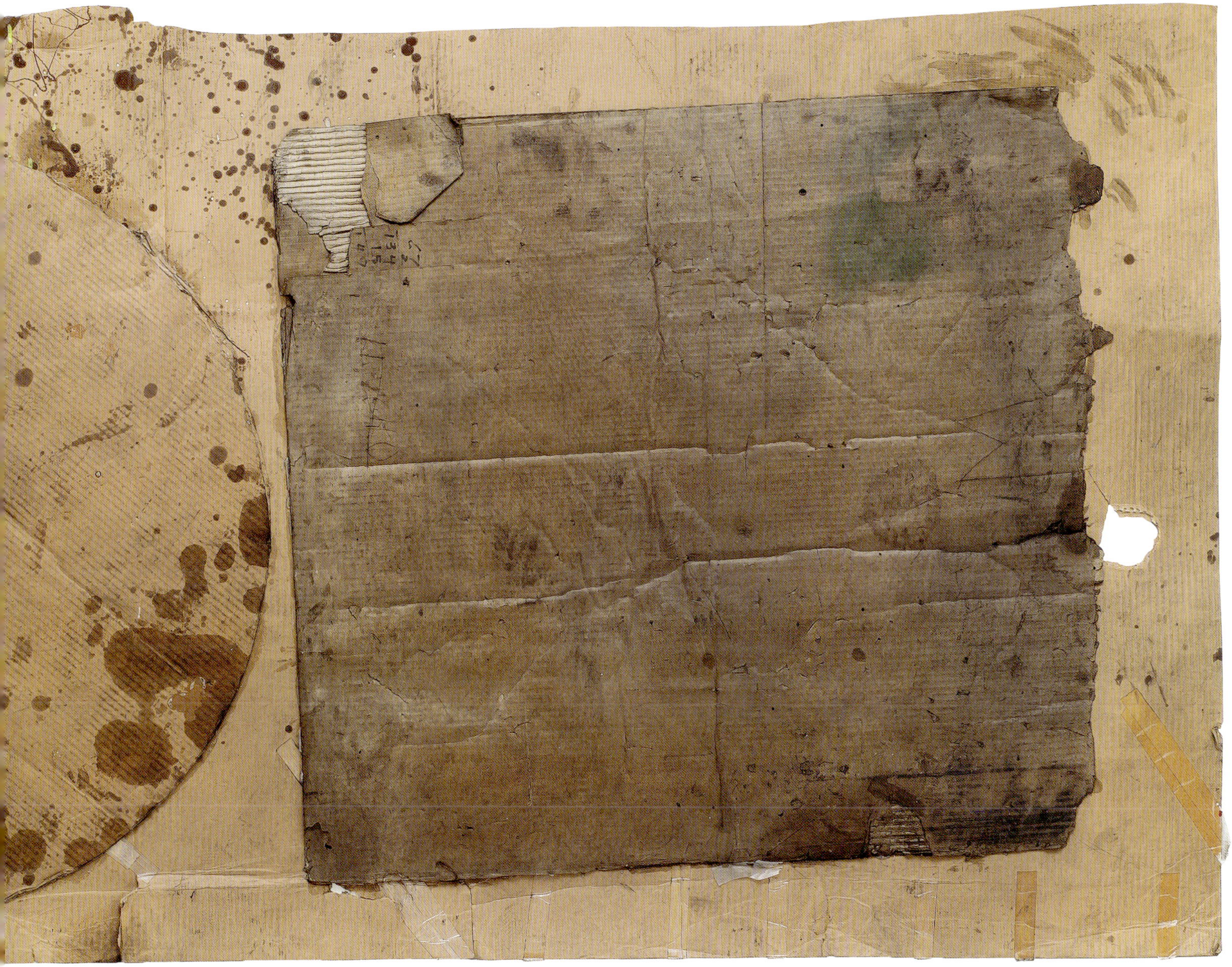

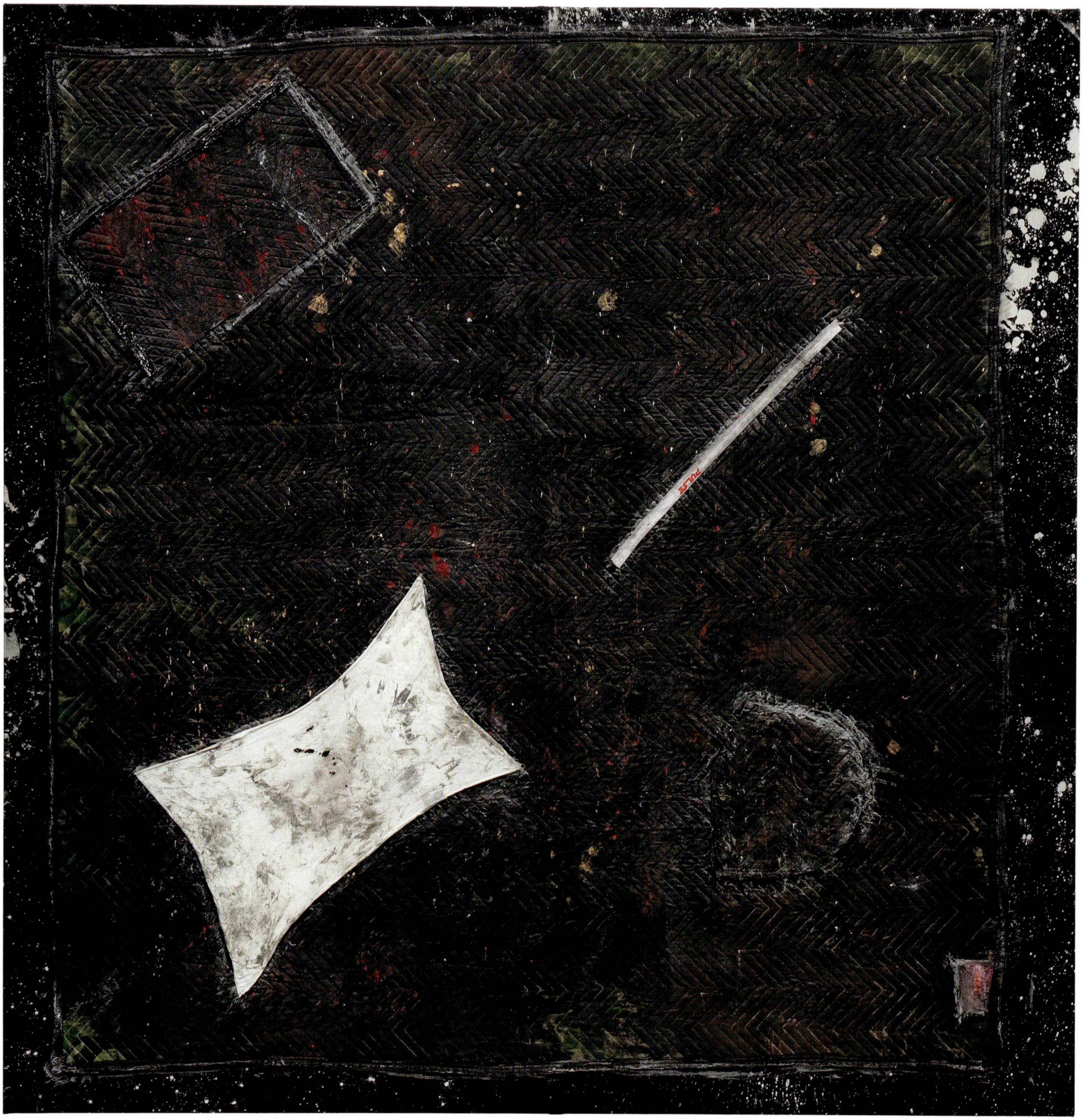

BC (3950), 2012
Fabric, paint, glue, and bleached canvas on panel

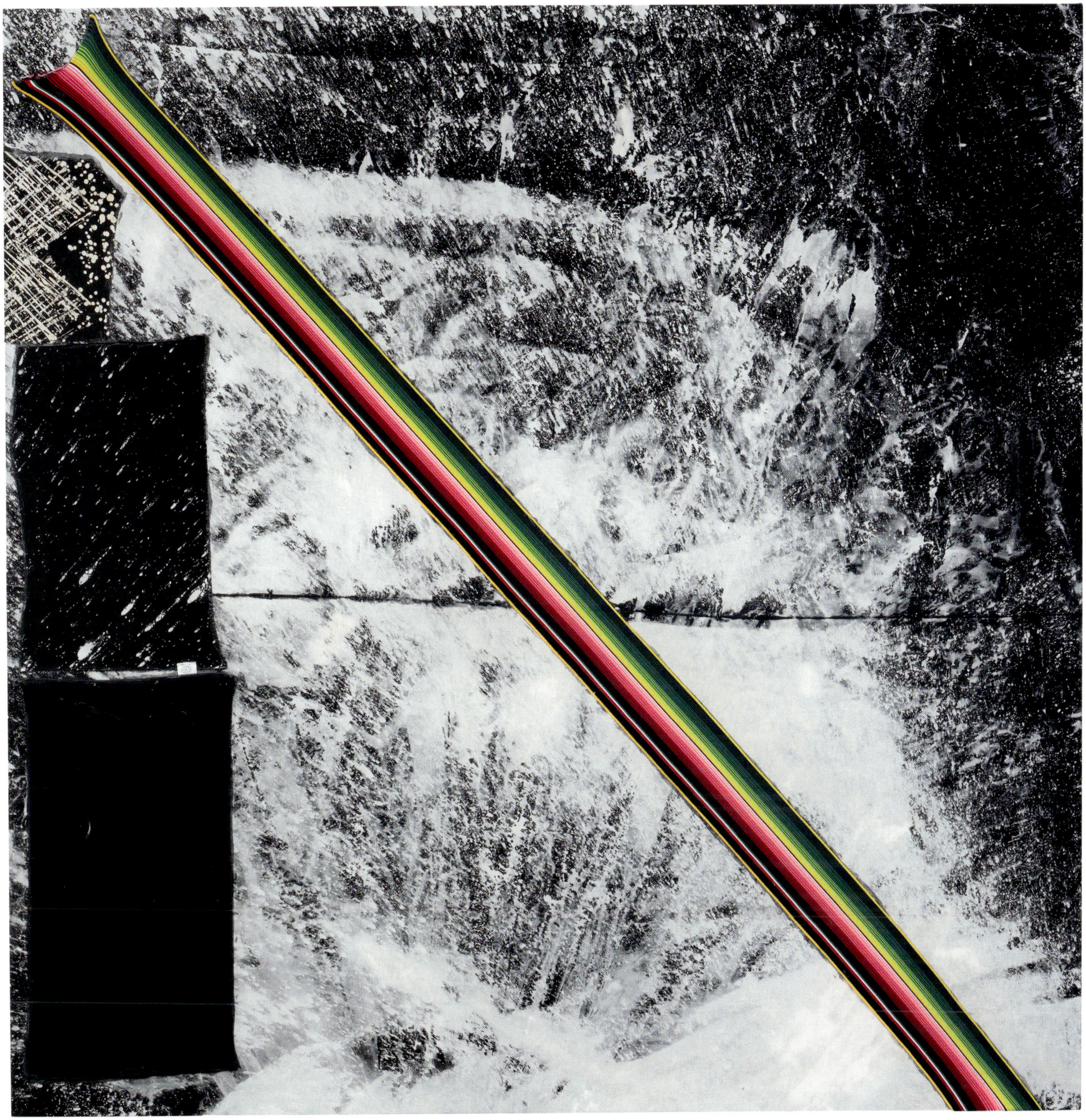

BC (5289), 2014
Fabric, glue, and bleached canvas on panel

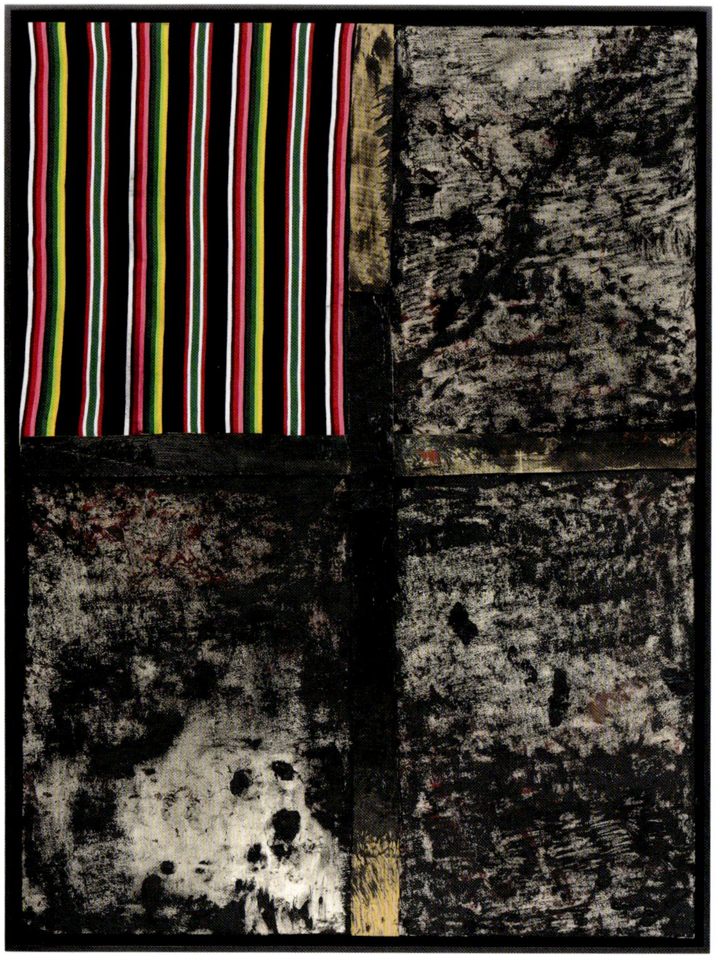

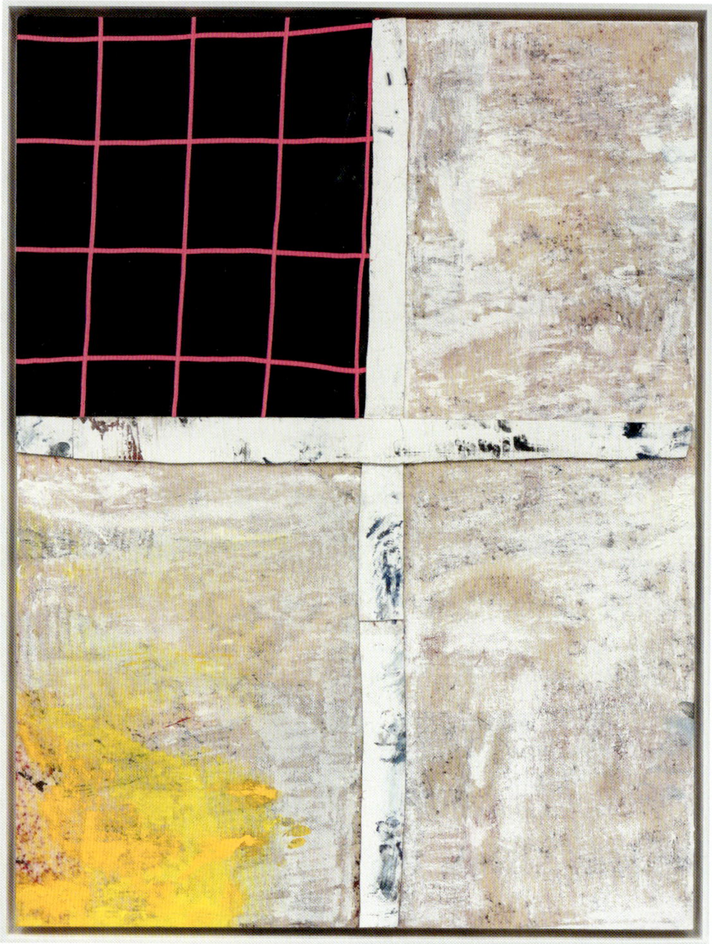

Left:
ENGULFED COROLLA, 2017
Acrylic, oil, elastic, and cardboard on canvas

Right:
HOT FLAT LIGHT, 2017
Acrylic, oil, elastic, and cardboard on canvas

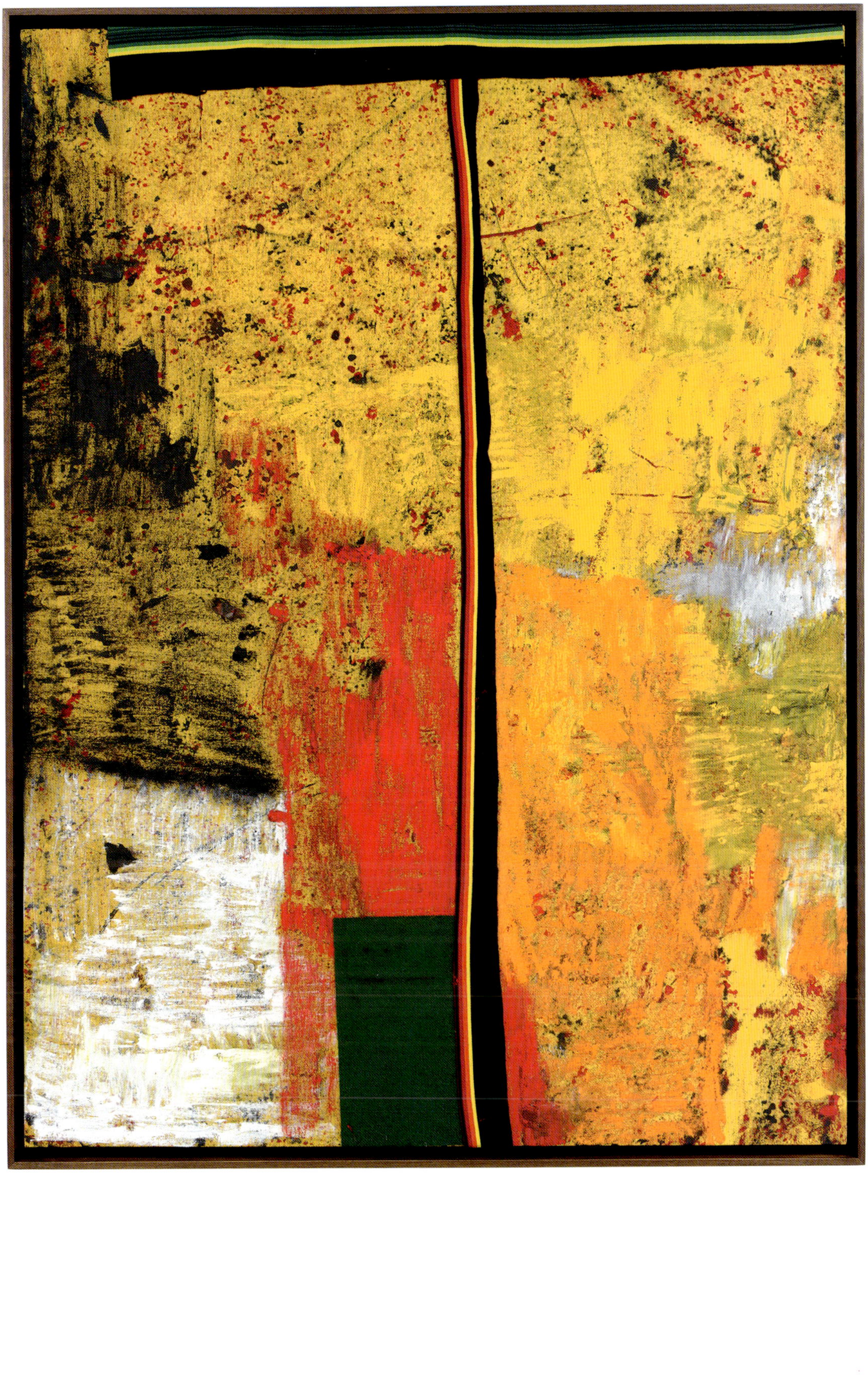

CRUX.YELL., 2016
Acrylic, oil, elastic, and fabric on canvas

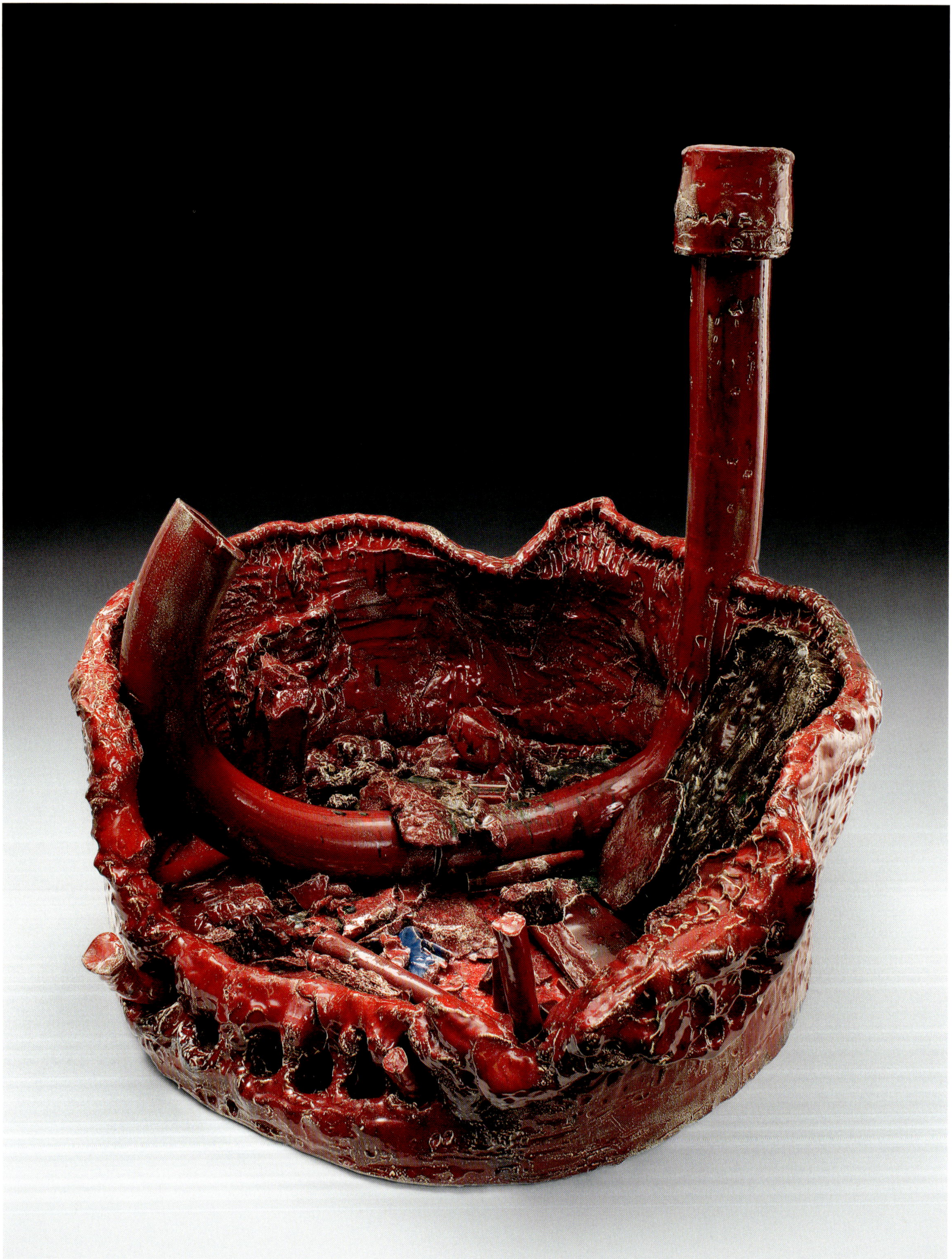

Ceramics

RUBY'S longstanding engagement with ceramic sculpture began when he enrolled in a free-form clay class at a community art center while a student at the School of the Art Institute of Chicago. Influenced by his mother's collection of West German pottery and dishware and interested, at first, in exploring the notion of art therapy, Ruby fostered a sustained fascination with the associations called forth by working with clay and the medium's capacity for expressing gesture with a sense of immediacy. In his nonutilitarian ceramics, Ruby often executes amateur tropes with a well-developed sense of material, history, and process. He interrogates various received forms—vessels such as ashtrays or basins—and brings them into the realm of sculpture through an acute sense of display. Indeed, ceramics are symbolically resonant within Ruby's multidisciplinary practice: images of kilns recur throughout, for example, emblematic of ideas of material transformation central to his work.[1]

Ruby's early ceramics are thickly glazed, anthropomorphic objects, heavily worked by hand. For example, *Blue Angel* (2007) is a pockmarked blue and red, basket-like object with connected protuberances. Ruby's extensive series of numerically titled, nonfunctional ASHTRAYS are modeled on those vernacular receptacles, though they are often narrative containers rather than idealized forms: *ASHTRAY 141* (2010), for example, is a shallow, turquoise blue object that holds suspended what appears to be a toxic orange puddling liquid. Ruby has also transposed the formal qualities of these ceramics in other media, such as the bronze *Hiker (4949)* (2014), which depicts the handworked characteristics of a medium associated with craft in one of sculpture's most vaunted materials.

Since 2009, Ruby has made a series of large-scale ceramic Basins that he fills with broken or discarded material. He calls the works Basin Theology, and they evoke the mortar and pestle of an earlier series. Ruby collects in his studio all of his past mistakes from working in ceramic: those broken remnants of objects that fracture in the firing process, markers of the failure of previous efforts. By reusing them in this way, Ruby says, "I am smashing all of my previous attempts, and futile, contemporary gestures, and placing them into a mortar, and grinding them down with a blunt pestle."[2] This sense of material reclamation is a central tenant of Ruby's work and Basin Theology works represent the studio's function as a "dig site." Each Basin is displayed on a low plinth so that the viewer looks down into the object from above. Some Basins point to specific locations in their titles and appearance, such as the matte black *Basin Theology/La Brea 2* (2011) that recalls the collected debris, fossil deposits, and natural asphalt of the La Brea Tar Pits in Los Angeles. Others are invested with narrative, such as the oblong form of *Basin Theology/STYX BOAT* (2017), which alludes to the boat that ferries the dead to the afterworld in classical mythology. Ceramic sculptures like the Basins remain central in Ruby's output, for their dynamic ability to express material and conceptual concerns.

—J. D.

1. See collages such as *Kiln #1* (2005) [p. 34] or *Girl in Kiln* (2004) [p. 38] or *STOVE 3* (2012) [p. 146].
2. Sterling Ruby, "APOLOGETICS, 2015," in *Sterling Ruby* (New York: Phaidon, 2016), 136.

***Basin Theology/The Pipe*, 2013**
Ceramic

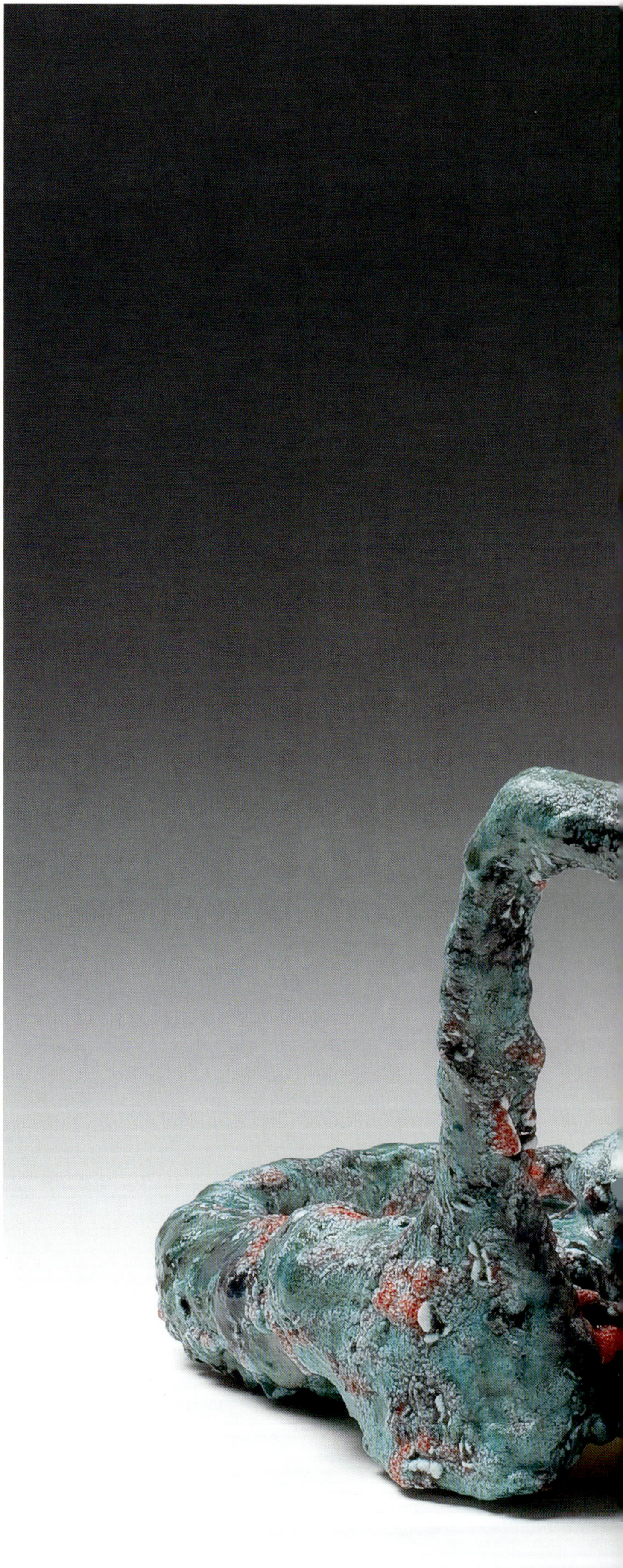

Blue Angel, 2007
Ceramic

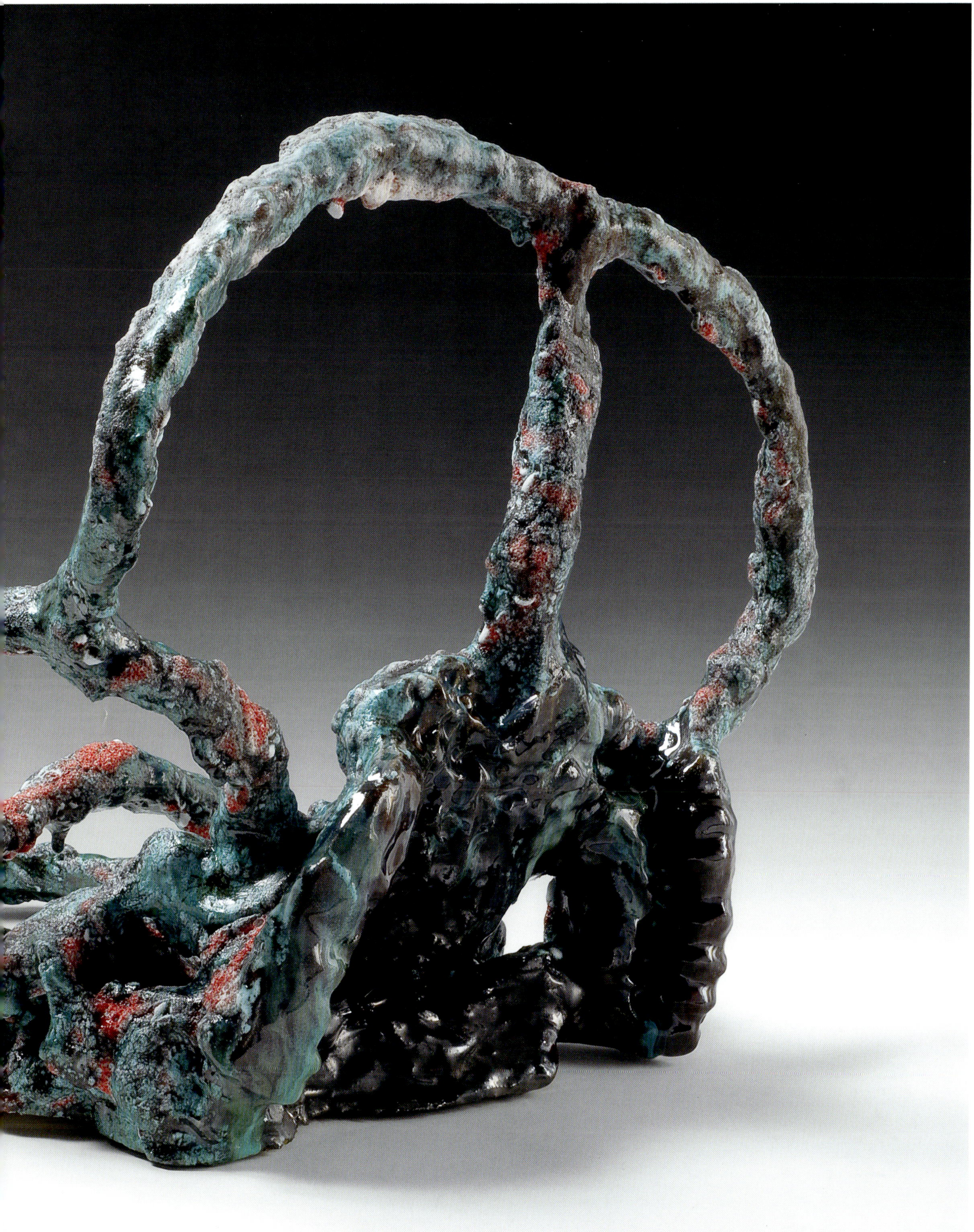

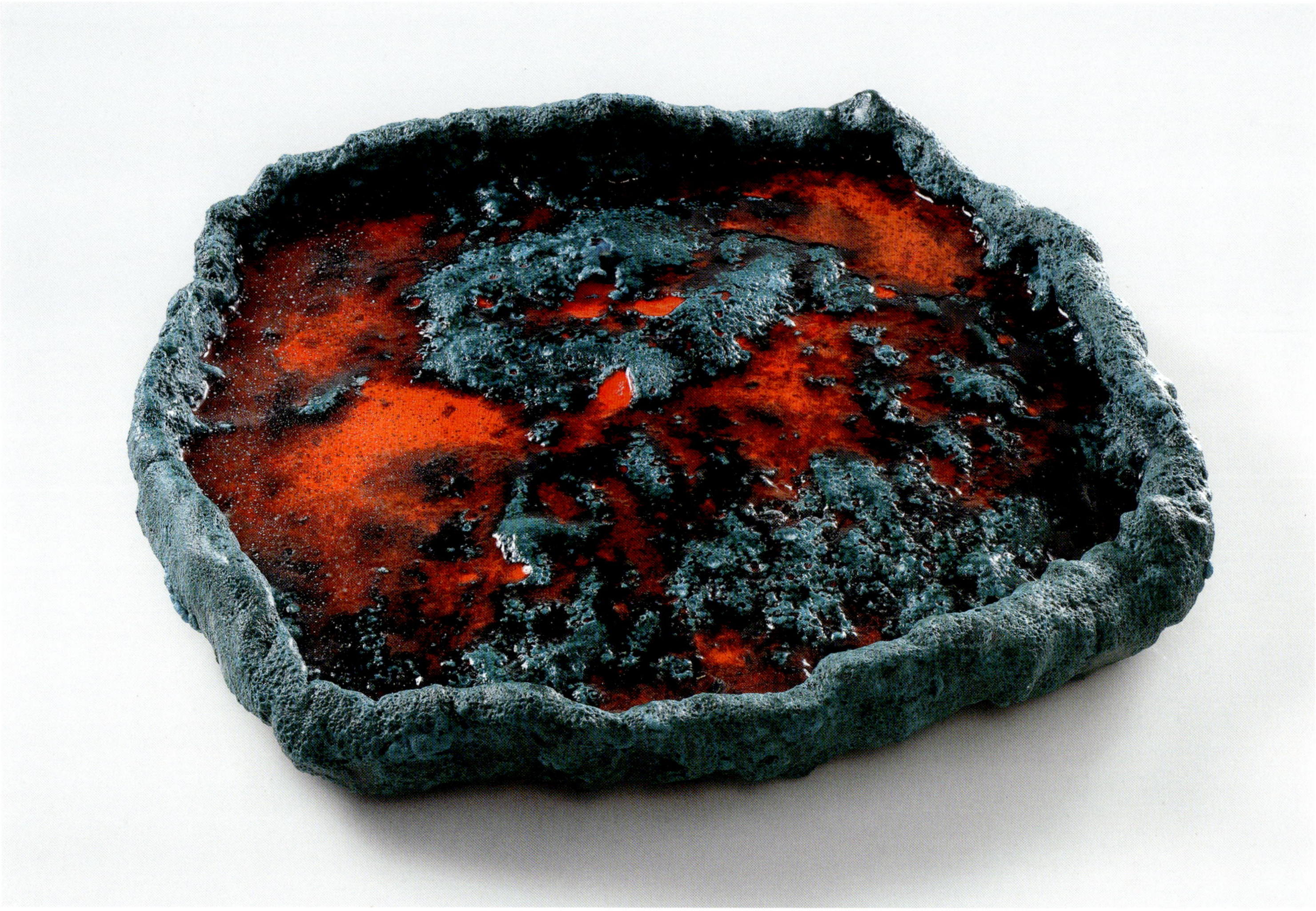

ASHTRAY 141, 2010
Ceramic

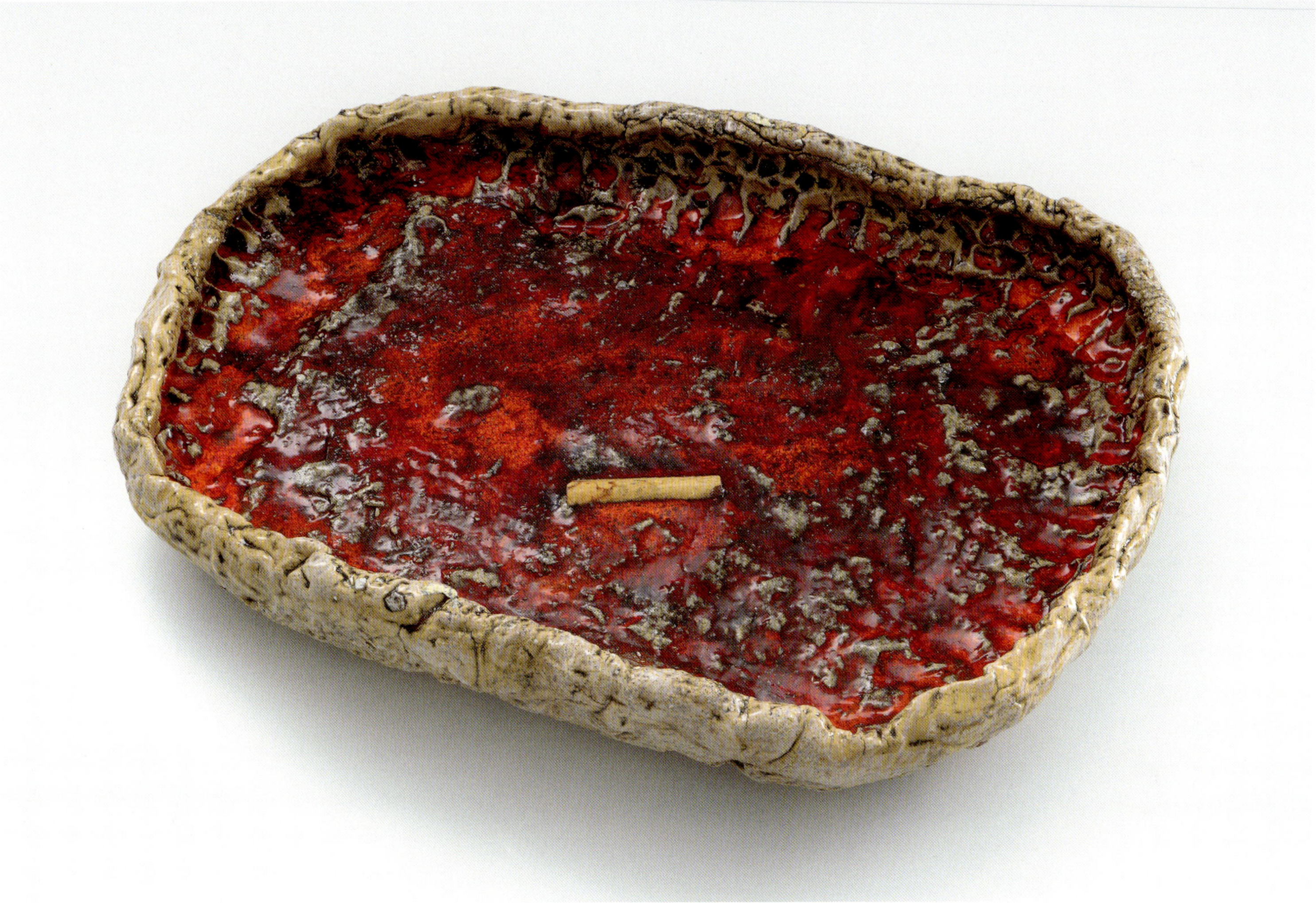

ASHTRAY 465, 2018
Ceramic

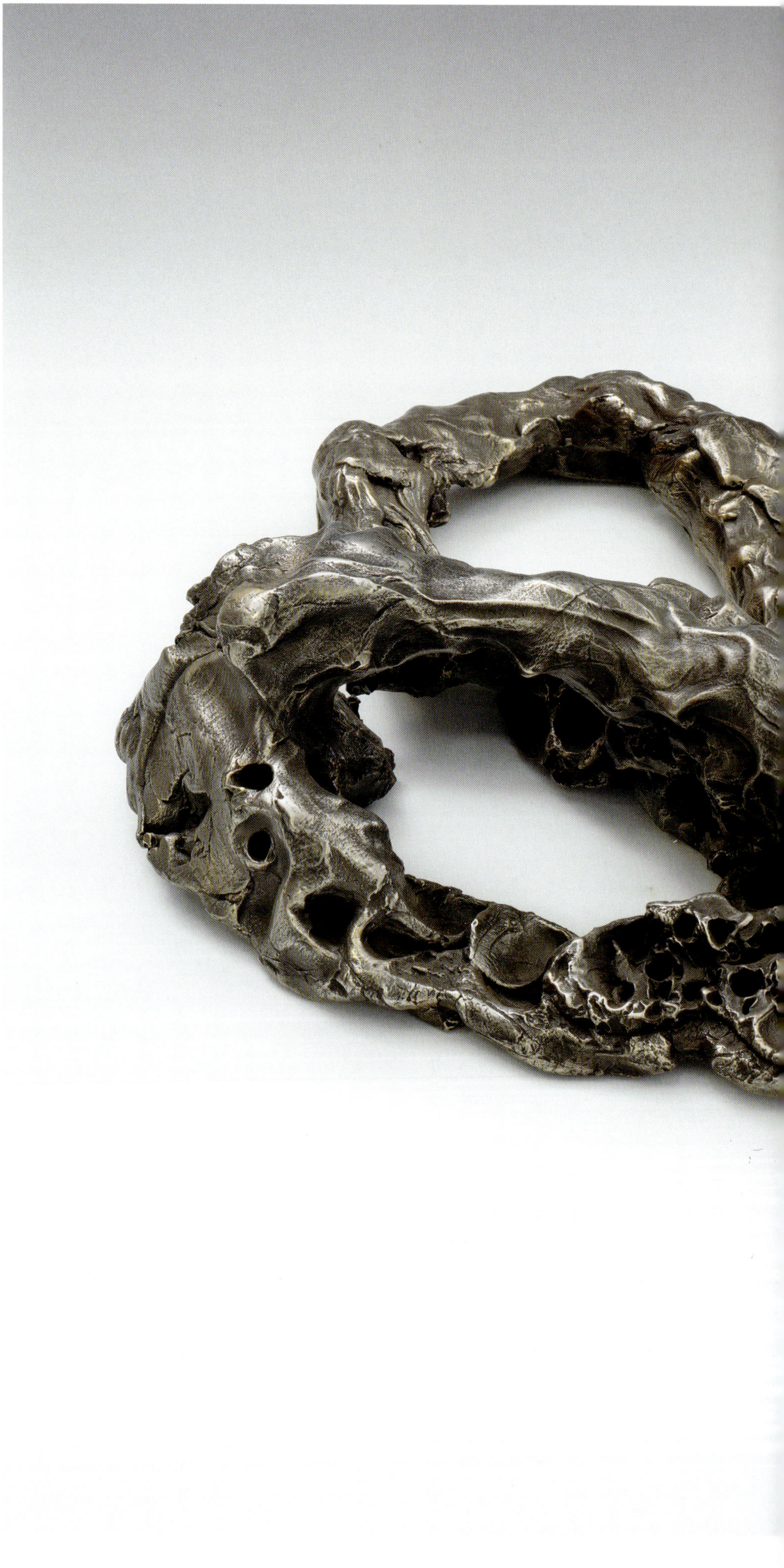

ACTRESS 2, 2010
Bronze with silver nitrate patina

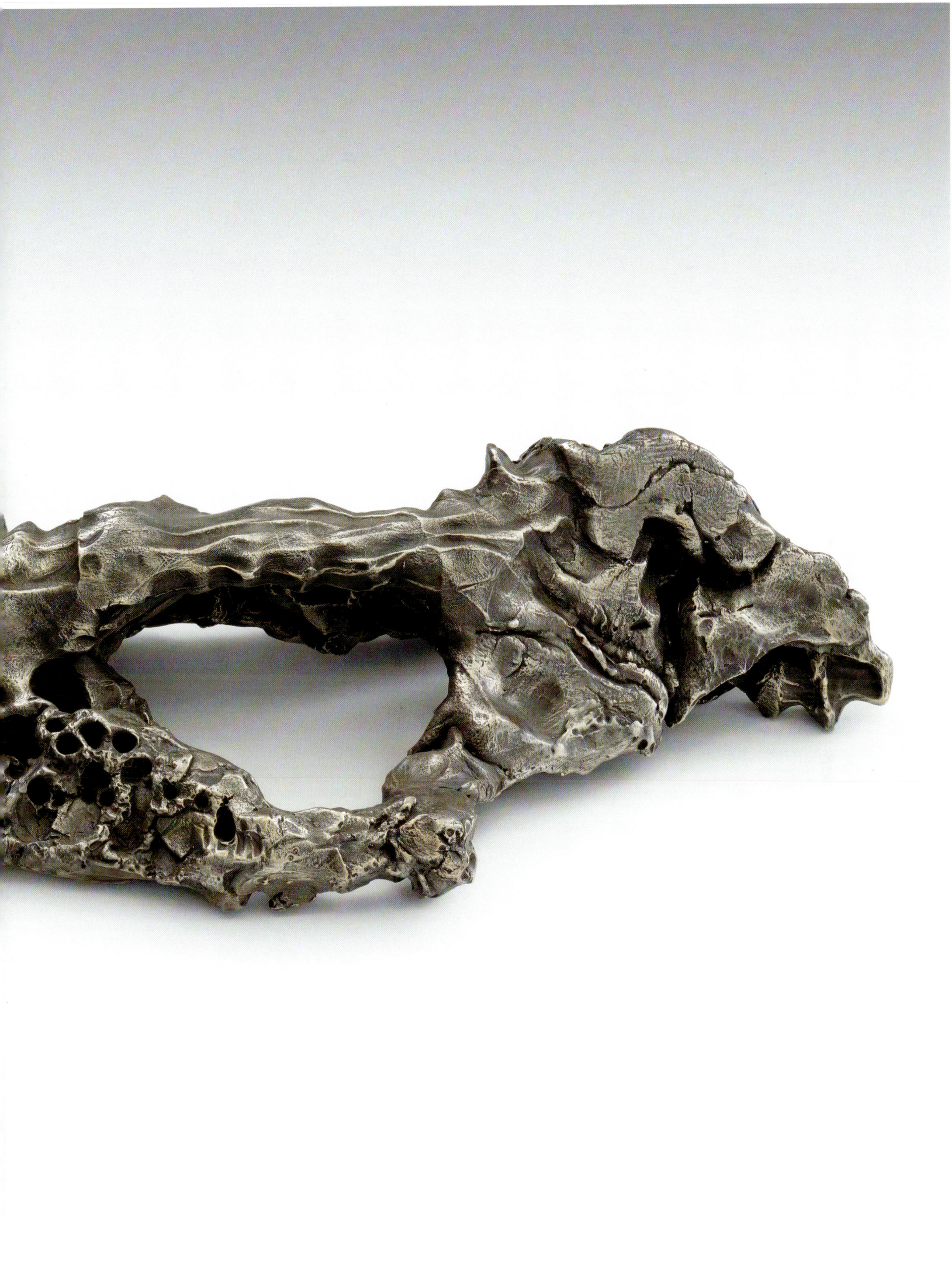

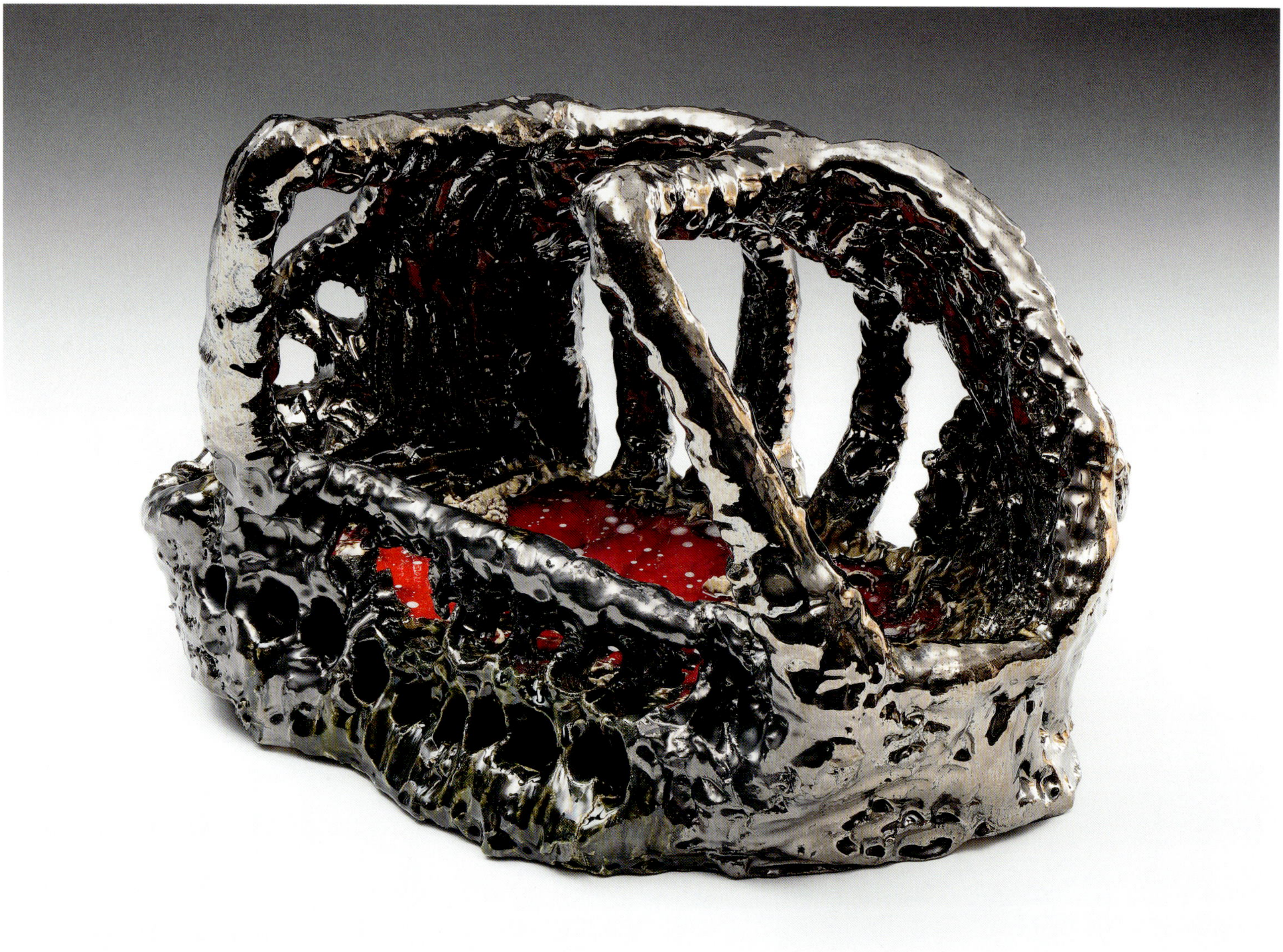

Modern Brass/Ketamine User, 2012
Ceramic

Opposite:
Bishop Score 2, 2013
Ceramic

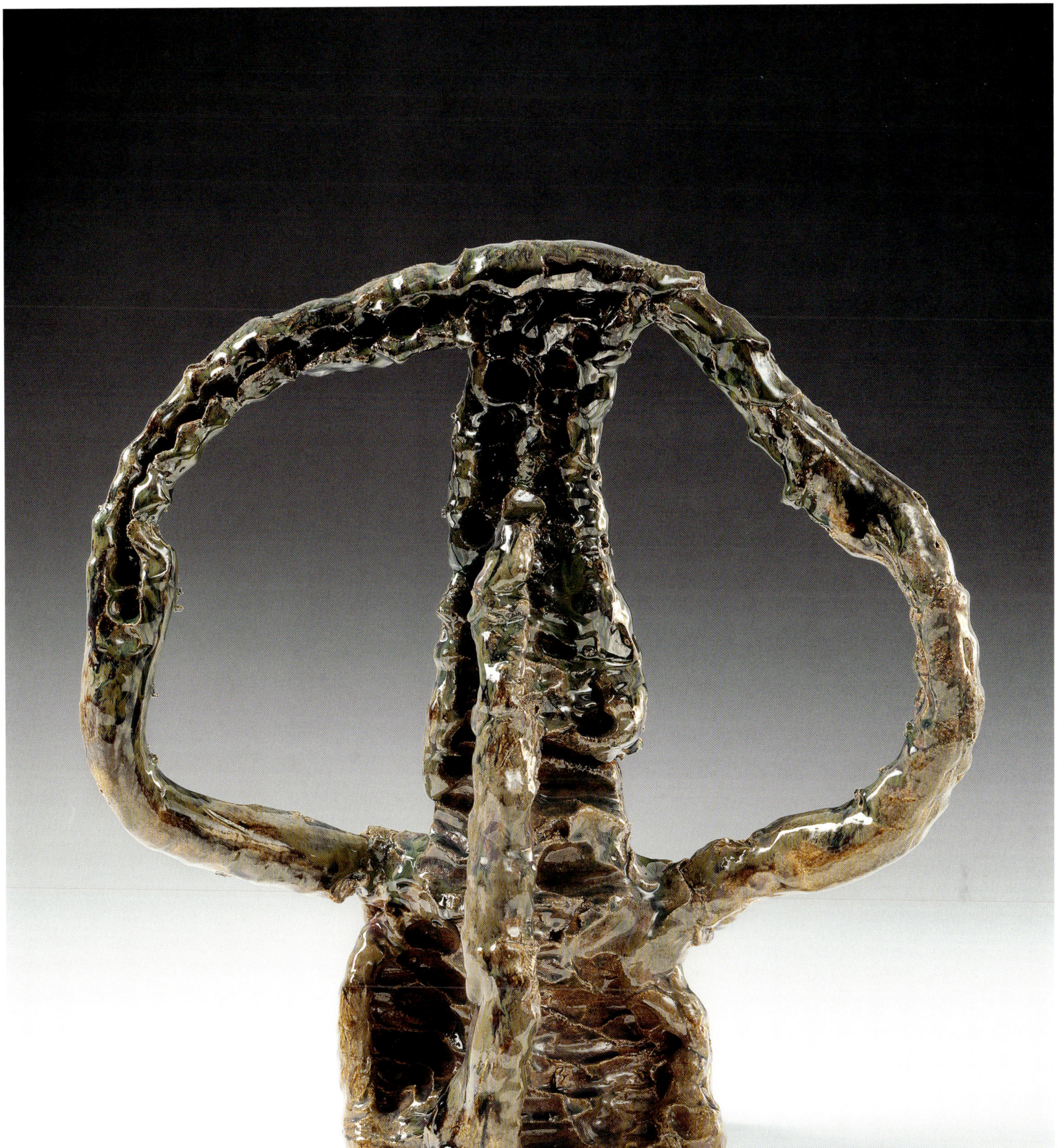

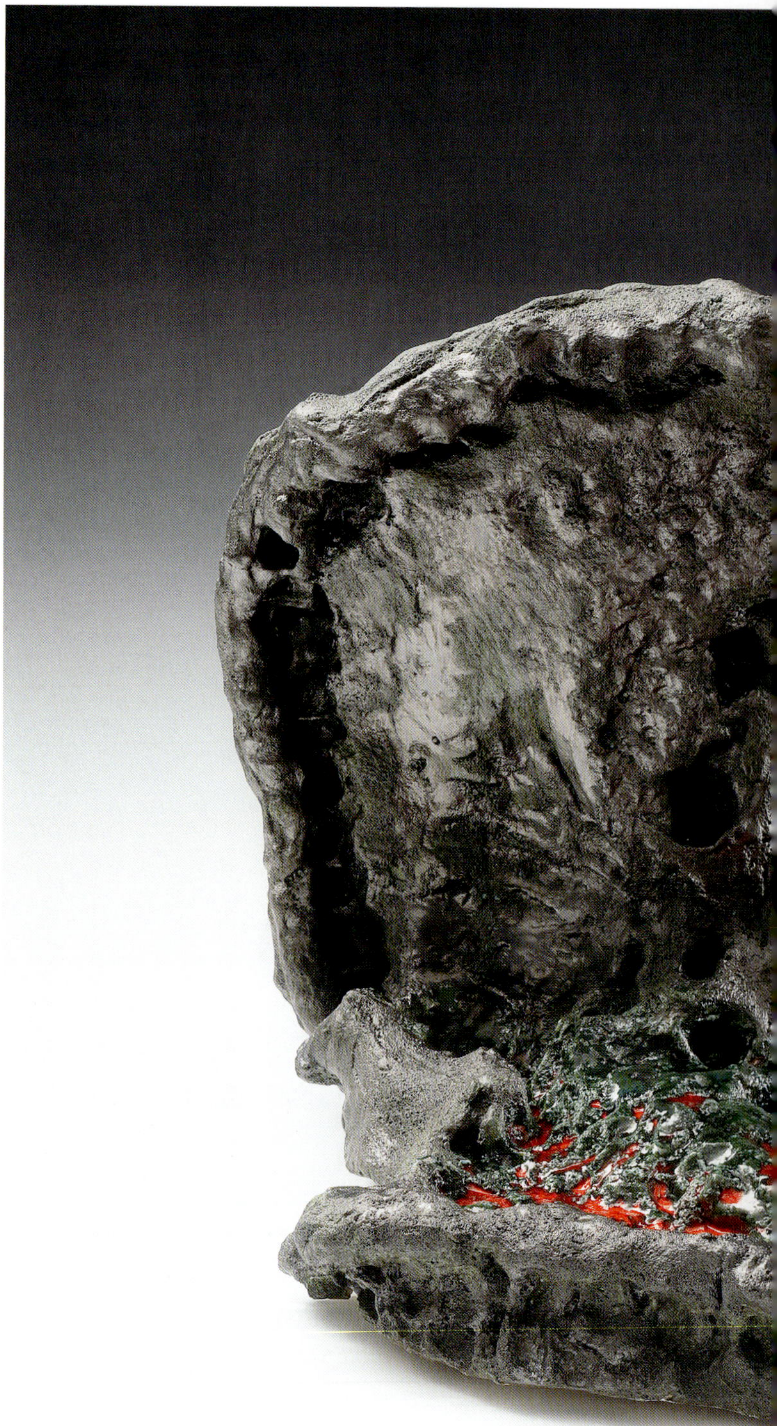

Drive-Thru Pewter Facial, 2010
Ceramic

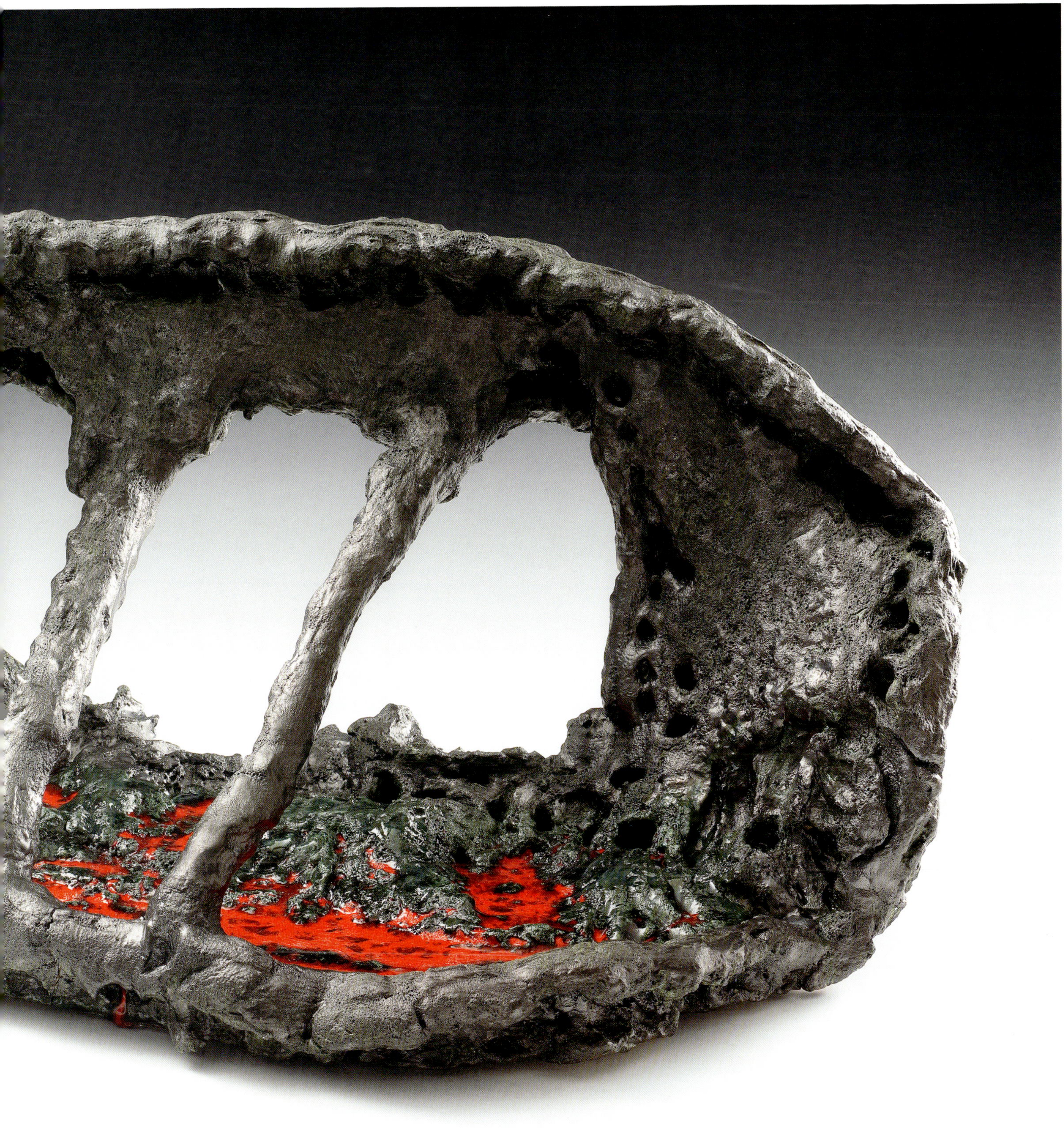

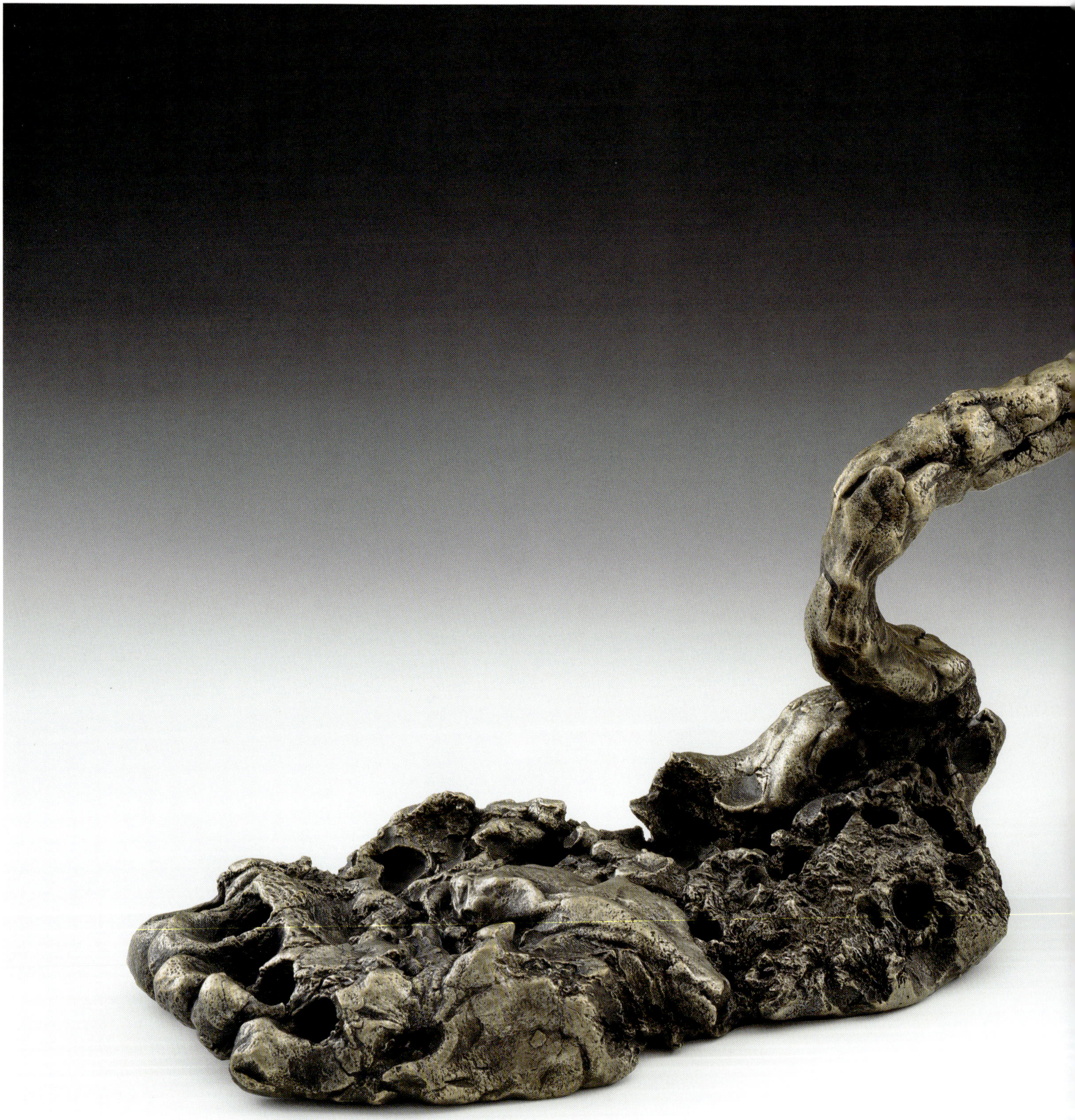

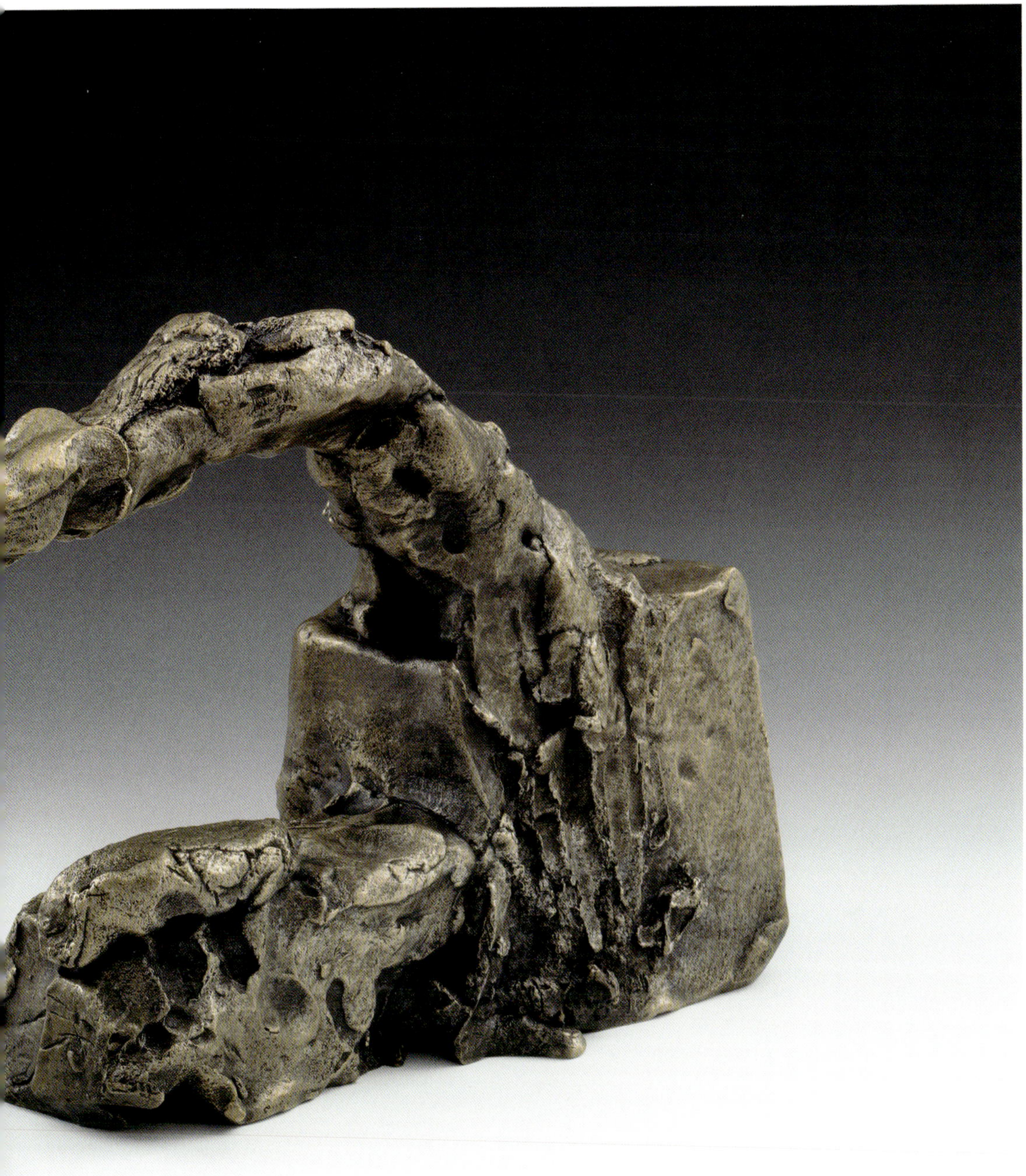

Hiker (4949), **2014**
Bronze with silver nitrate patina

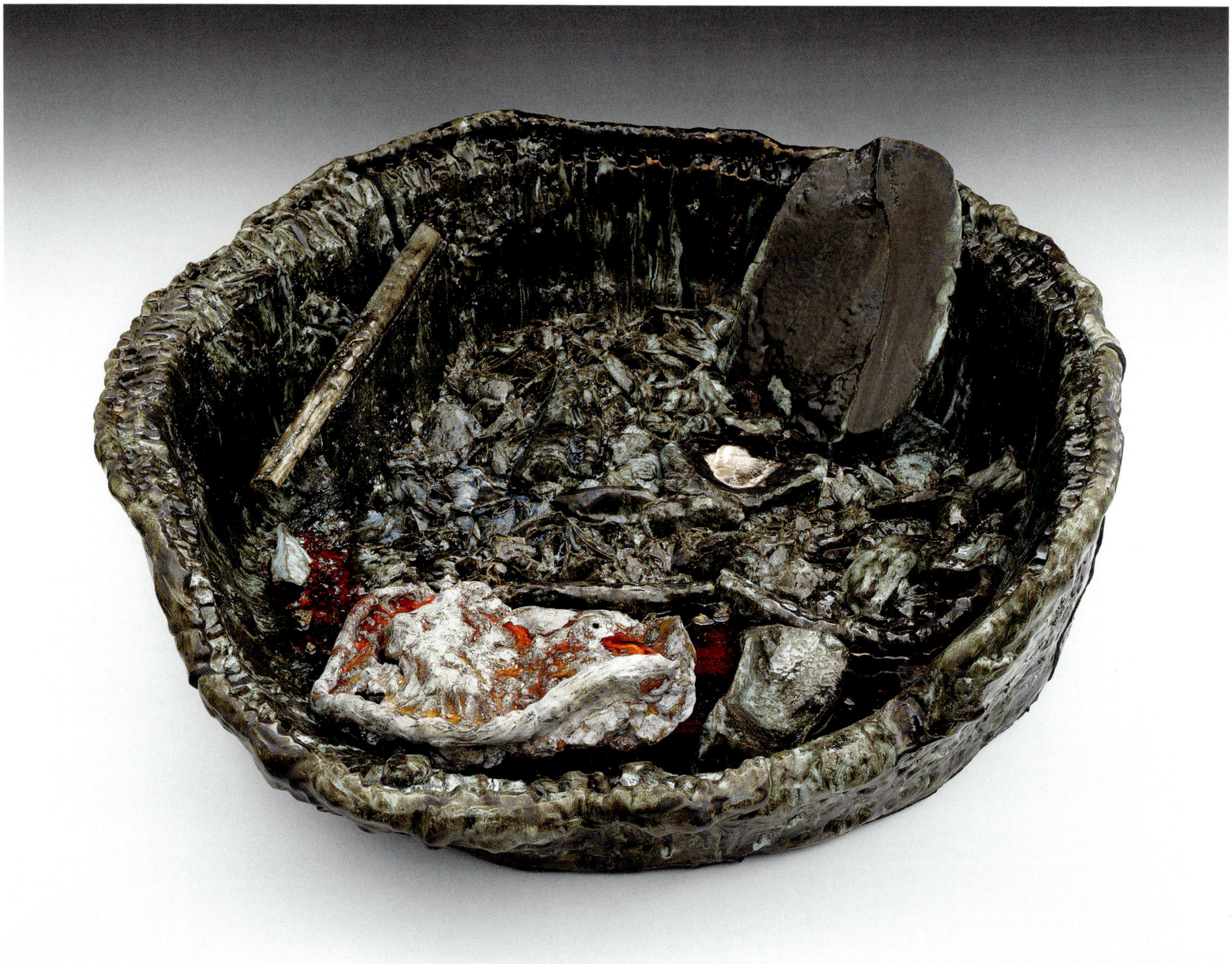

Basin Theology/CRYPTOCRYSTALLINE, 2016
Ceramic

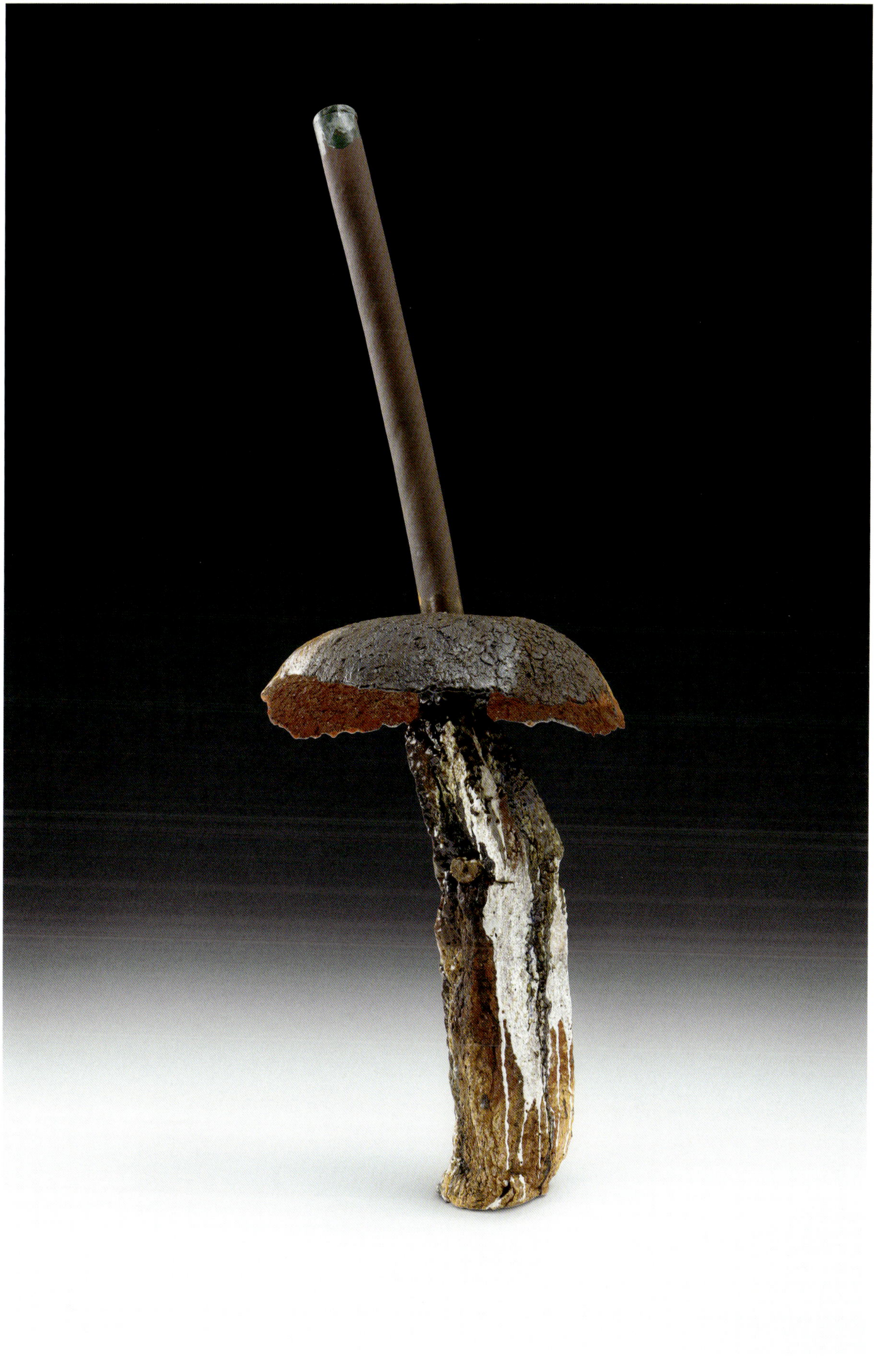

ANGLE OF DEPRESSION, 2017
Ceramic

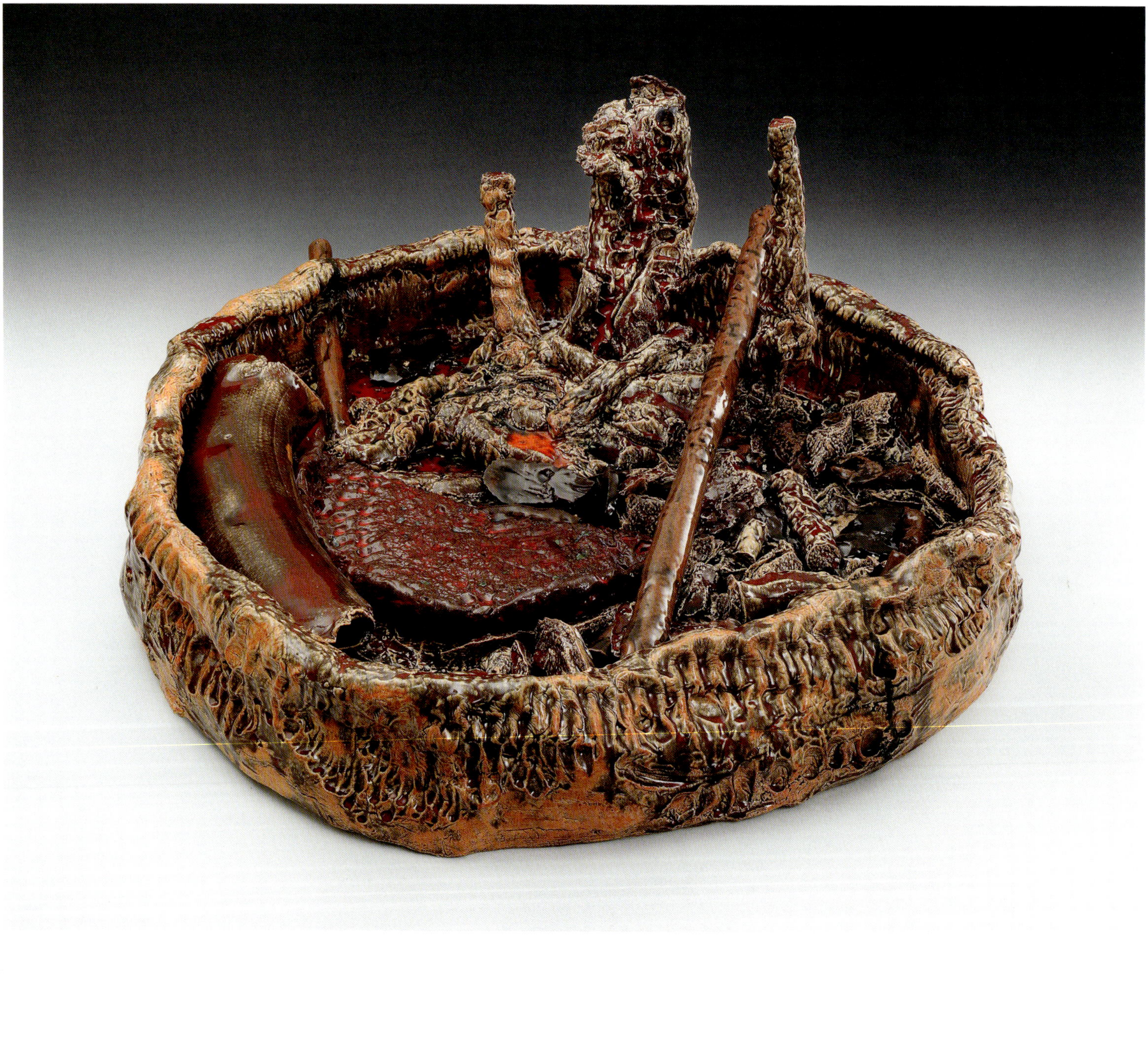

Basin Theology/Red Bull, 2013
Ceramic

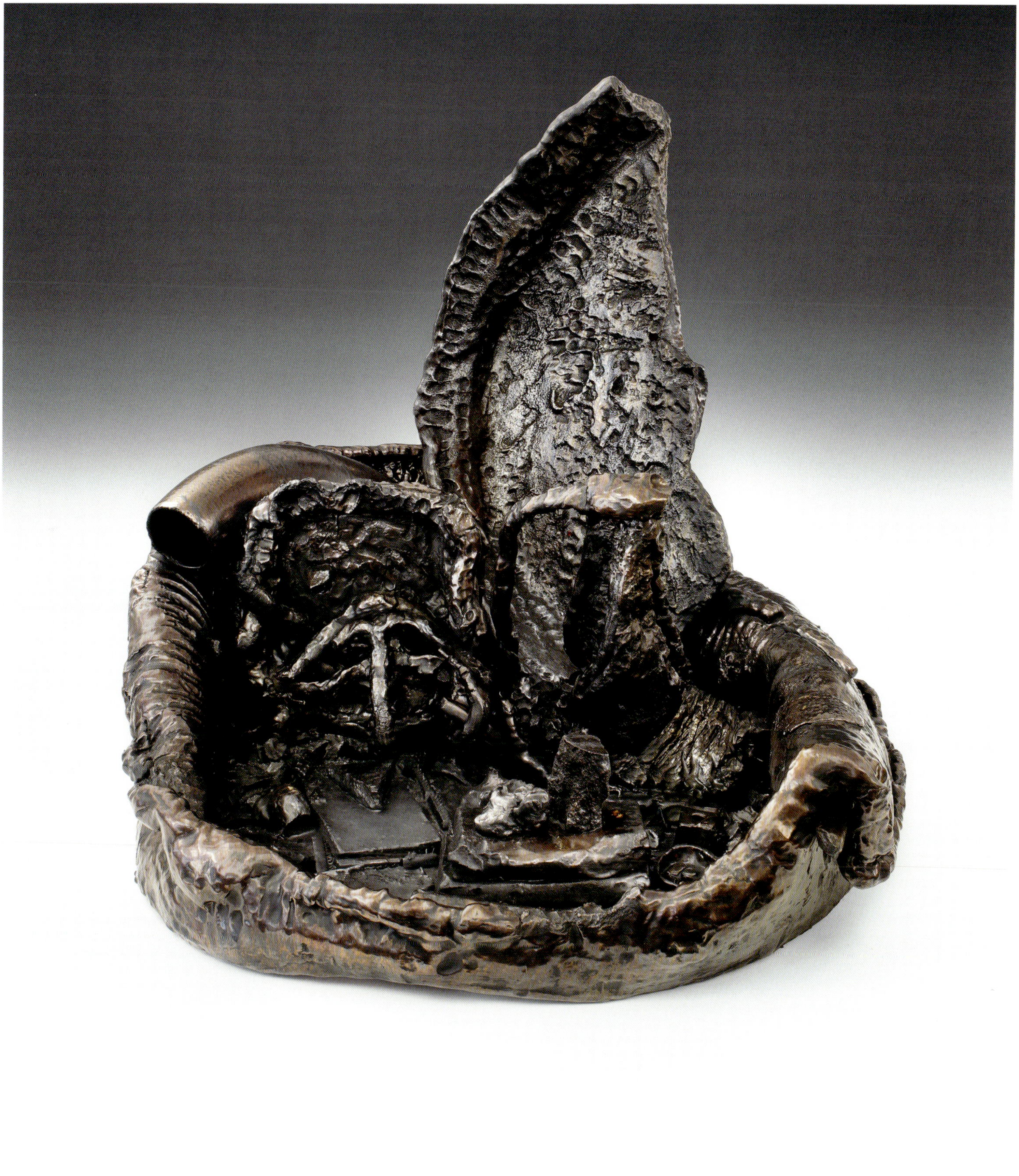

Basin Theology/Redox, 2013
Ceramic

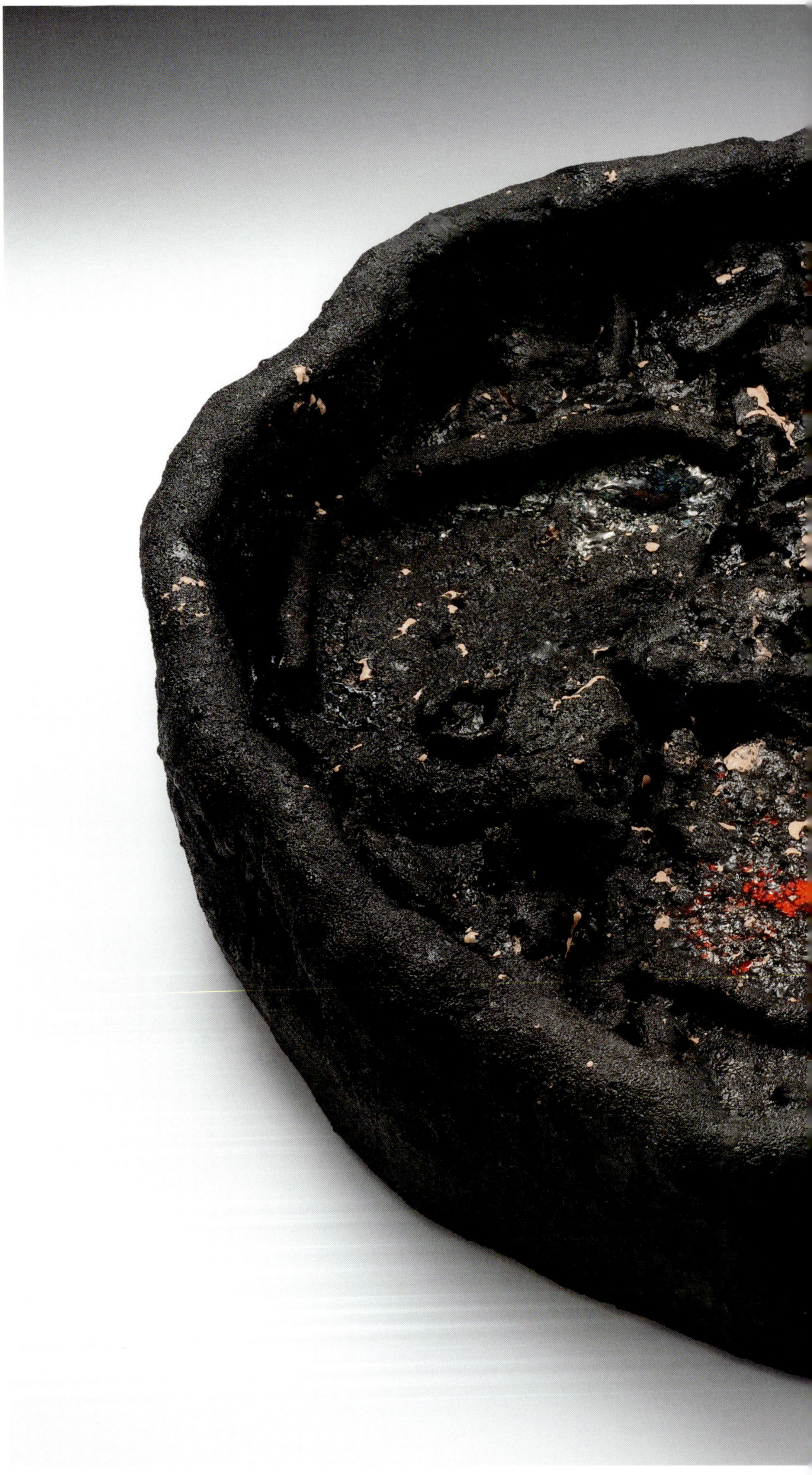

***Basin Theology/La Brea 2*, 2011**
Ceramic

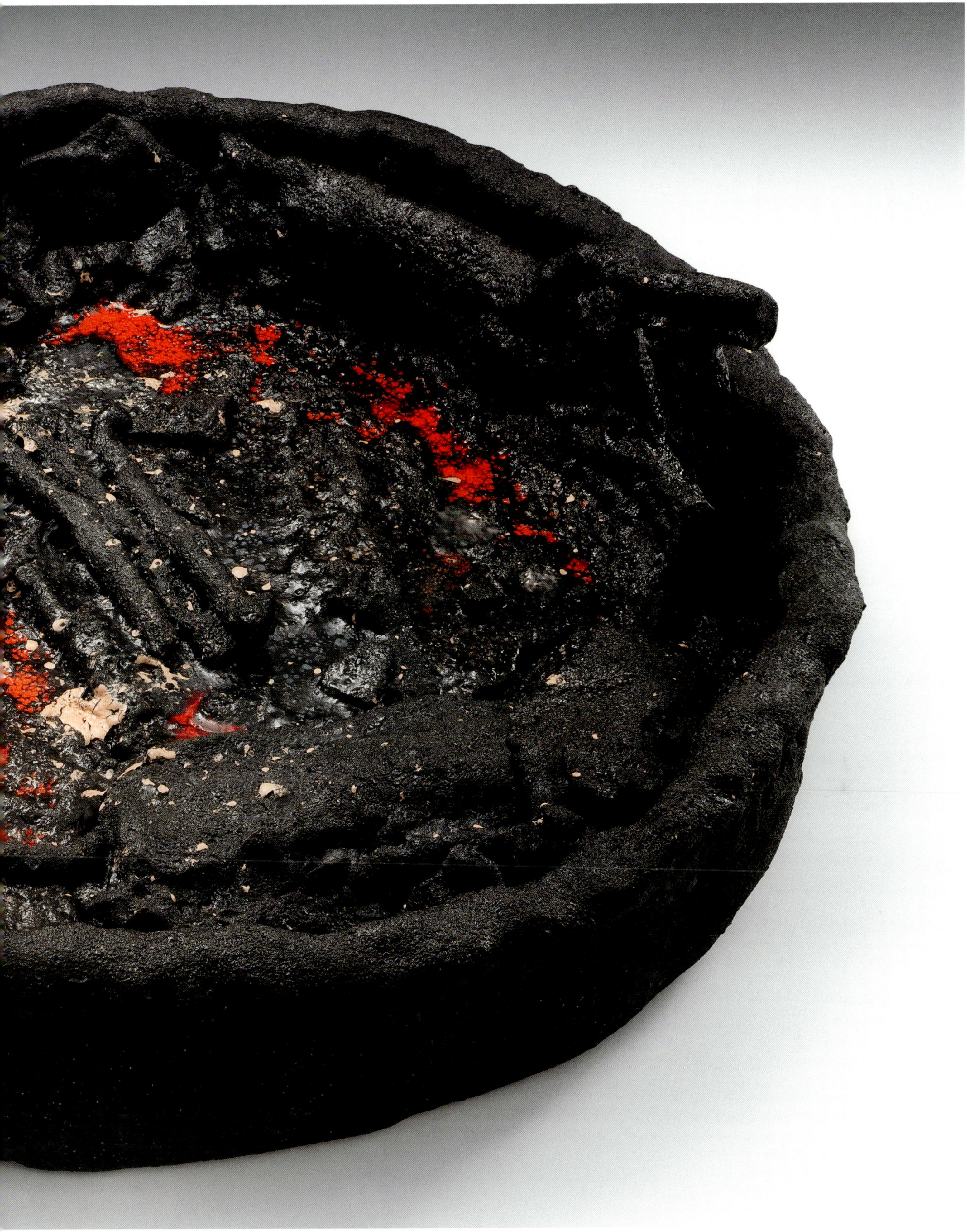

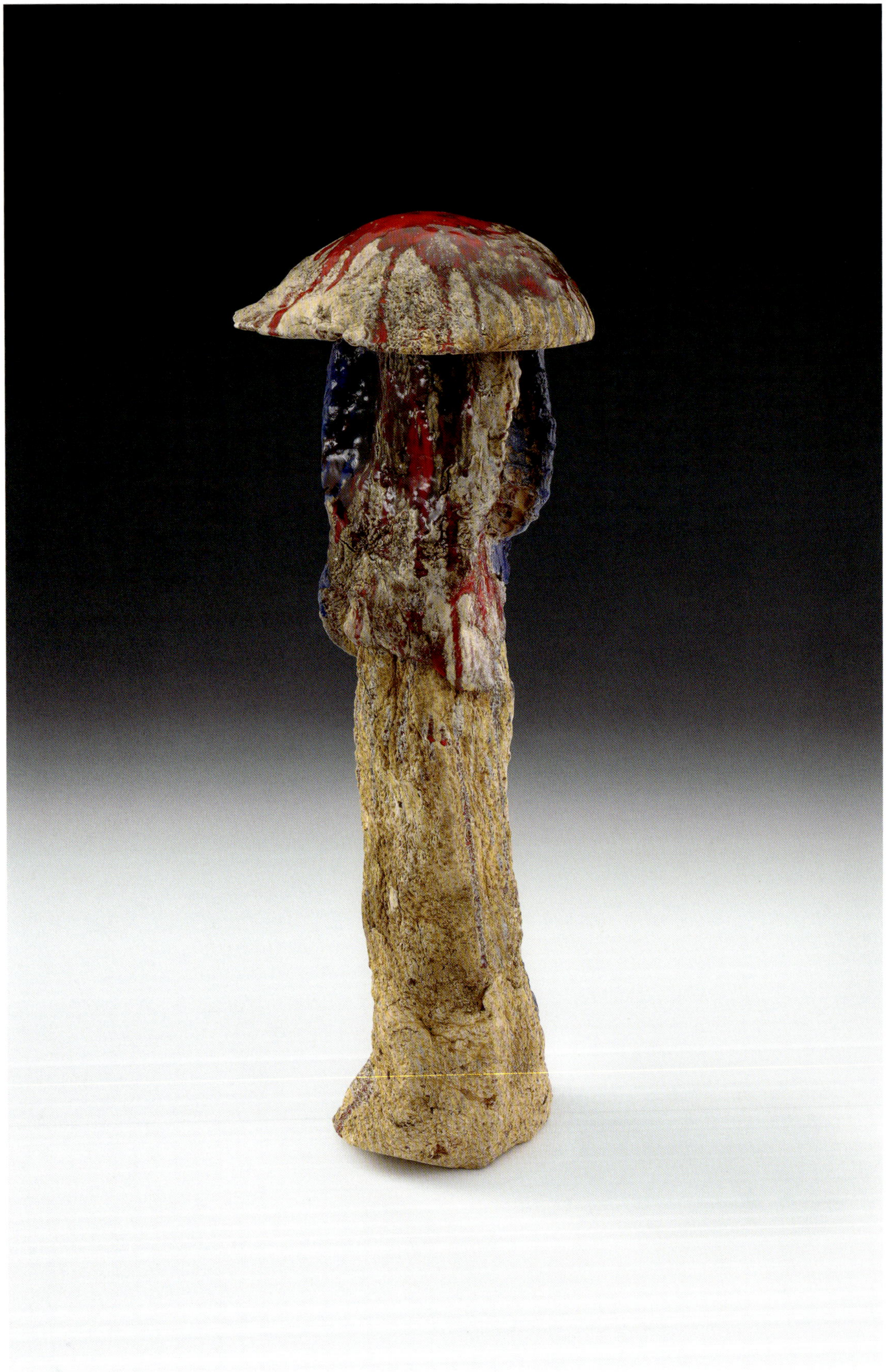

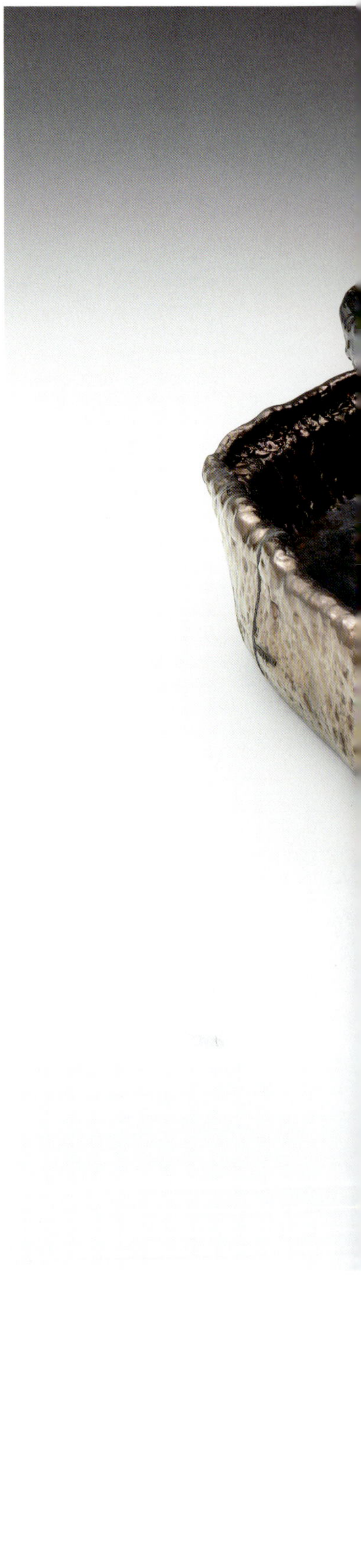

***TROOPER*, 2017**
Ceramic

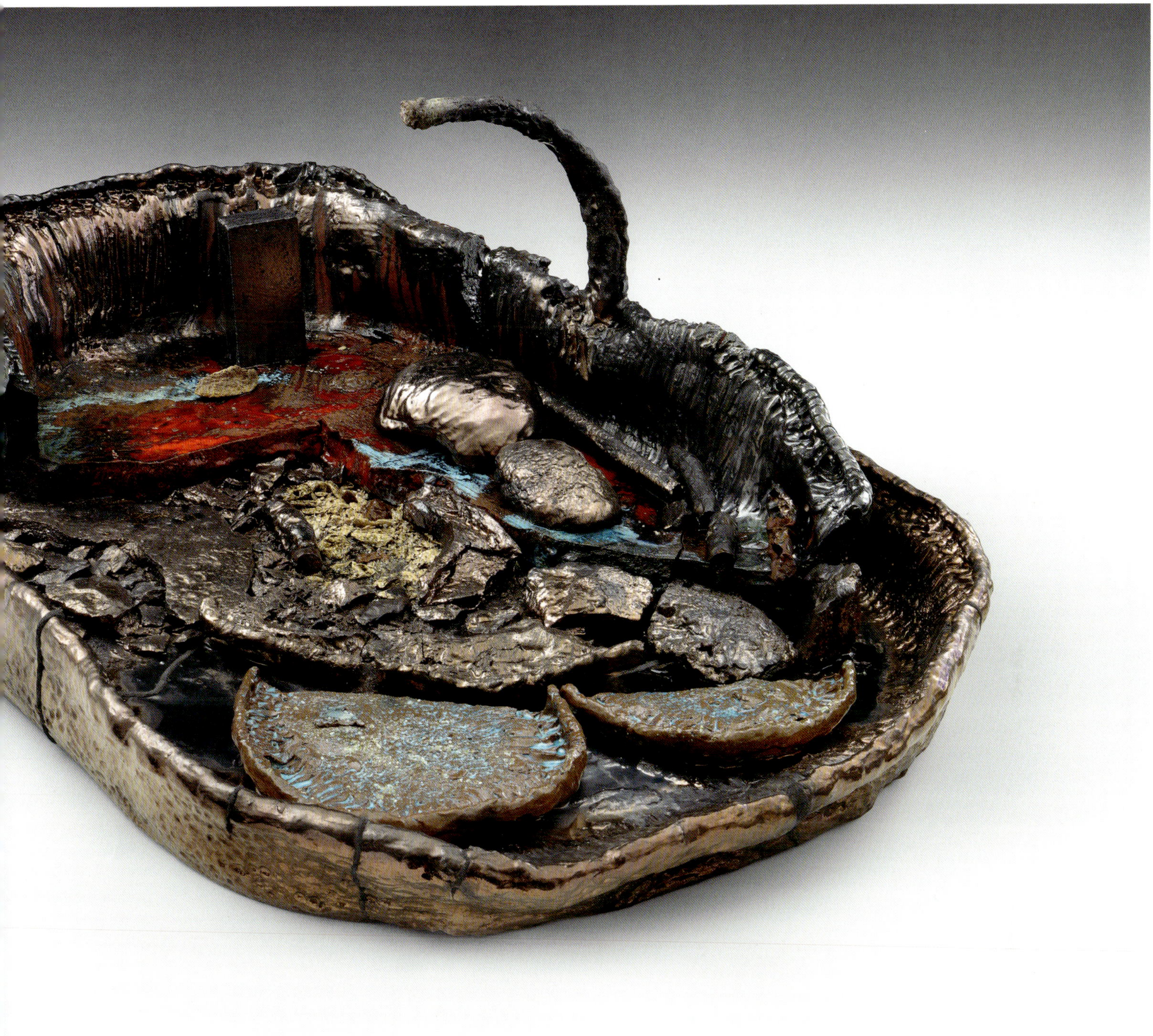

Basin Theology/STYX BOAT, 2017
Ceramic

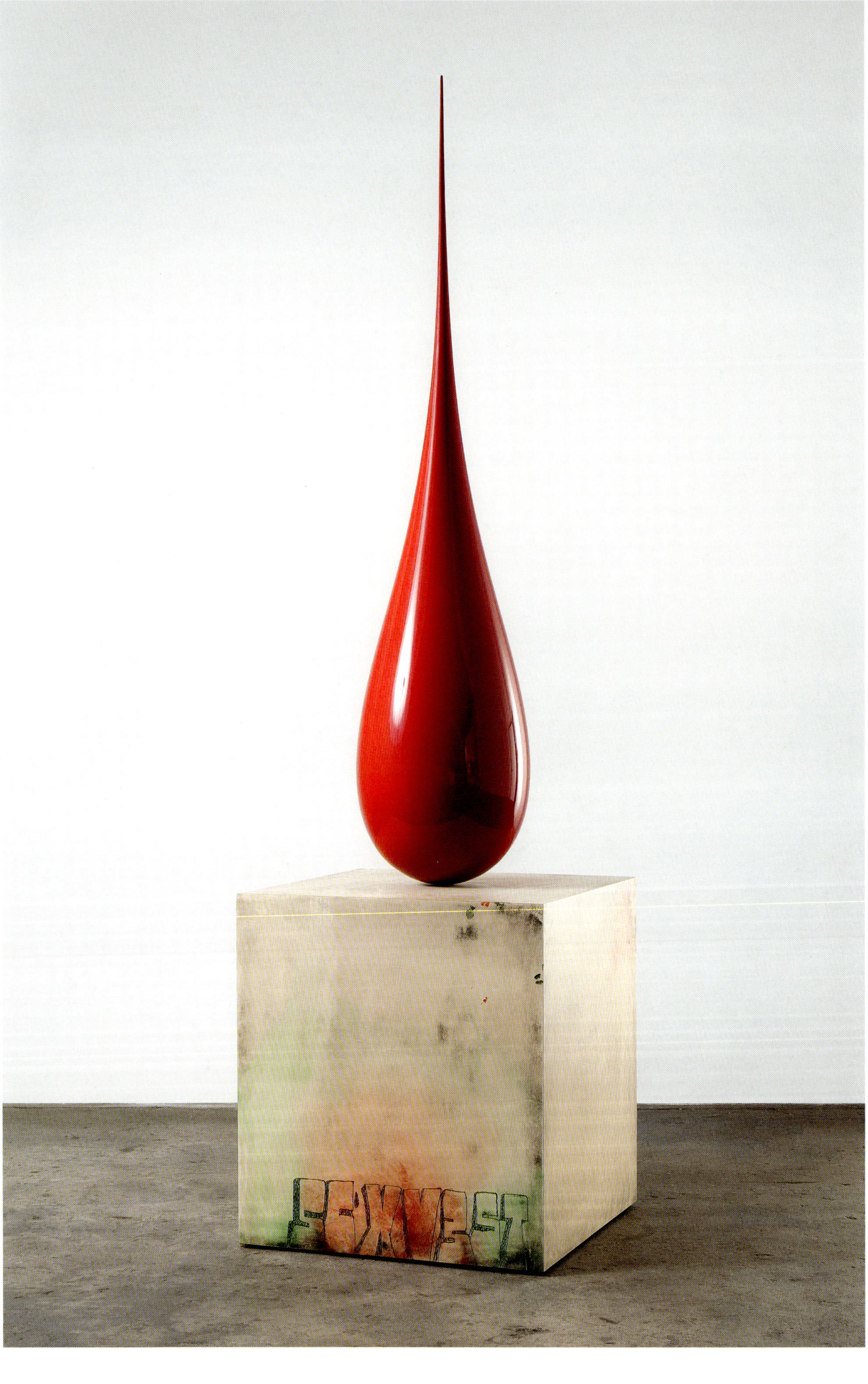

Geometric Solids, ACTS, and Alabasters

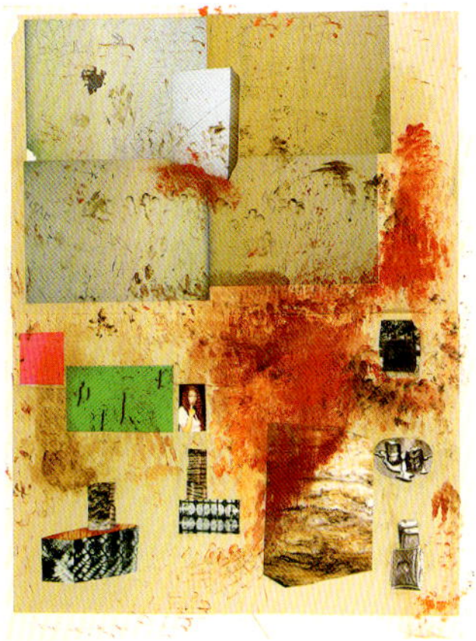

Fig. 1: *(4C) Study for Cubes, Codes, Crypts and Cosmetic*, 2006. Collage and paint on paper

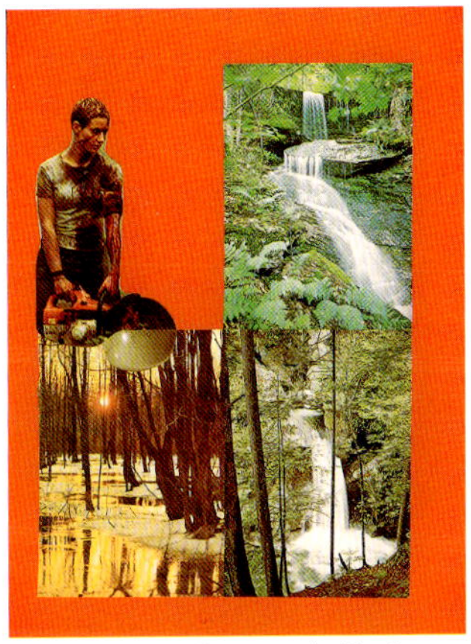

Fig. 2: *Absolute Contempt for Total Serenity #2*, 2005. Collage on paper

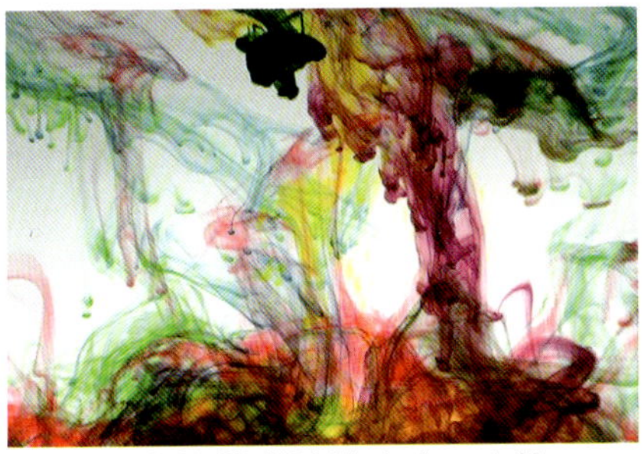

Fig. 3: *Dihedral* (still), 2006. Single channel video (color, sound; 8:06 minutes)

AN EARLY antagonism toward minimalism in Ruby's work developed out of his reading of its restrictive nature and its problematic ties to a brand of masculine authority. As Ruby's interrogation of the movement evolved along multiple fronts, he began to perceive the "unitary forms" of minimalism as analogous with institutional architectures—such as super-maximum security prisons—both reliant upon structures of discipline and control. Ruby maps this equivalency in several bodies of work, with text from *Anti-Print 3* (2005) framing his overriding concern: "FINISH ARCHITECTURE. KILL MINIMALISM. LONG LIVE THE AMORPHOUS LAW."

Ruby's series of geometric solids, formica monoliths in different shapes and orientations that Ruby often tags with spray paint or otherwise inscribes, evince his approach to grappling with the historical legacy of minimalism in sculpture. *Big Grid/DB Deth* (2008), for example, is an anthropomorphic, white formica and wood construction with cutout, look-through "eyes" that Ruby defiles with black spray paint and various inscriptions. Etched under the eyes of the sculpture are drops, recurring symbols in Ruby's work. From the early drawing *Crystal Cryer* (2001) [p. 36] to a series of soft sculptures, the drop references blood or teardrops, including the teardrop prison tattoos below the eyes that signify that the wearer has committed murder, suffered a long sentence, or lost a loved one, among other things. Monolithic forms appear in Ruby's collages as well, at times with wall-mounted Donald Judd sculptures compared with cells from supermax prisons, or in the equation of minimalist geometries with crypts, as in *(4C) Study for Cubes, Codes, Crypts and Cosmetic* (2006) [fig. 1].

Another three of Ruby's early collages feature an image of a bloodied and emboldened Cécile de France defiantly wielding a cut-off saw—taken from her role as Marie, the protagonist of the horror movie *High Tension* (2003)—juxtaposed with several images of natural landscapes against an orange background. Each titled *Absolute Contempt for Total Serenity* (2004–2005) [fig. 2] the collages suggest a particular aversion toward such unspoiled images of the natural landscape. Ruby subsequently began making a series of sculptures he calls ACTS (Absolute Contempt for Total Serenity), which feature different configurations of clear urethane blocks colored with dye and balanced on treated formica. The pigments are suspended in each clear urethane block, fixed in between liquid and solid states of matter, in a way that recalls both Ruby's video *Dihedral* (2006) [fig. 3] and his series of cast acrylic alabaster sheets. While the formica volumes suggest the geometric solids of minimalism in banal designer colors, Ruby employs aggressive gestures to disrupt the uniformity of the configurations he assembles. The volumes are again spray painted, smudged, or inscribed with graffiti-like segments of language or symbols. Like the other geometric solids, the ACTS sculptures convey what the artist Richard Hawkins has described as Ruby's consistent "antipathy towards austerity"[1] through bodies of work that systematically destabilize programmatic aspects of minimalism.

—J. D.

1. Richard Hawkins, "Sterling Ruby: Long Live the Amorphous Law," *Flash Art*, October 2006, 80, https://flash---art.com/article/sterling-ruby-2/.

SCXV3ST/BD, **2012**
Fiberglass, wood, spray paint, and formica

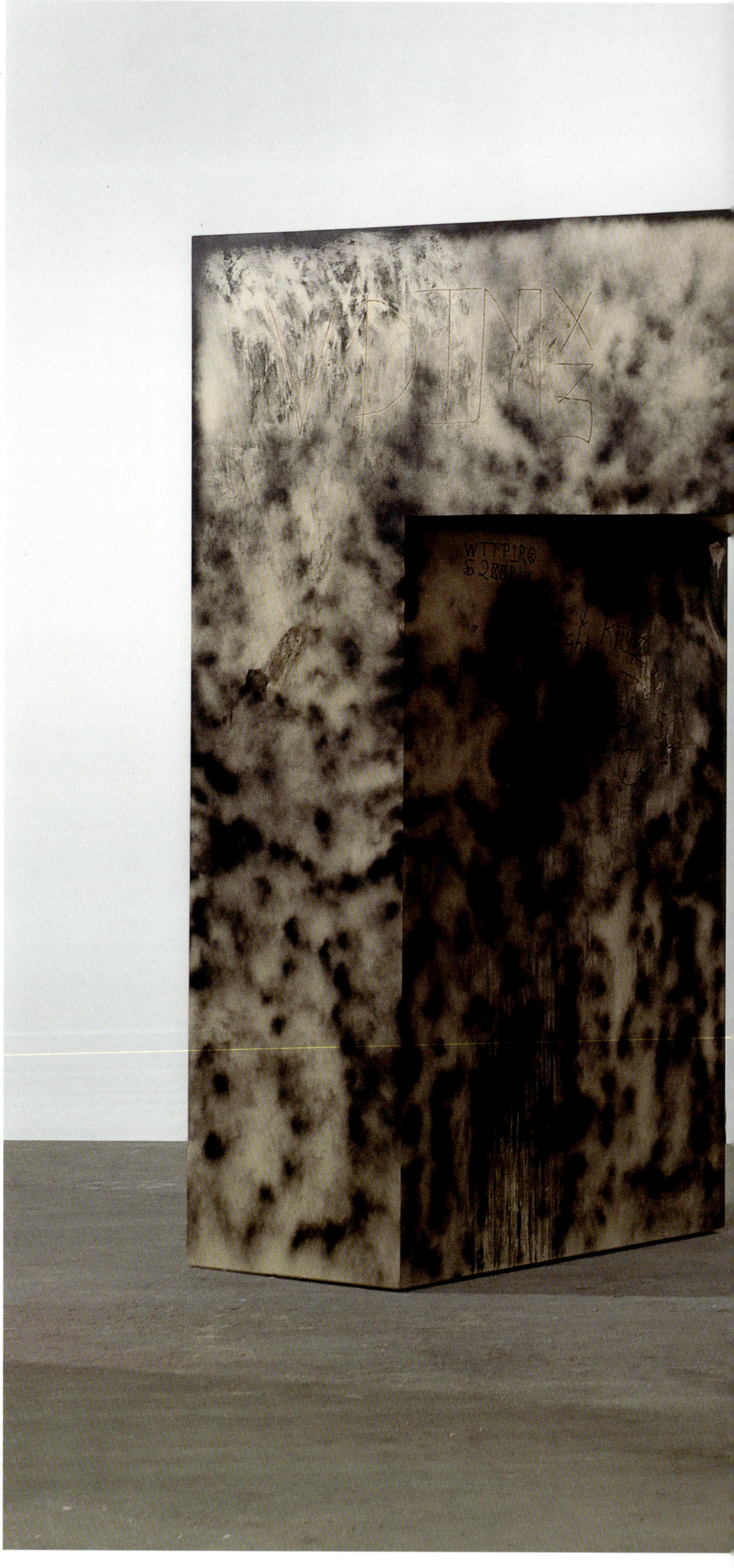

ZEN RIPPER, 2008
Formica, spray paint, and wood

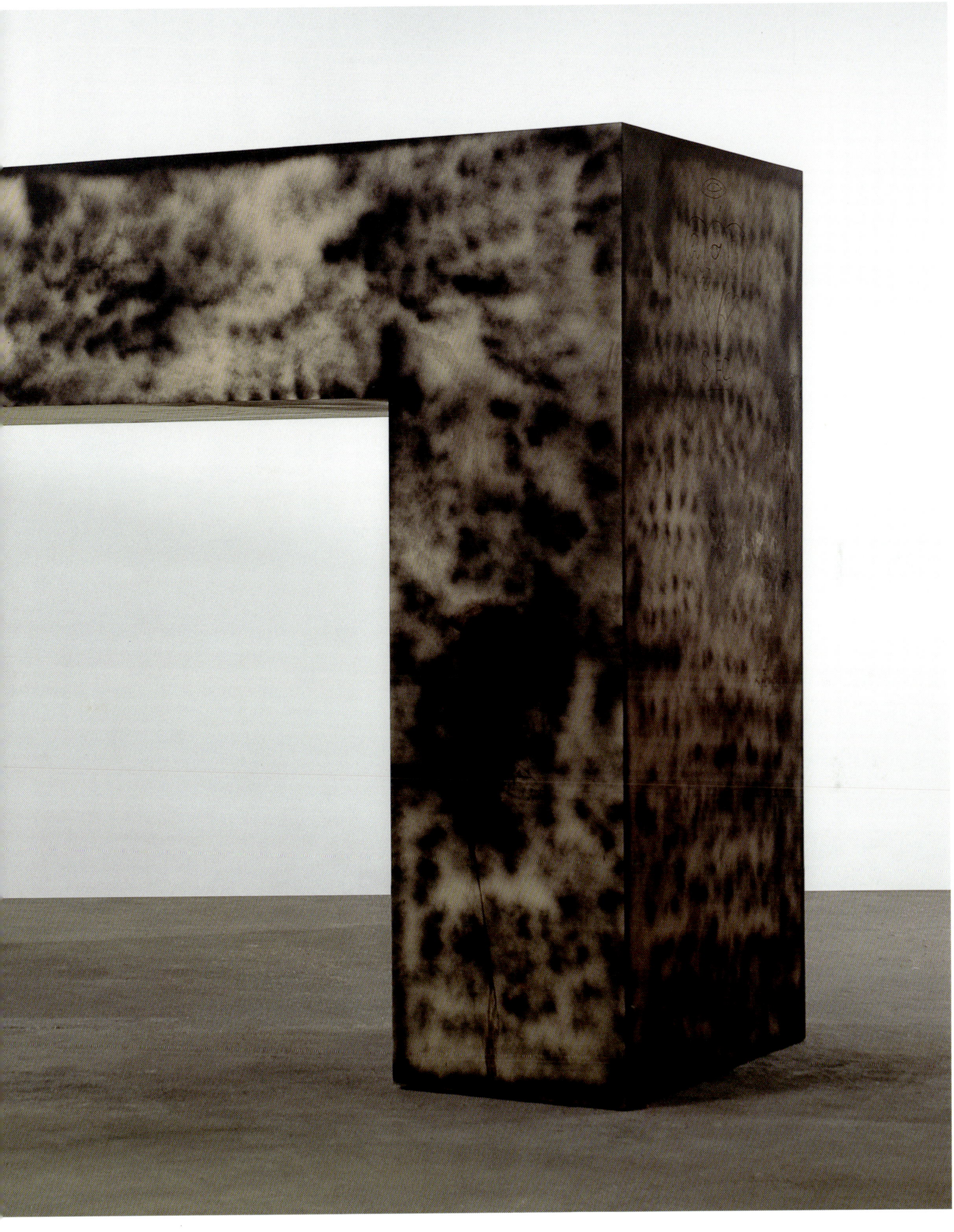

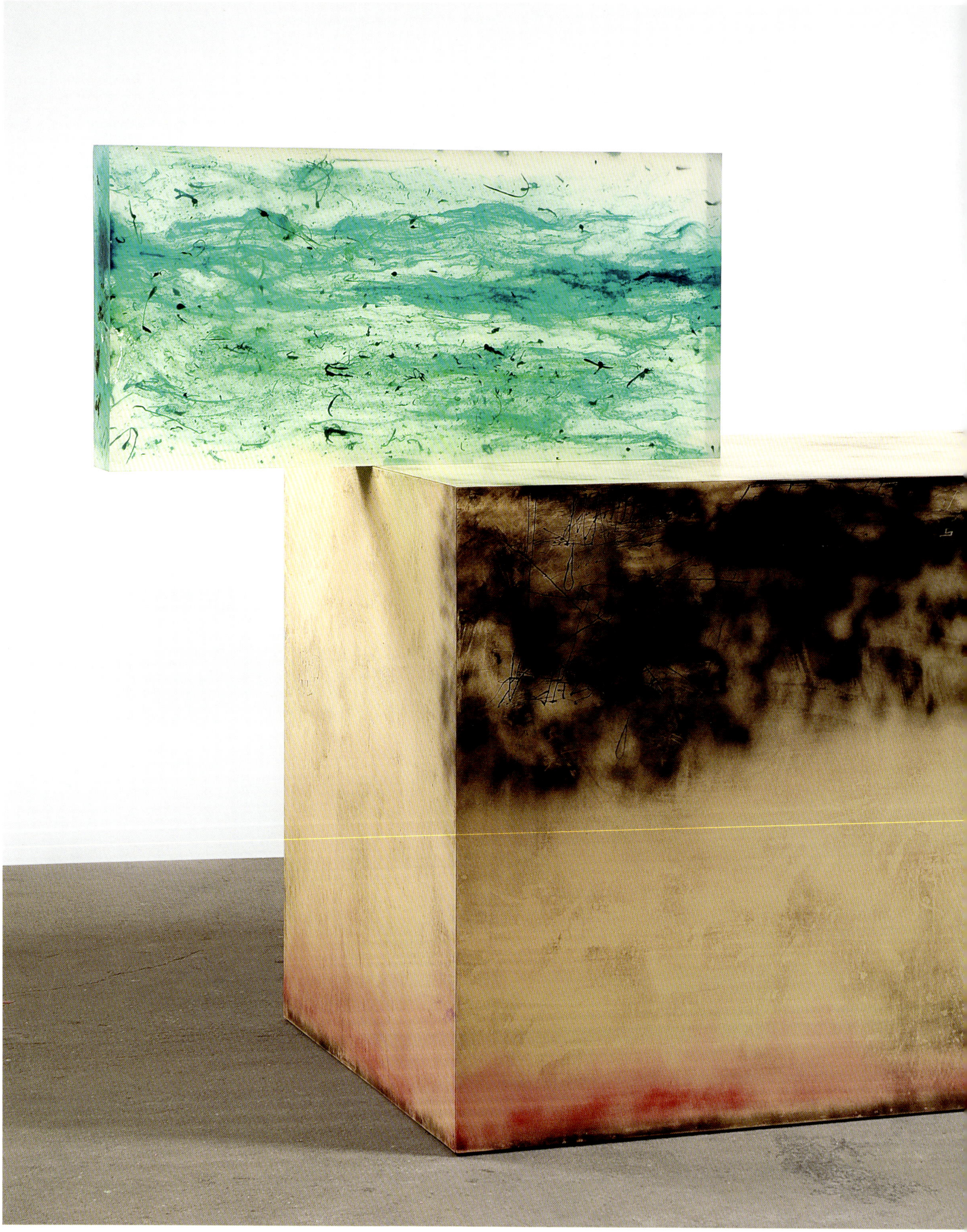

ACTS/ 187 DREAMER, 2009
Clear urethane block, dye, wood, spray paint, and formica

Next spread:
Installation view, *SUPEROVERPASS*, Foxy Production, New York, 2007

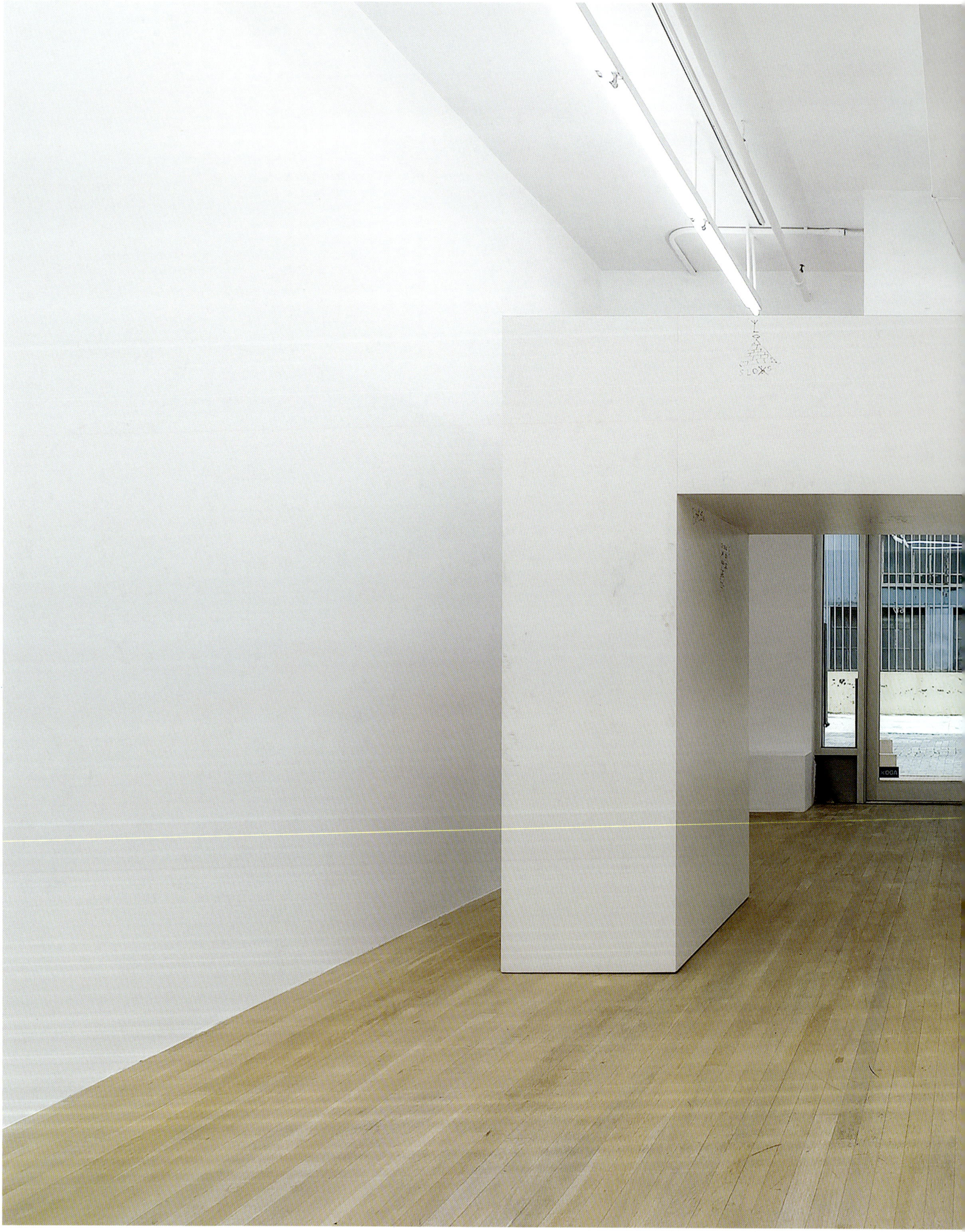

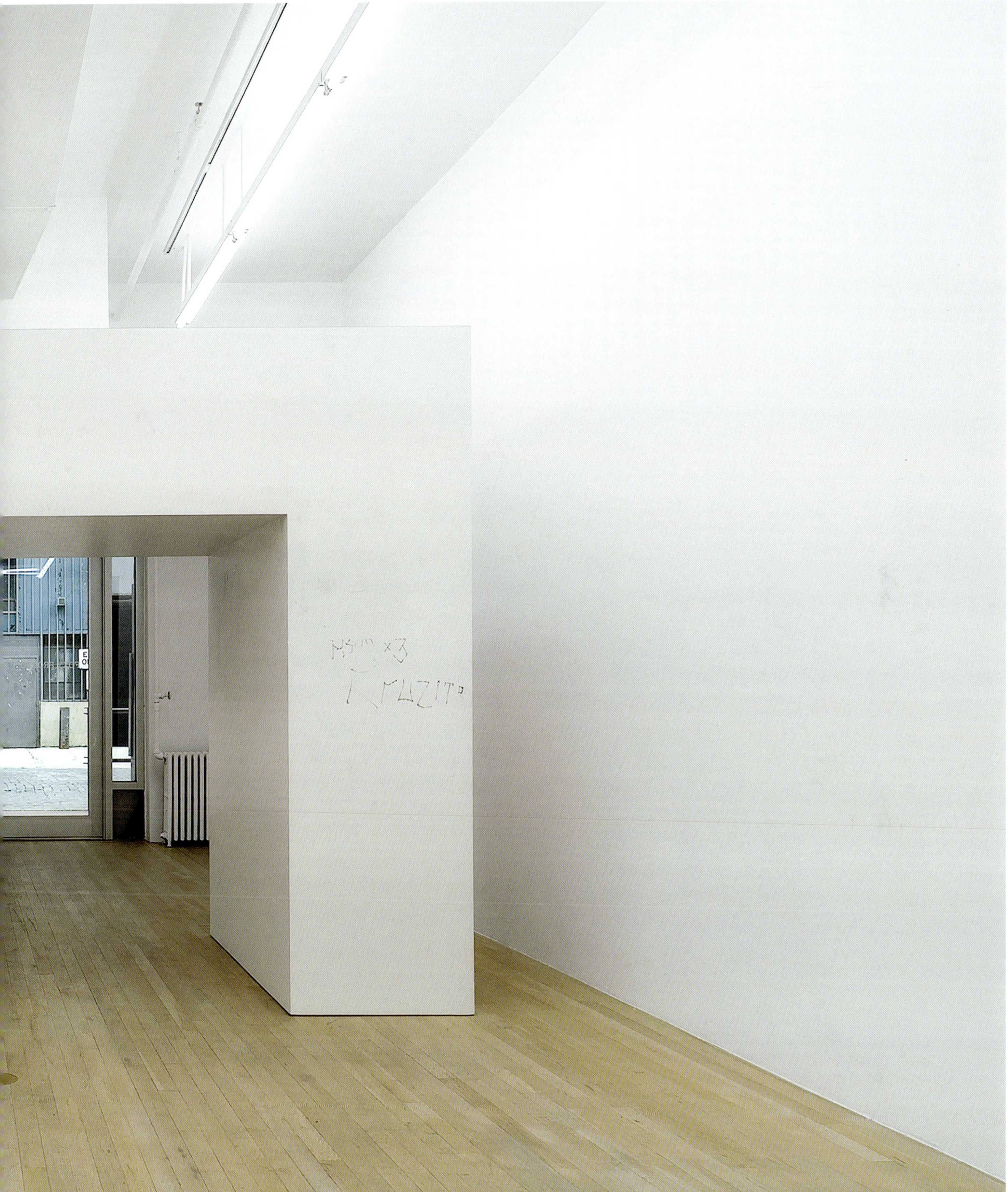

Big Grid/DB Deth, 2008
Formica, spray paint, and wood

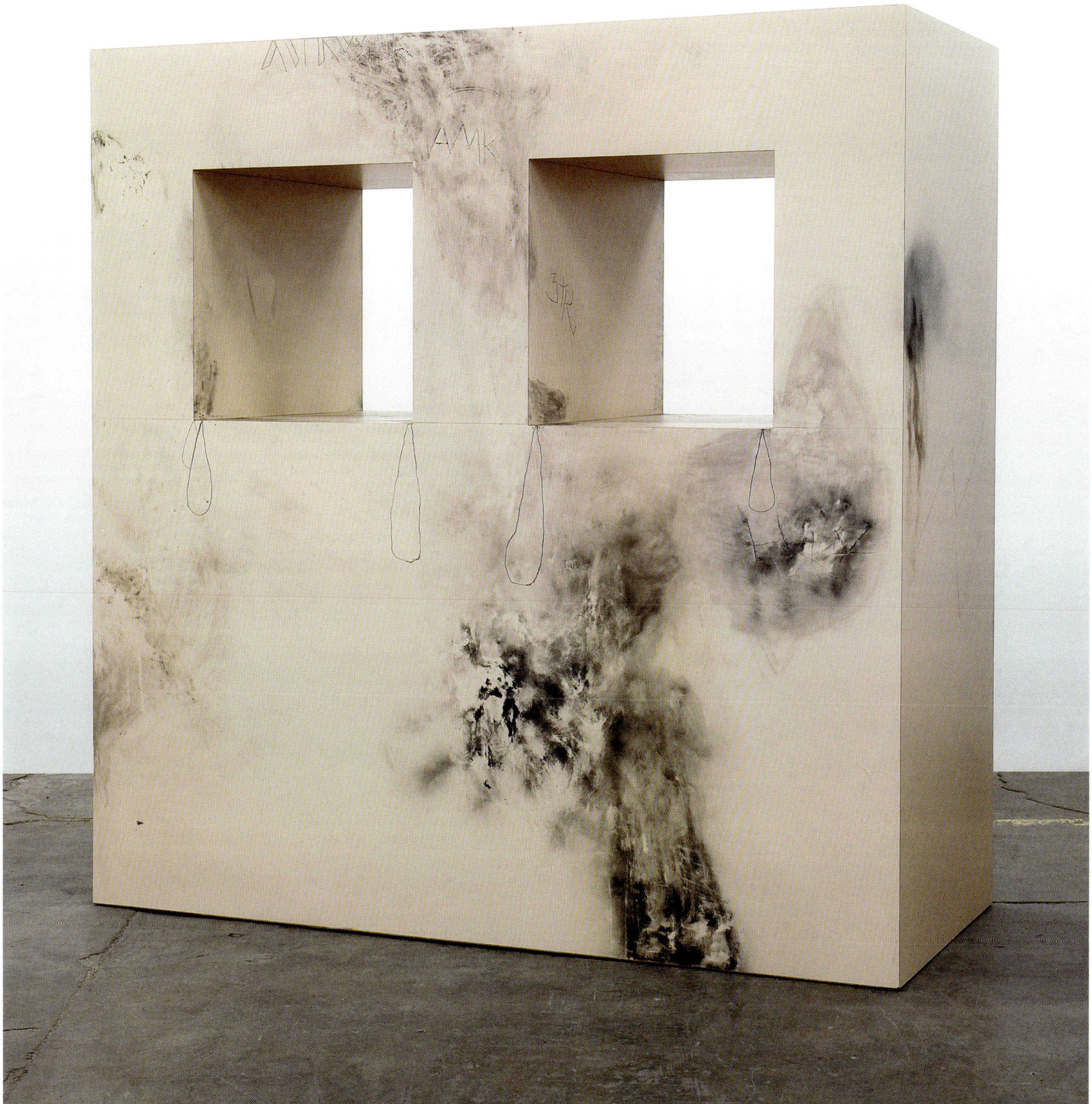

ACTS/WS ROLLIN, 2011
Clear urethane block, dye, wood, spray paint, and formica

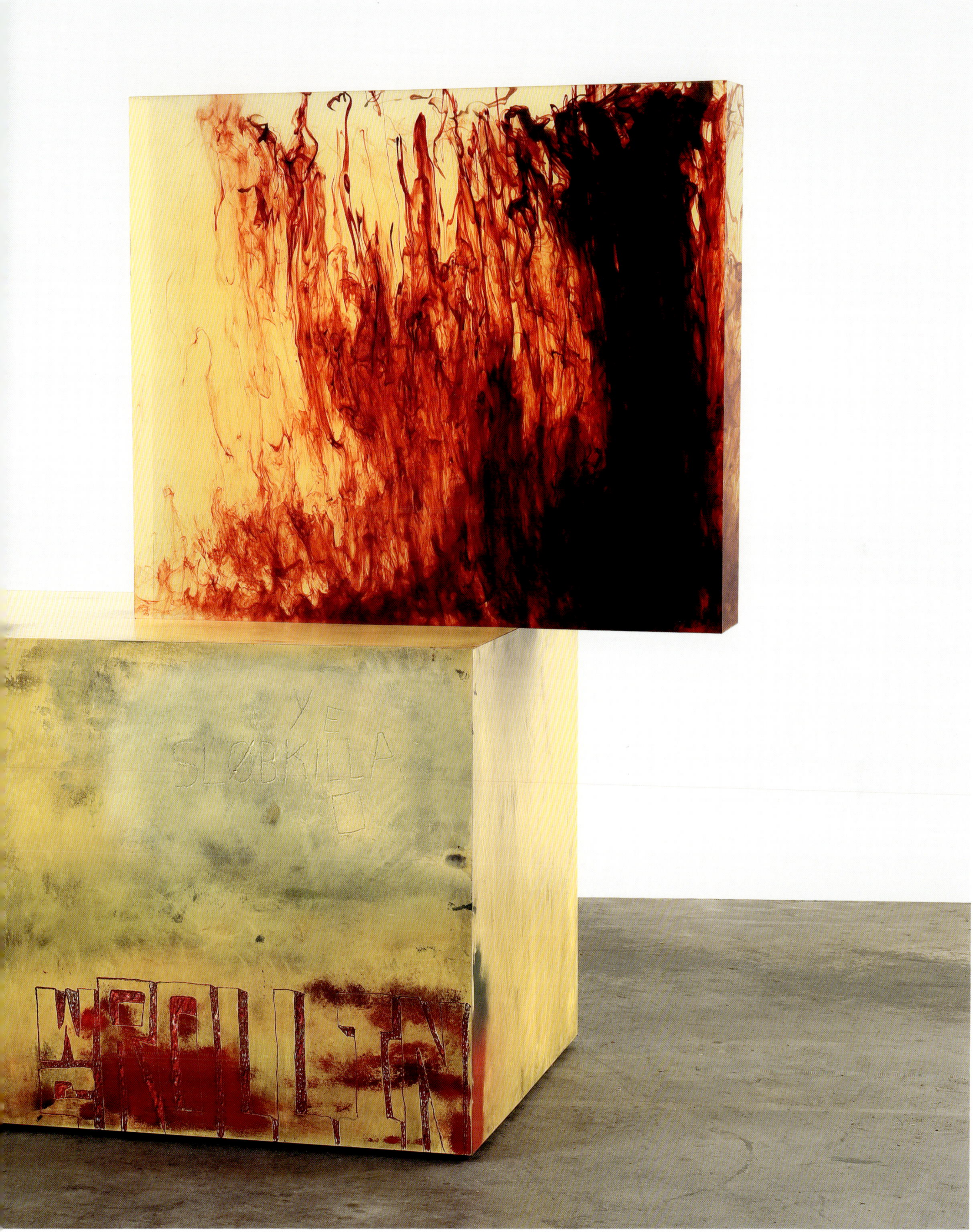
YE
SLØBKILLA

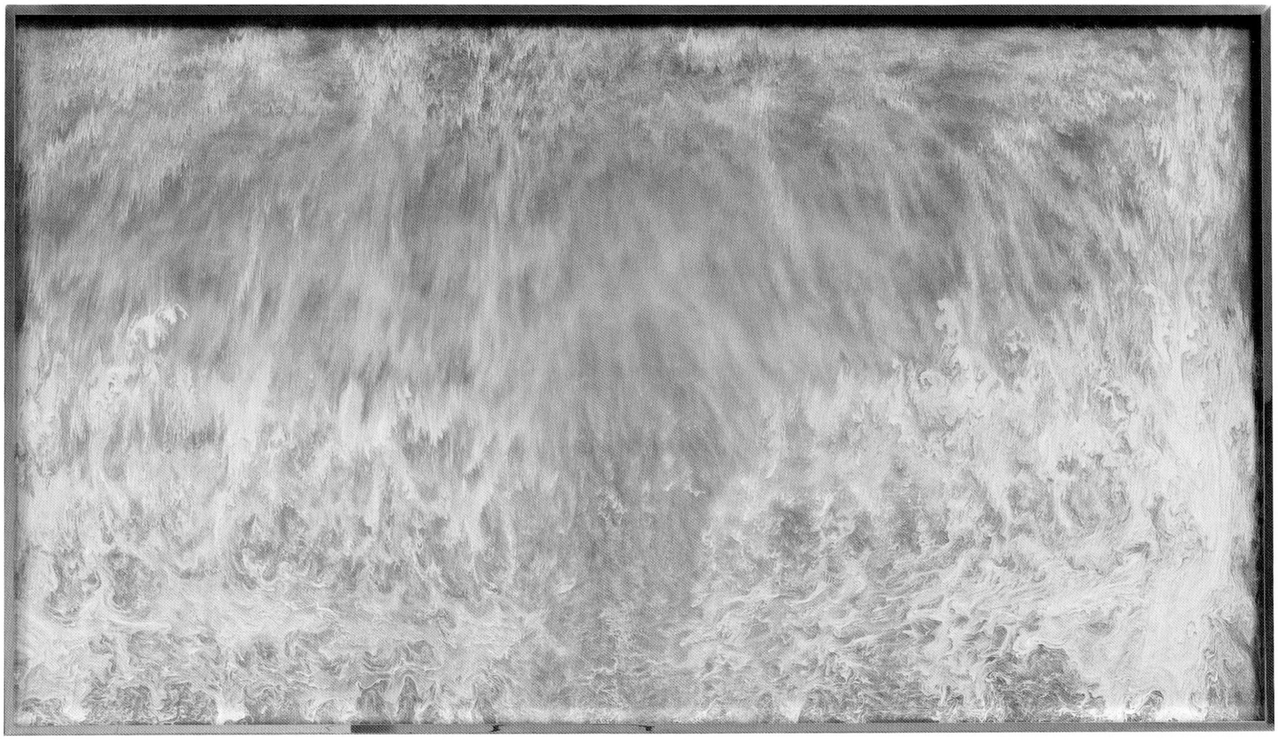

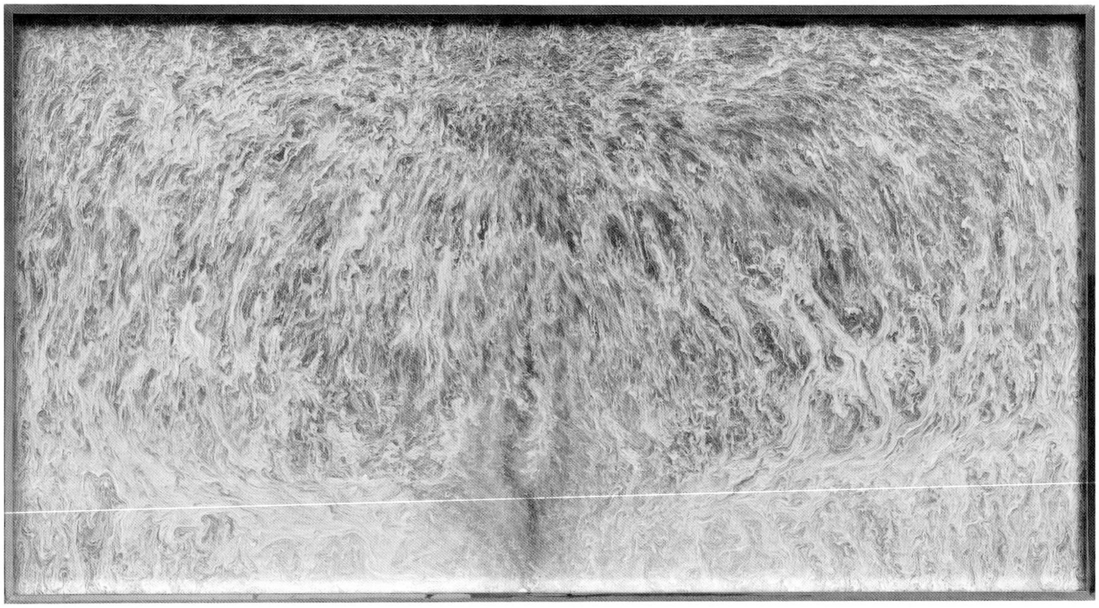

Opposite, top to bottom:

***Alabaster SR10-16*, 2010**
Acrylic

***Alabaster SR08-2*, 2008**
Acrylic

Top:
***Alabaster SR11-58*, 2011**
Acrylic

Bottom:
***Alabaster SR11-63*, 2011**
Acrylic

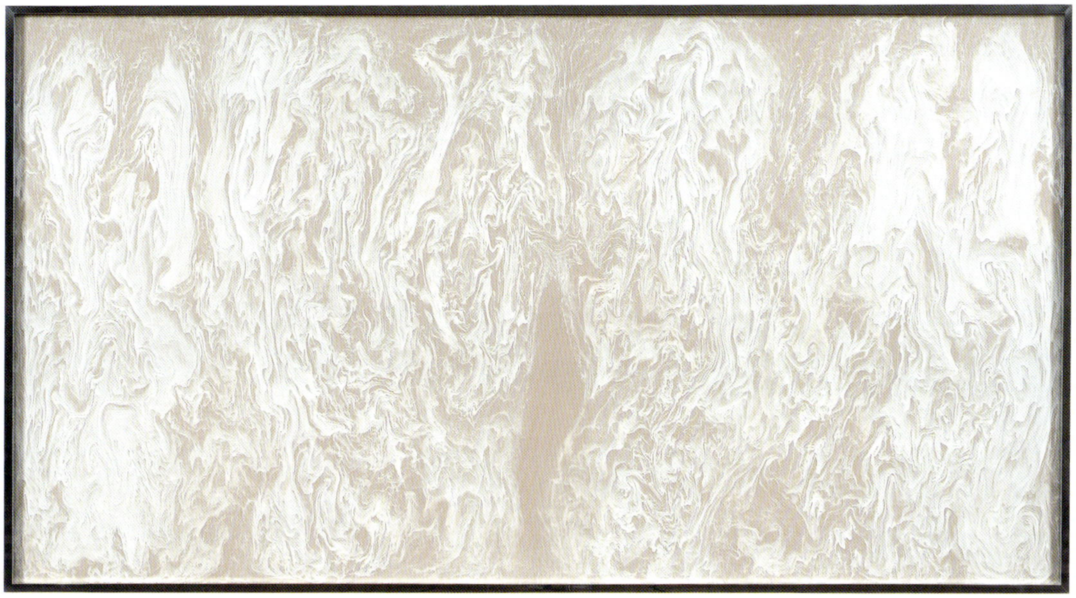

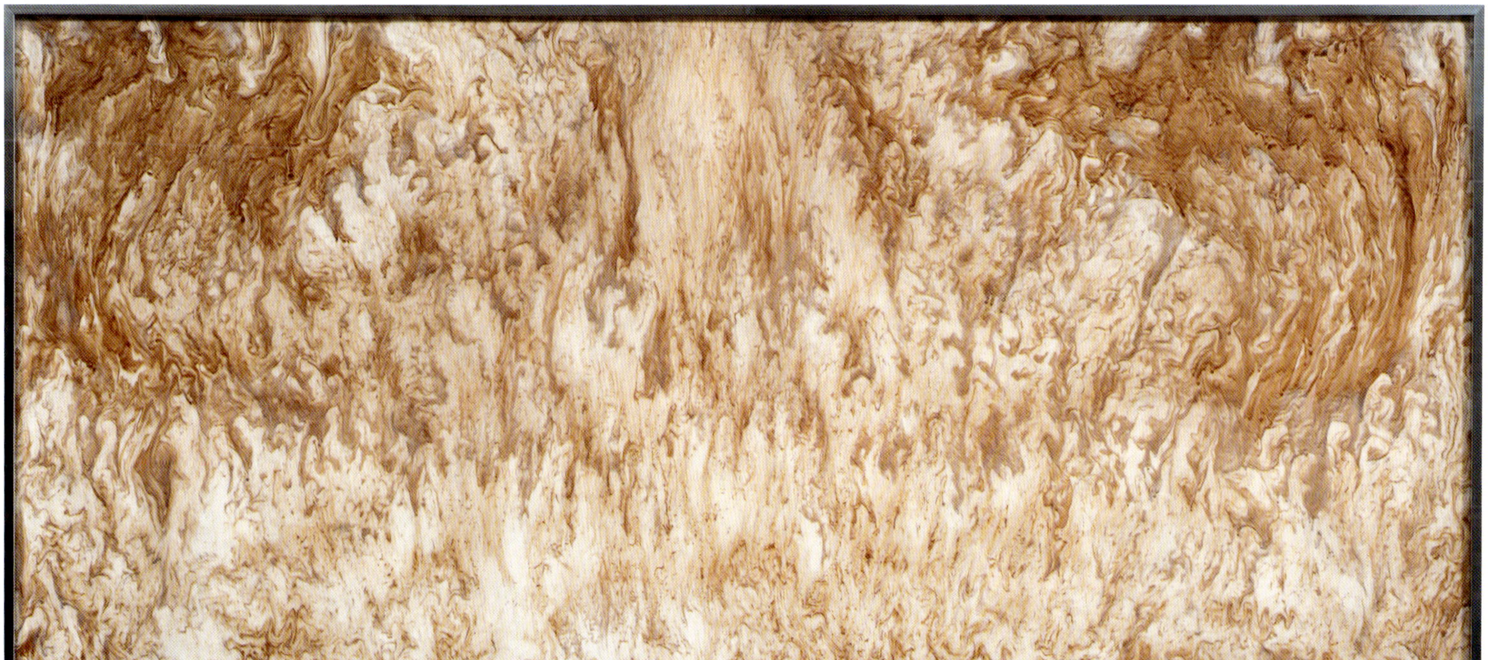

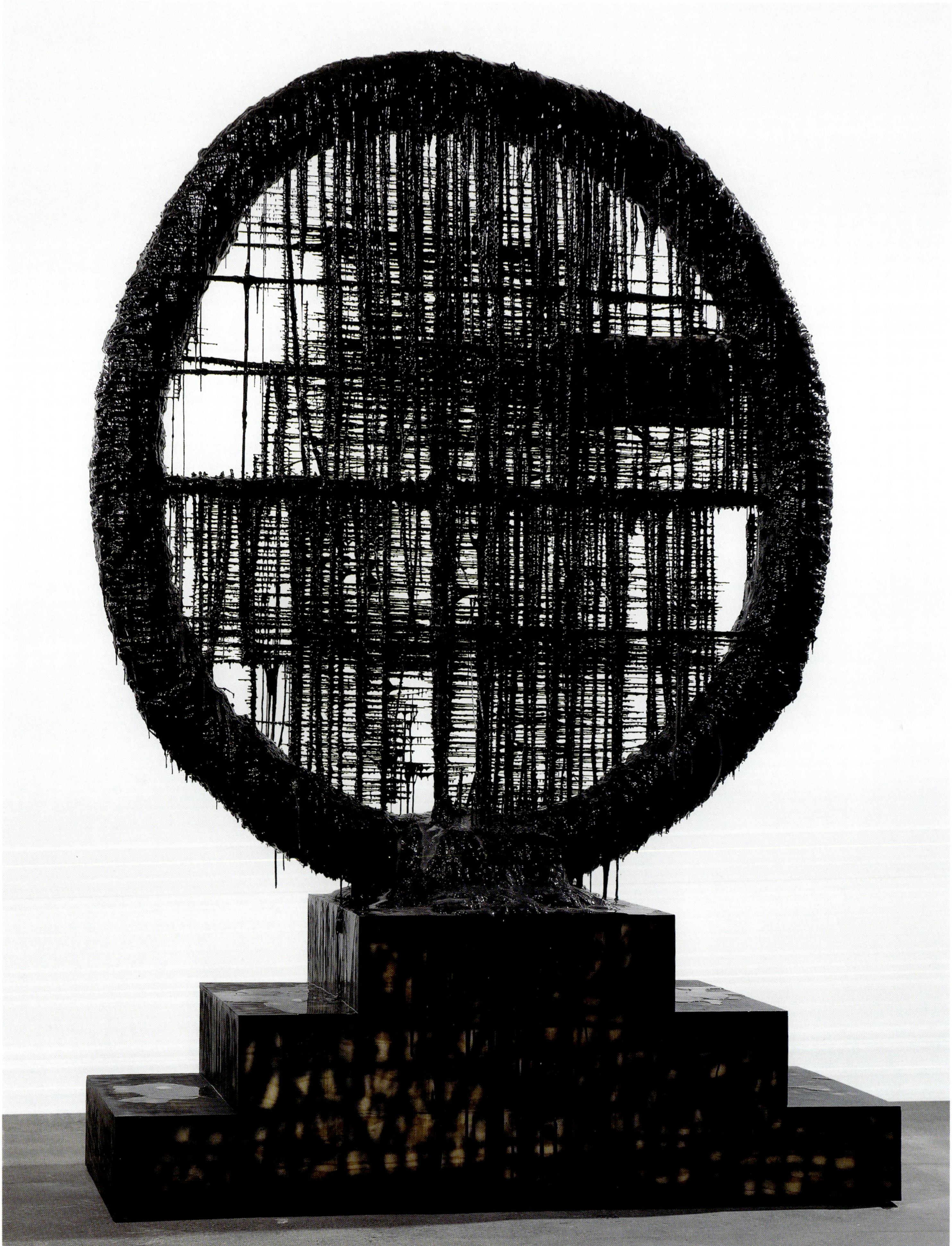

Urethanes

AFTER MAKING ceramic sculptures and working with the practical limitations of scale particular to electric car kilns for several years, Ruby started making monumental, "scale-less" poured urethane sculptures around 2005. Over the course of several months, Ruby pours liquid urethane over an object from above in small batches, working quickly before the noxious urethane solidifies. This labor-intensive process is repeated until the dense layers of urethane achieve a desired visual effect, such as the irregular grid of labyrinthine drips hardened within the negative space of an upright, gate-like circular object in *Black Star/Prostitute's Bolster* (2007). Here, the urethane appears like overlapping, individually drawn lines that preserve the expressive nature of each drop, creating a petrified structure that entombs a bolster within its framework. As a final step, color is applied as a kind of tinting dye with glossy coats of clear urethane, such that each sculpture appears wet, as if still in formation.

Other urethane sculptures explore this process using different formal configurations. Two works bare the spray-painted insignia "CDCR," the initialism for the California Department of Corrections and Rehabilitation. In *BASIN CDCR* (2011), for example, an elongated wood and PVC appendage extends out of a circular basin affixed in layers of red, black, and blue urethane on a low formica plinth. As in other of these works, the wooden element acts like a crutch that supports the anthropomorphic phallic extremity, delimiting the sense of powerful masculinity implied by the monumental form.

Naturally occurring outcrops such as stalagmites appear frequently in Ruby's collages, such as in *Nails, Mammary, Stalagmites* (2010) [p. 43]. Though Ruby had been experimenting intermittently with poured urethane Stalagmites since 2002, it was five years later that he settled on the recognizable form of his Monument Stalagmites—tall, upright accumulations supported by a wooden crutch on a low formica plinth. In his work, the stalagmite—a type of rock formation that arises from the floor of a cave due to the drip of calcareous water—often stands for the "amorphous law" that counters the institutionalization of the rigid geometries of minimalism.

For the Stalagmites, denotation implies narrative possibilities for abstract sculptures. In *Monument Stalagmite/The Shining* (2011), for example, "THE SHINING" is written in bright orange, outlined in black on the wooden support. The cascading, deep red color of the object then takes on the quality of blood, alluding to the infamous scene in Stanley Kubrick's 1980 film adaptation of Stephen King's novel *The Shining* (1977) when a torrent of blood pours from an elevator in the Overlook Hotel. The subtitling of each Monument Stalagmite carries forward similar associations found in much of Ruby's works in a towering sculpture that inhabits, often with violent intensity, museum architectures.

—J. D.

Black Star/Prostitute's Bolster, 2007
PVC pipe, urethane, wood, aluminum, and spray paint

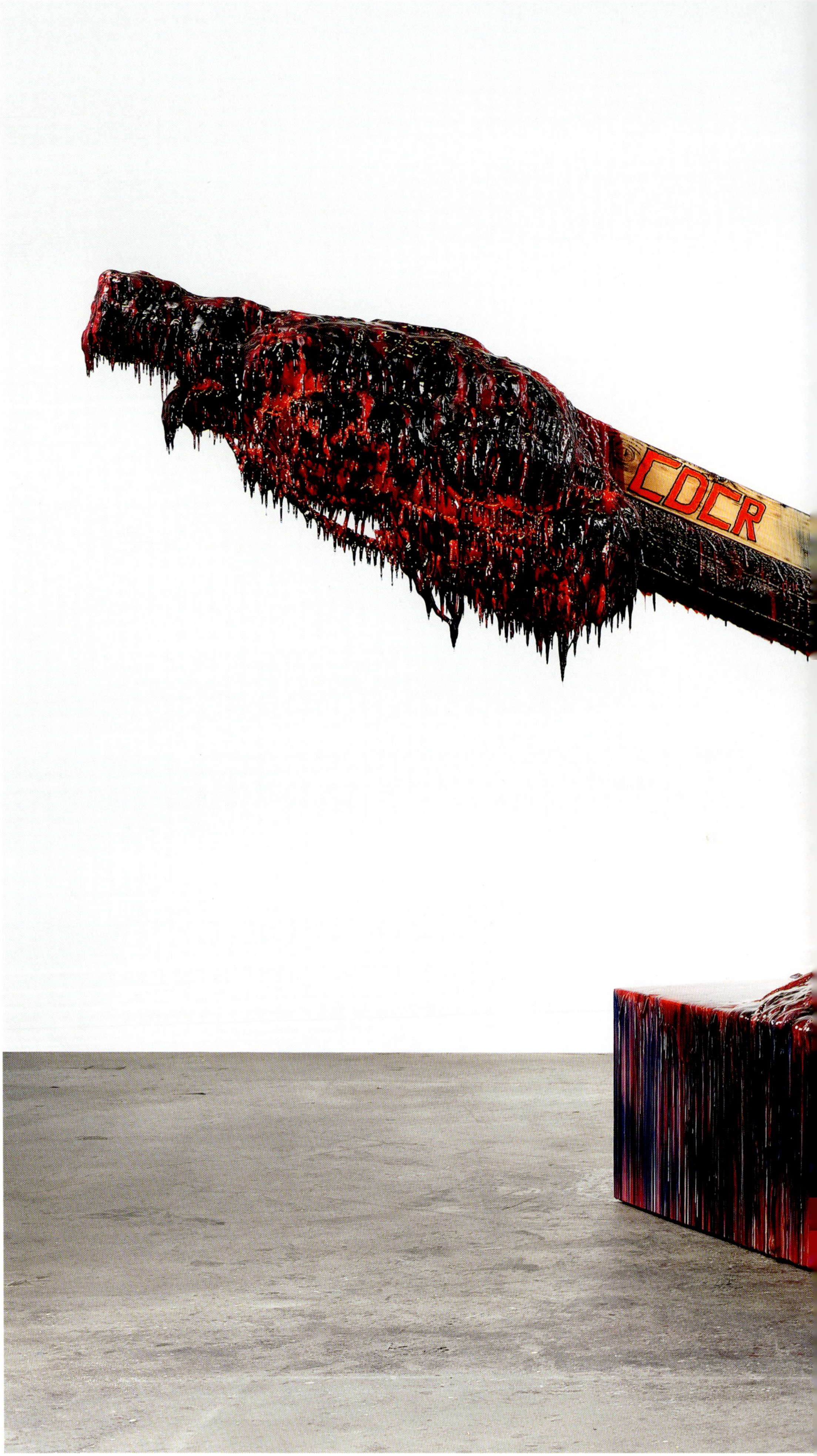

BASIN CDCR, 2011
PVC pipe, foam, urethane,
wood, spray paint, and formica

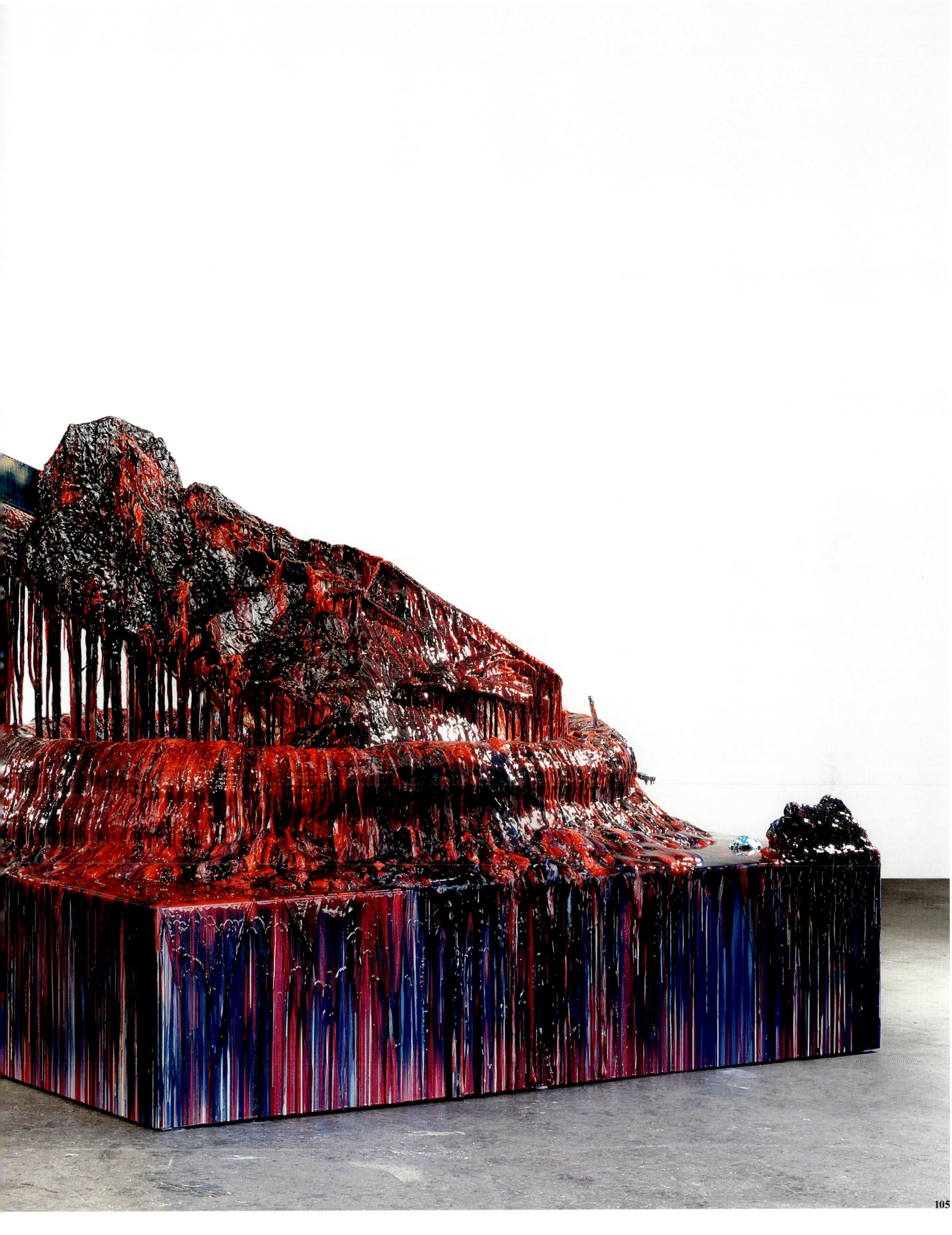

American Risk, 2009
PVC pipe, foam, urethane, wood, spray paint, and formica

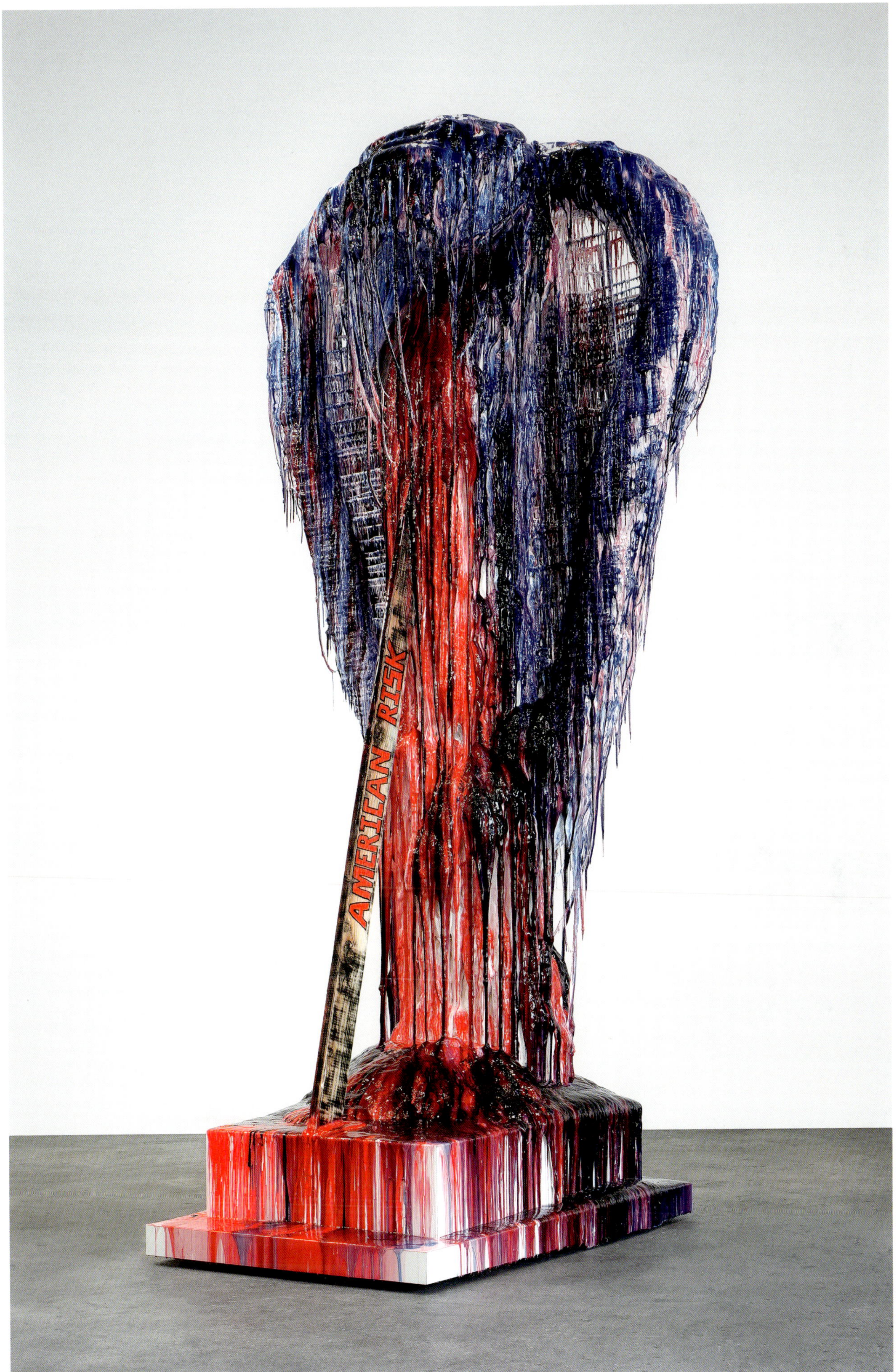
AMERICAN RISK

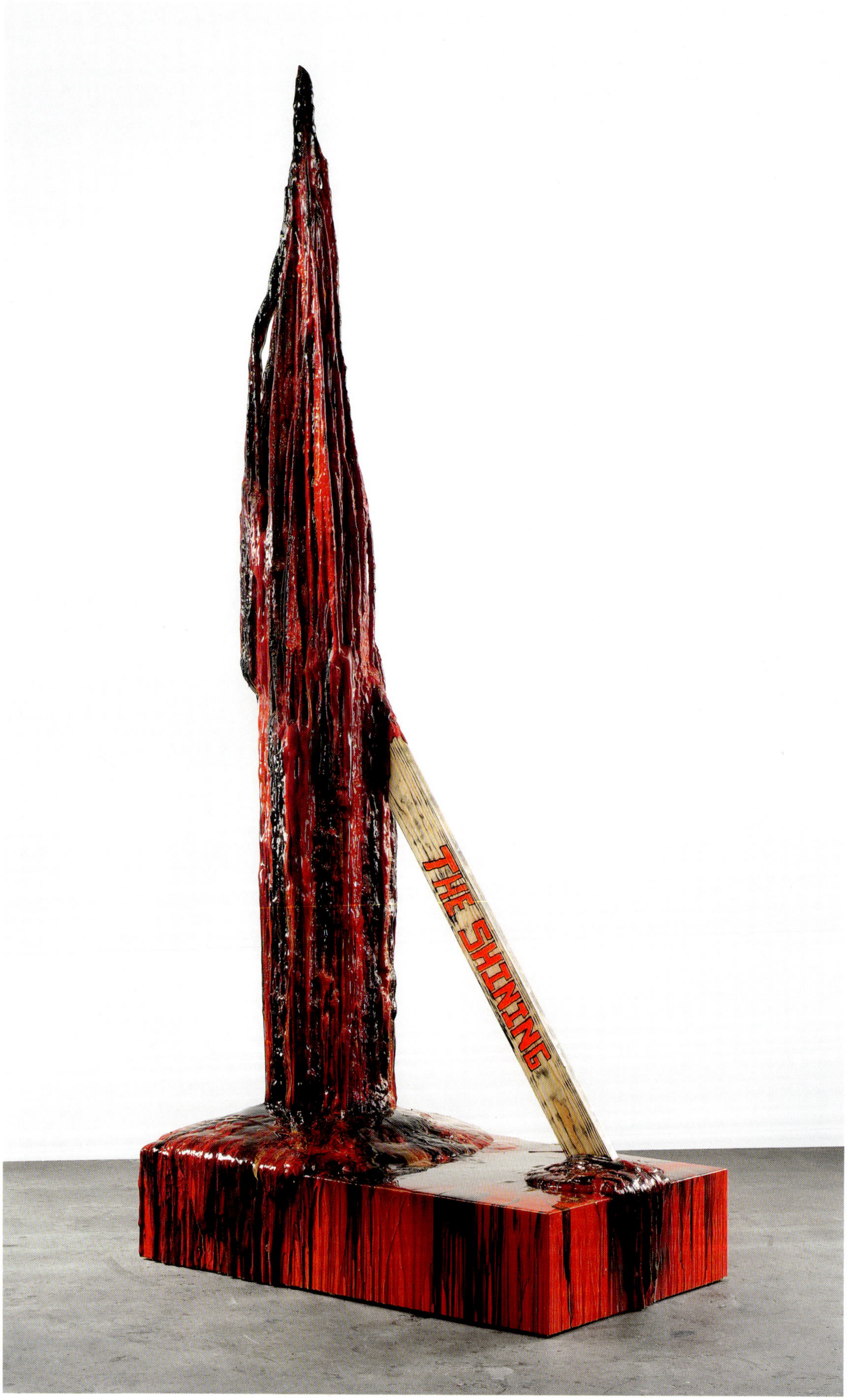
THE SHINING

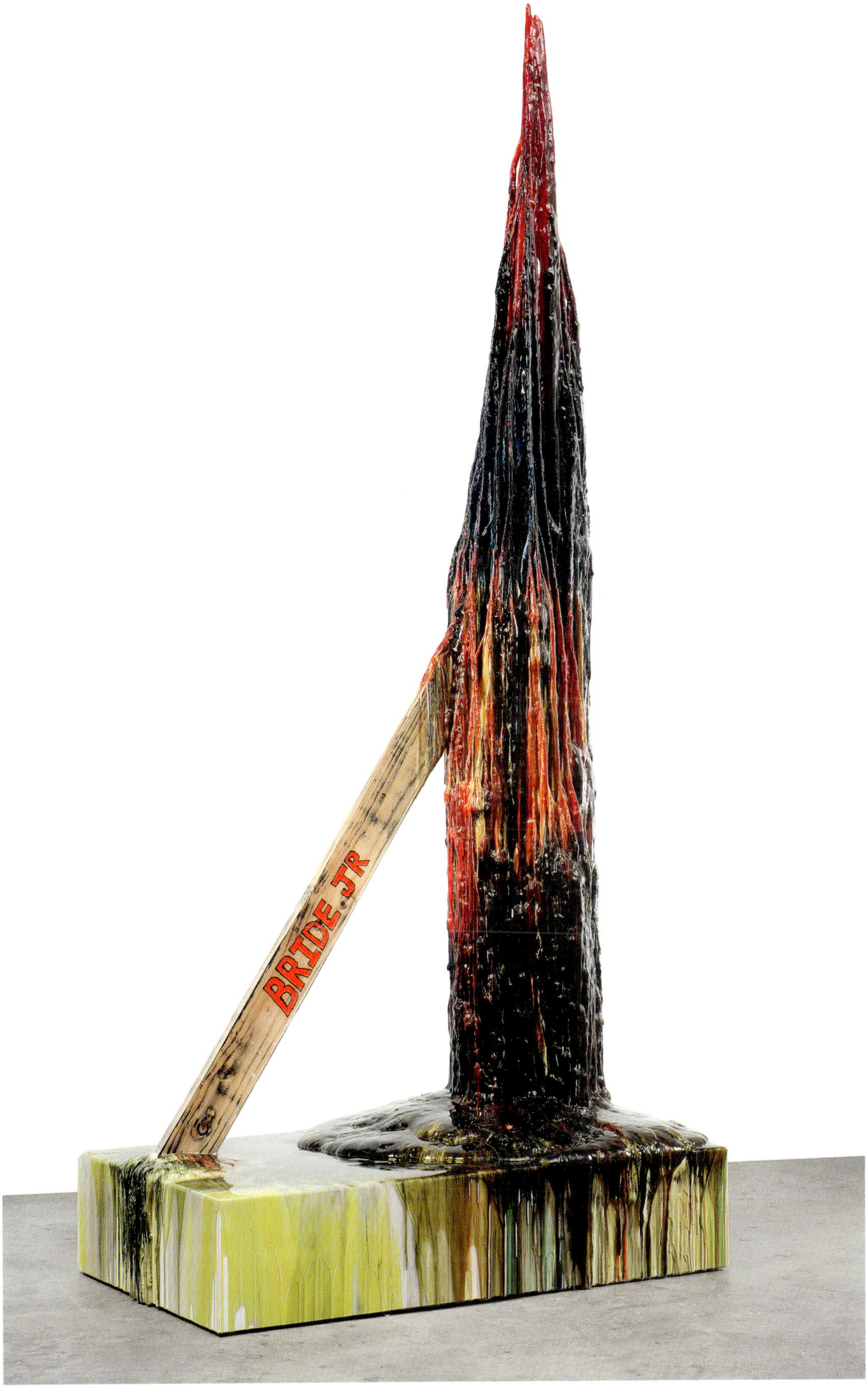

Opposite:
***Monument Stalagmite/The Shining*, 2011**
PVC pipe, foam, urethane, wood, spray paint, and formica

Right:
***Monument Stalagmite/Bride Jr.*, 2011**
PVC pipe, foam, urethane, wood, spray paint, and formica

Monument Stalagmite/Baseline, 2008
PVC pipe, foam, urethane, wood, spray paint, and formica

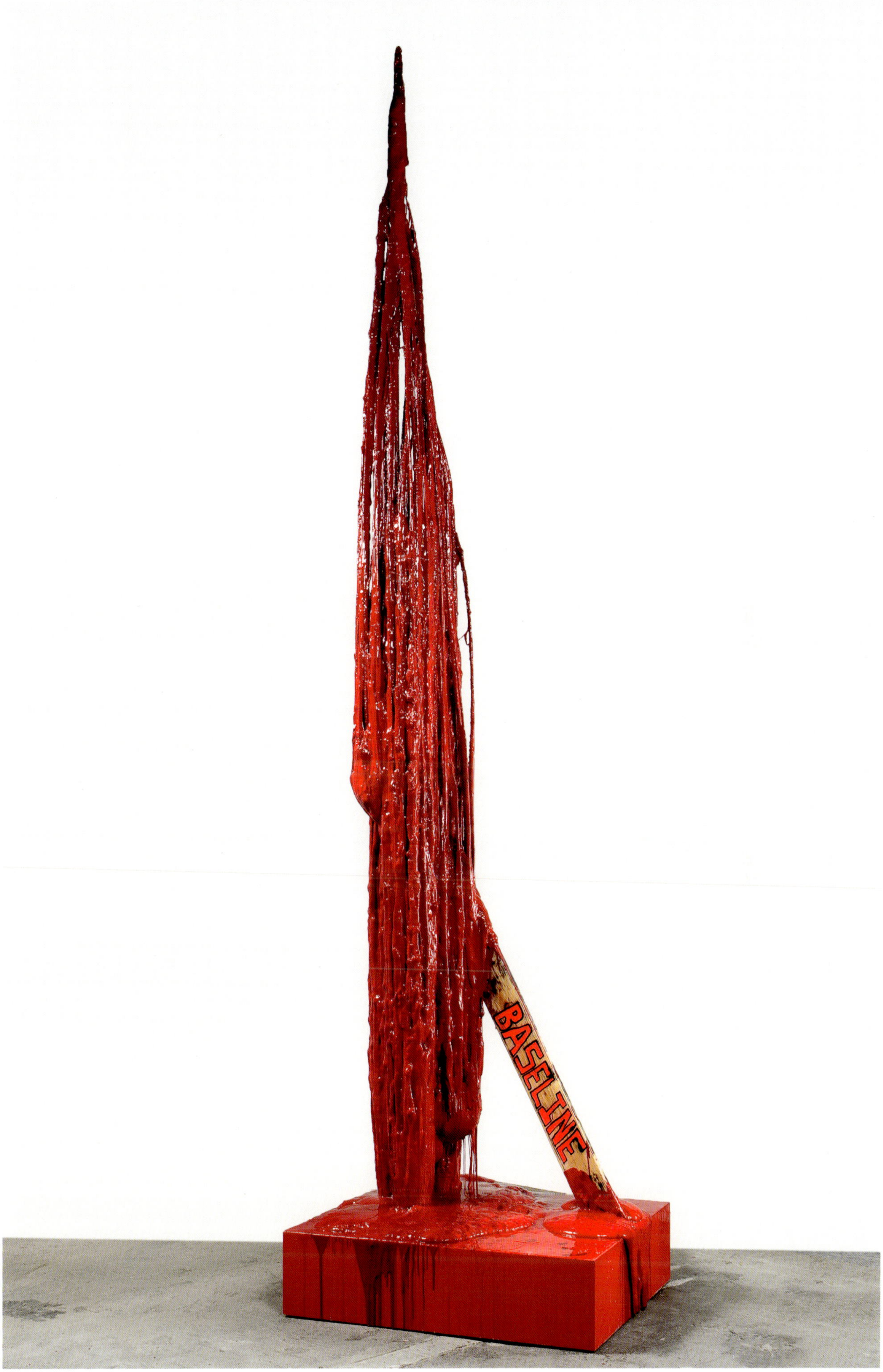
BASELINE

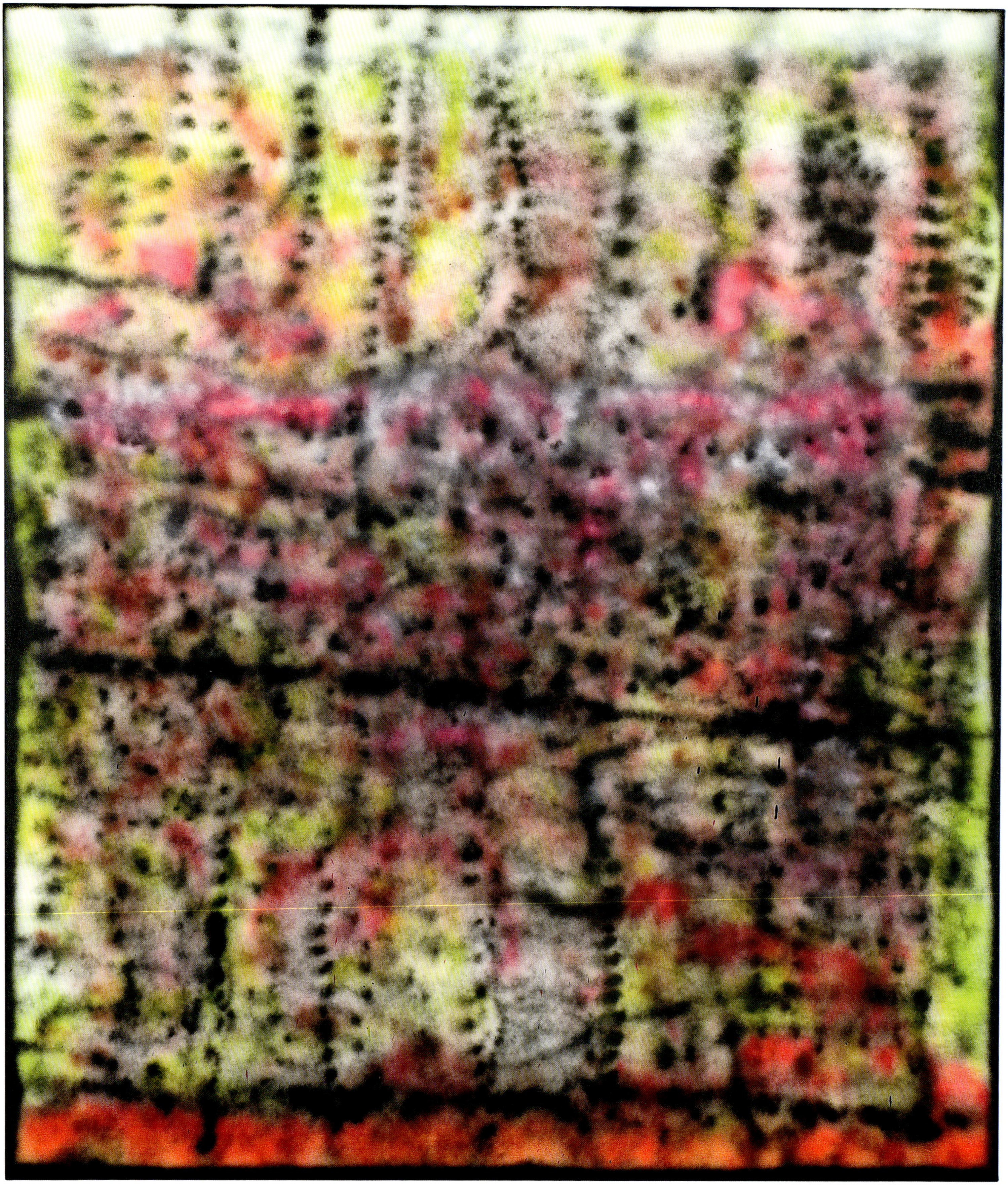

SP04, 2007
Spray paint on canvas

SP

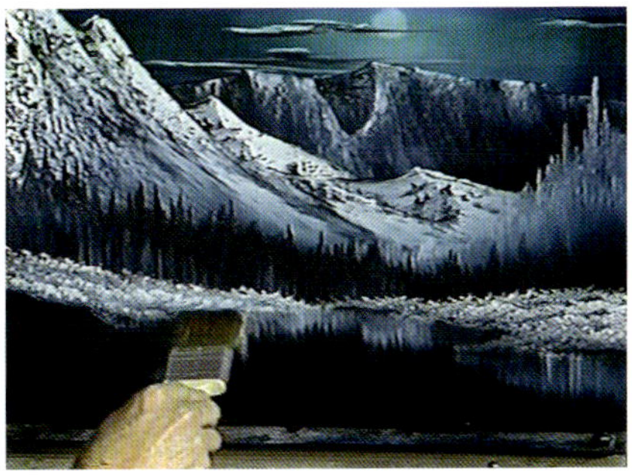

Fig. 1: *Landscape Annihilates Consciousness* (still), 2002.
Single channel video (color, sound; 11:40 minutes)

SPRAY PAINT is one of Ruby's signature materials. He began implementing a variety of spray-painting techniques in his work in different media around 2003, to create a textured ground for his collages on paper, for example, or as a means of tagging and defiling his inscribed formica sculptures. Ruby was introduced to aerosol art at a young age when he visited an exhibition of American graffiti at a museum in Rotterdam, and an interest in such forms of renegade expressivity developed thanks to his proximity to the Washington, DC punk scene. When he later moved to Los Angeles, Ruby was fascinated by spray-painted gang insignia and other territorial demarcations made by different groups who laid claim to neighborhoods in the city. Works like *ACTS/WS ROLLIN* (2011) [pp. 98–99] even incorporate the specific "hand-styles" of the Westside Rollin 60's neighborhood Crips. Ruby's use of spray paint explores the broad range of cultural, historical, and formal associations it elicits as a material often coded as transgressive and situated within particular, often vernacular, subcultures. In Ruby's hand, spray paint is a means to erode further outmoded distinctions between high and low art, with a material as corrosive as bleach when used to undermine aesthetic purity.

In 2007, Ruby made his first monumental spray paintings on canvas called SP. Each work is an atmospheric color field painting worked intensively by hand with an abstract lexicon of overlapping dots, drips, lines, and shapes. These paintings call to mind the abstract expressionist canvases of Mark Rothko as well the legacy of American landscape painting, though Ruby deploys these associations to radically different ends. In early spray paintings such as *SP04* (2007), Day-Glo patches of orange, yellow, and magenta are overpainted with patterns of black dots and lines that suggest years of overpainted graffiti on urban walls or abandoned homes rather than transcendental washes of color or pristine landscapes. The black mass of intersecting forms that buoys *SP49* (2008) is both architectural and bodily, faintly radiating shades of red, blue, and purple against a putrid yellow background. The SP paintings frequently evoke landscapes ravaged by environmental degradation. The encroaching darkness of *SP131* (2010) veils what appears to be a vivid sky impossibly colored by toxic pollution, just as the hazy admixture of fluorescent colors in *SP242* (2013) looks like a horizon shrouded by smoke from one of the wildfires that routinely ravages California. The viscous drips on the surface of many of these canvases were at first accidents when the paint can was emptying and started to sputter. Later the drips were embraced as a motif that cuts across the horizontality of the picture plane, alluding to rain or tears, as well as the stylized drips made by graffiti artists.

A particular perspective toward commodified forms of landscape painting is implied by an early video work titled, provocatively, *Landscape Annihilates Consciousness* (2002) [fig. 1]. Ruby alters found footage of landscape painter and television host Bob Ross, decoupling his voice from video of his hand executing a wintry landscape. His hypnotic voice repeats, mantra-like, a looped set of instructional phrases, until the process becomes perverse. Within this set of repetitious procedures, either the painter's subjectivity is defused or it disappears completely.

—J. D.

SP49, 2008
Spray paint on canvas

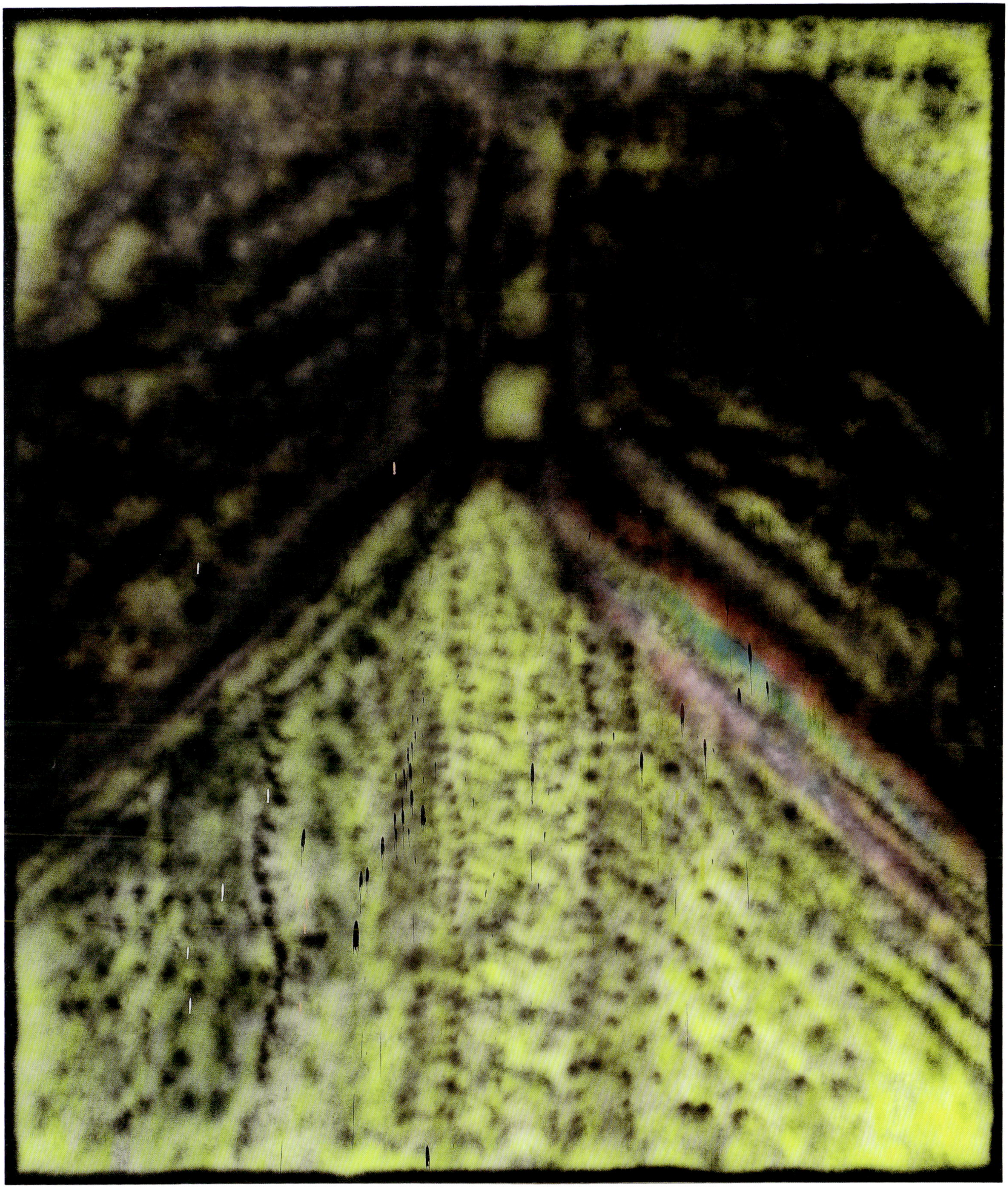

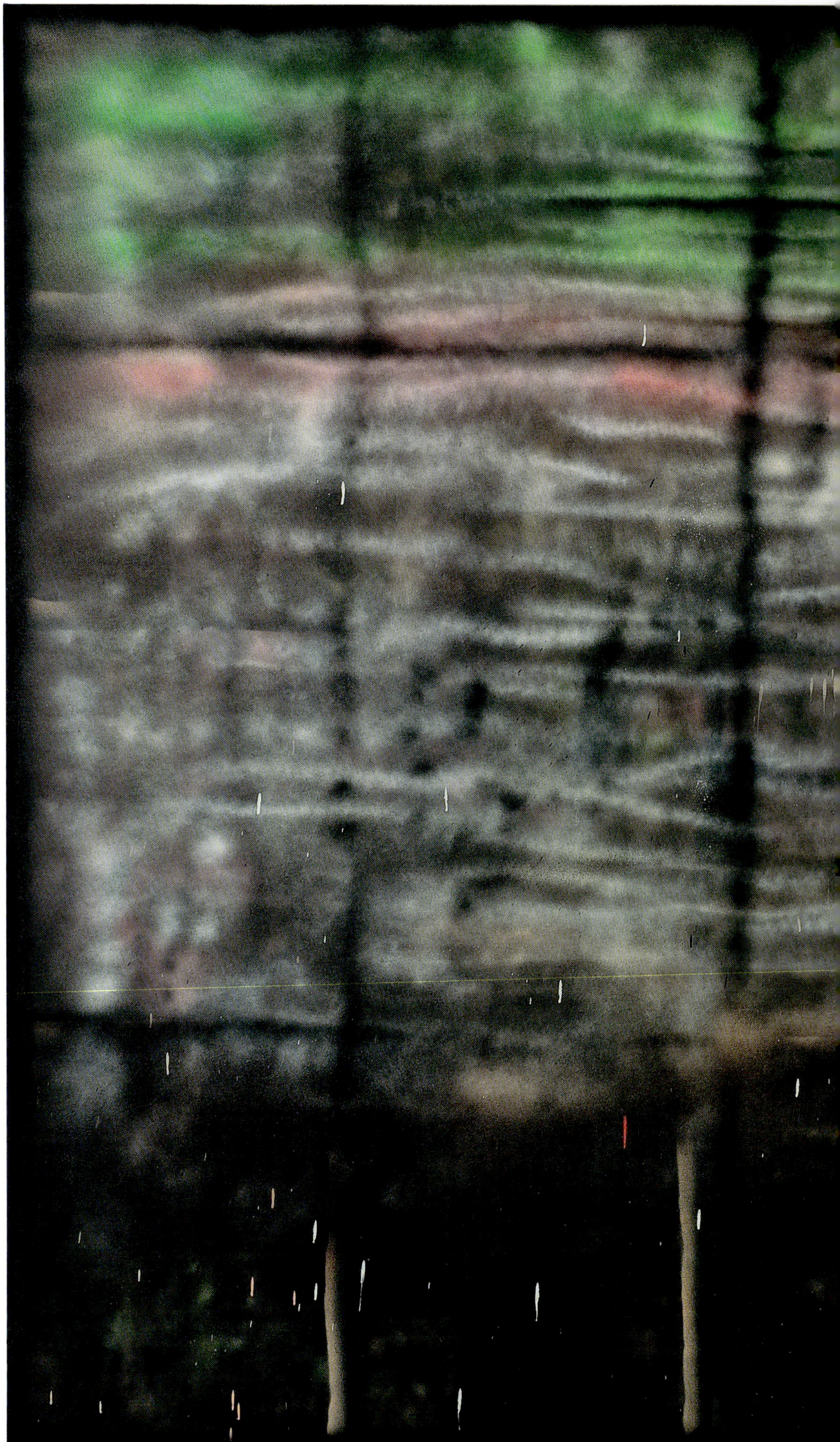

SP21, 2008
Spray paint on canvas

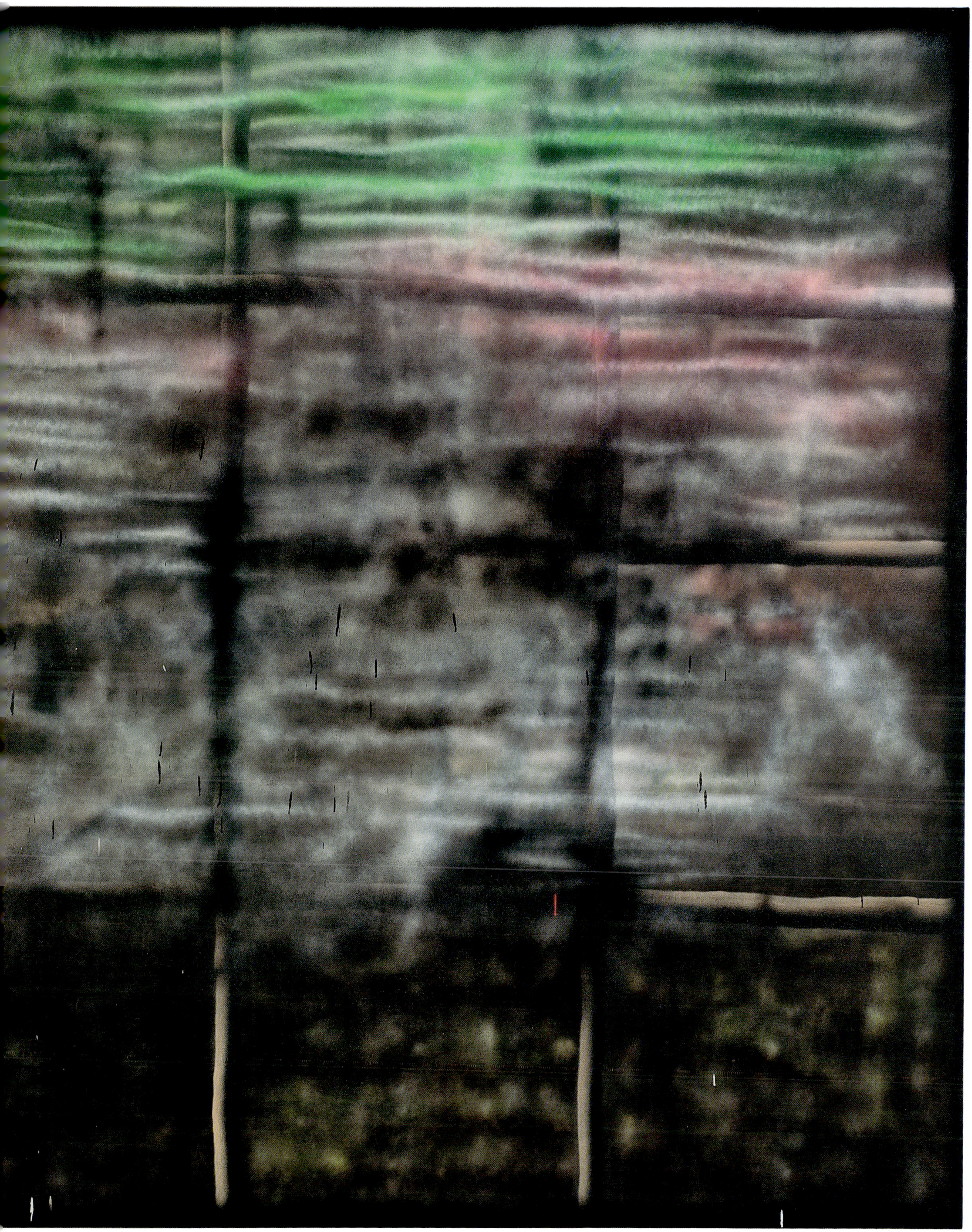

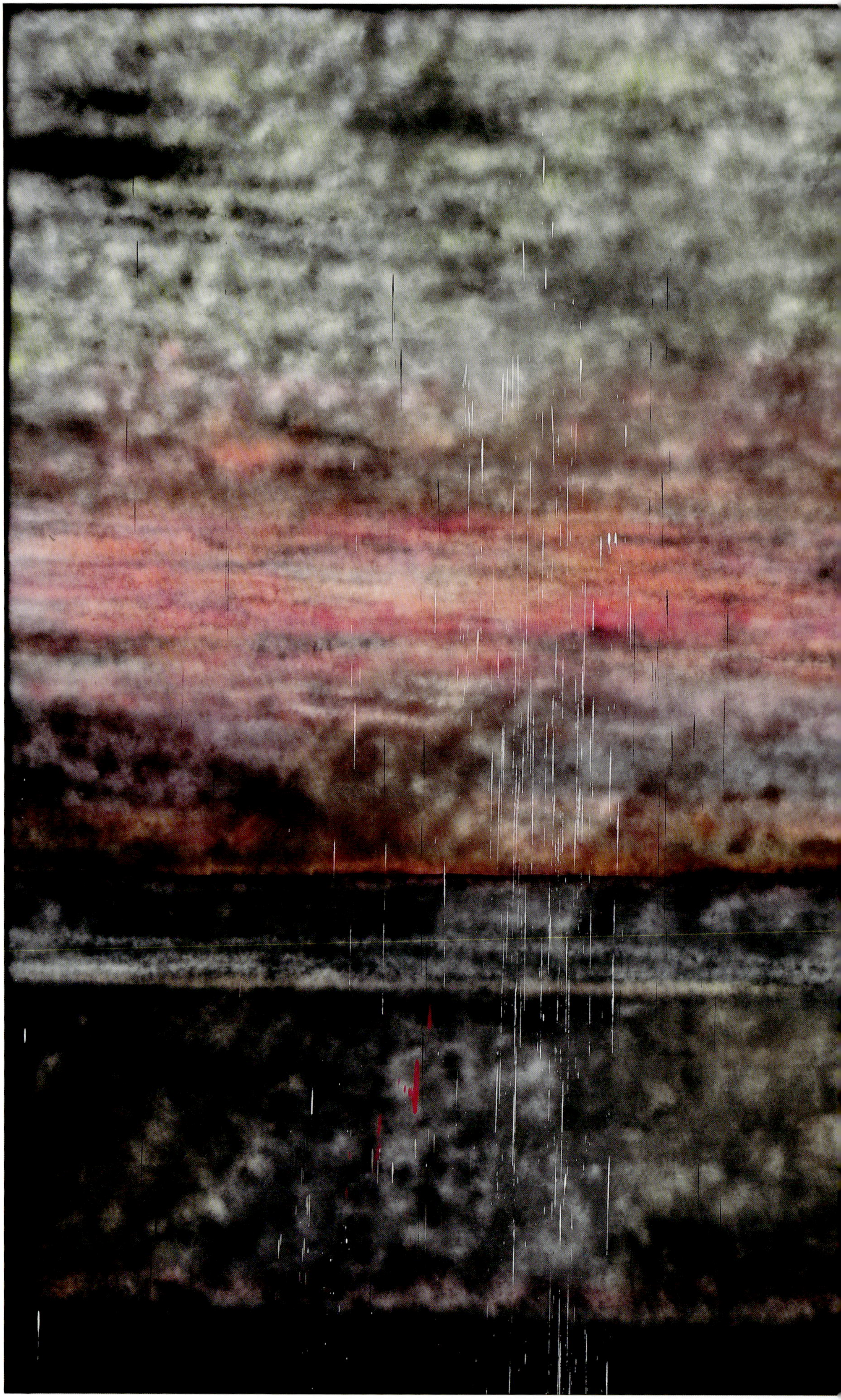

SP250, 2013
Spray paint on canvas

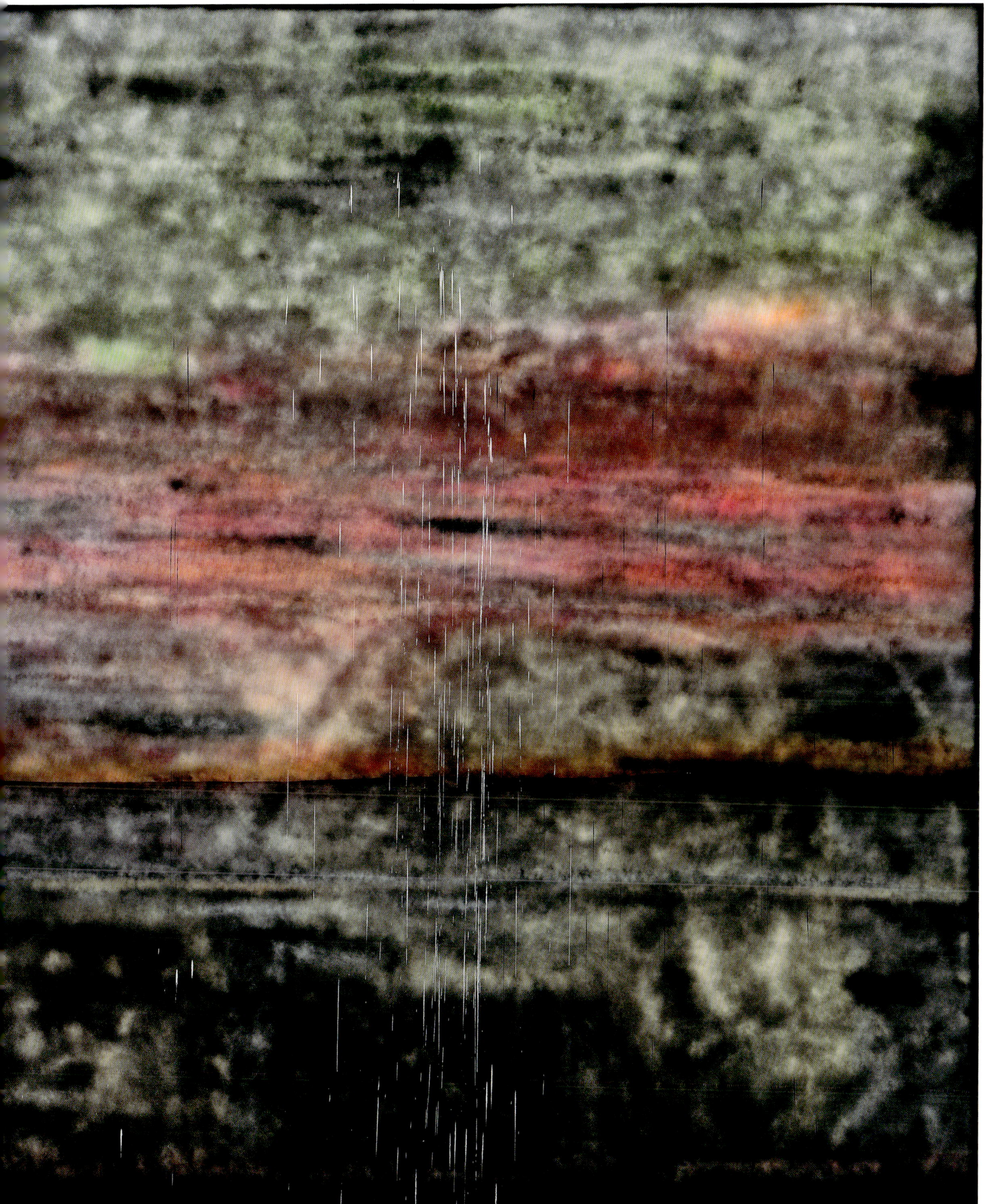

SP302, 2014
Spray paint on synthetic canvas

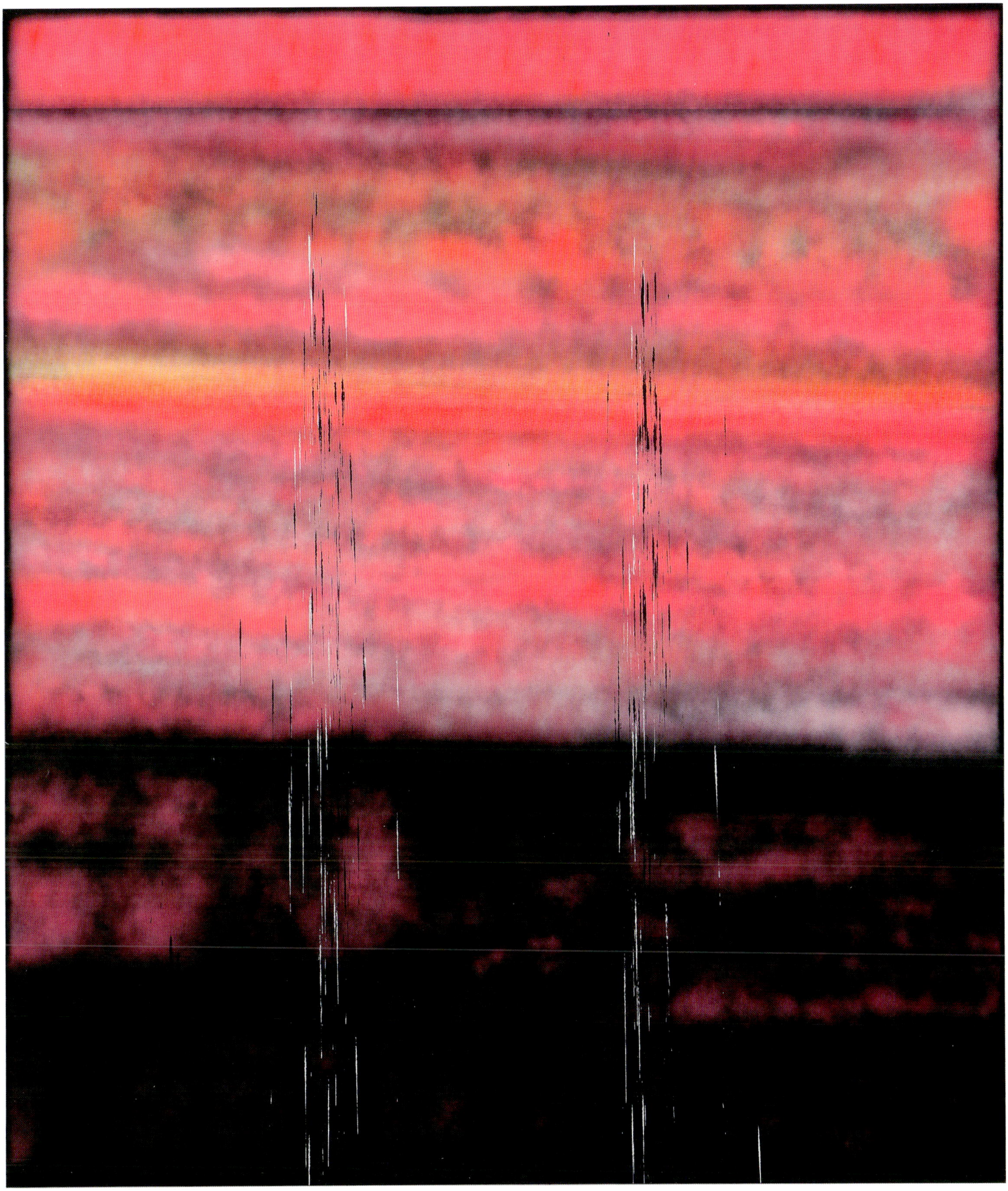

SP131, 2010
Spray paint on canvas

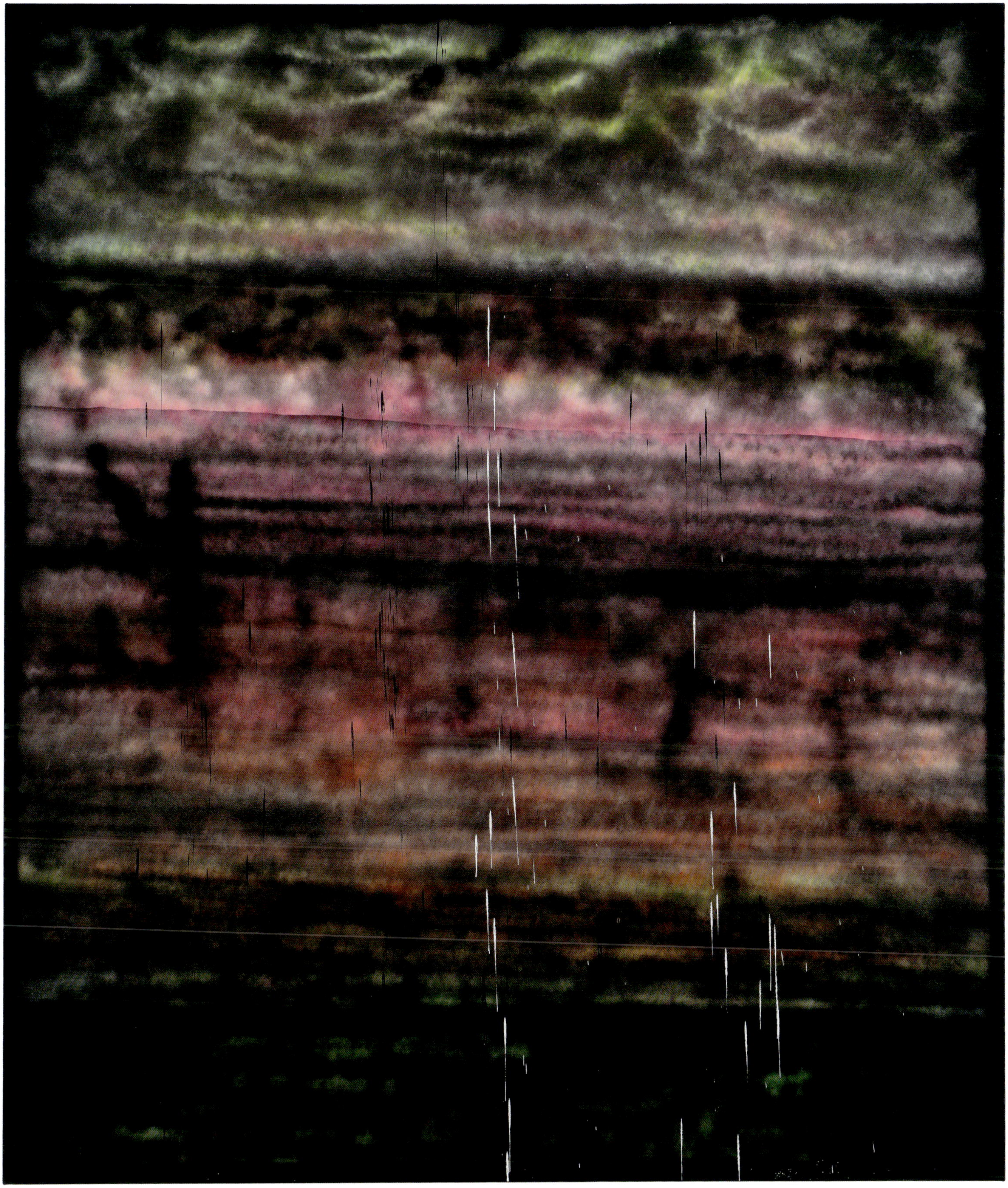

SP242, 2013
Spray paint on canvas

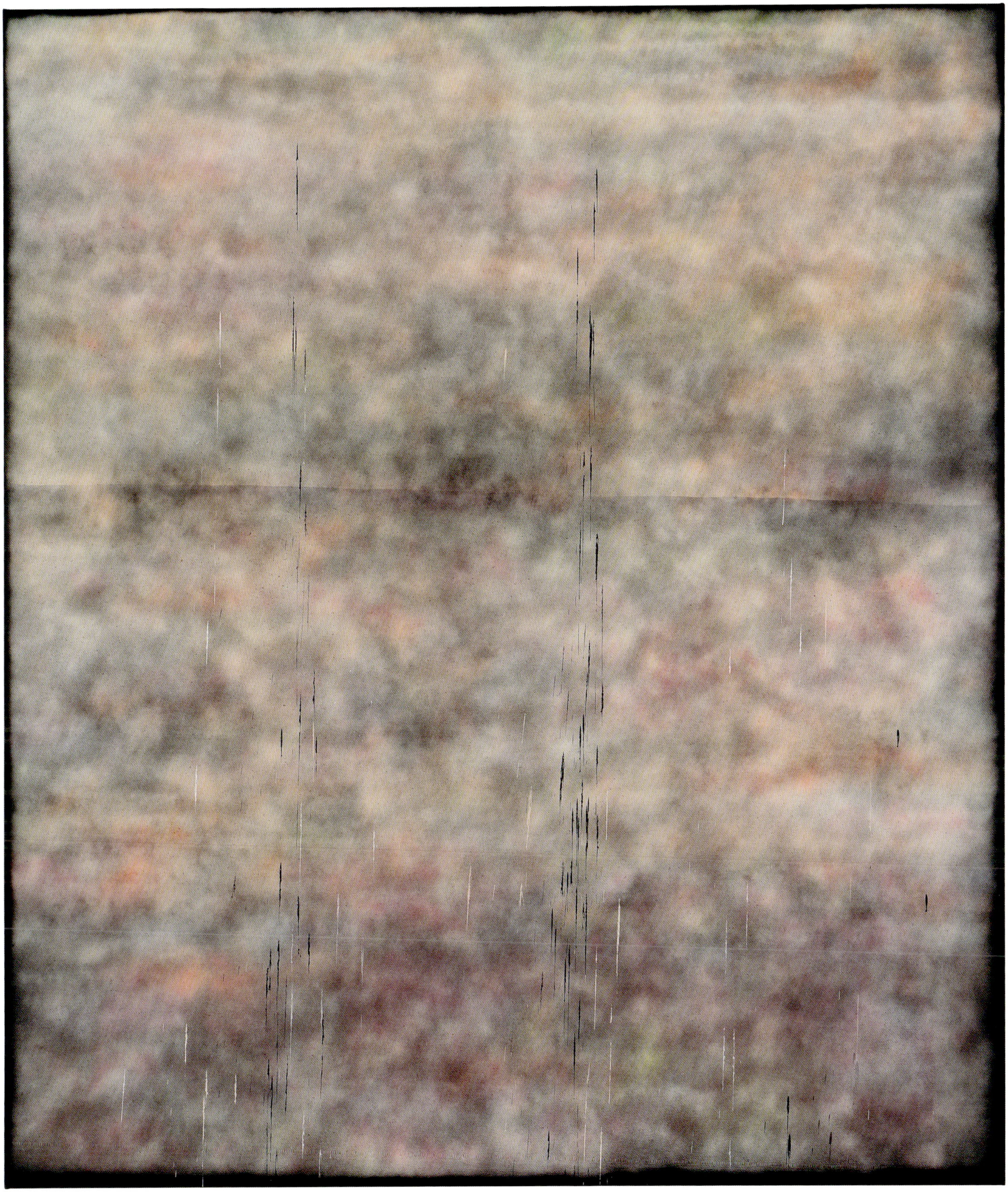

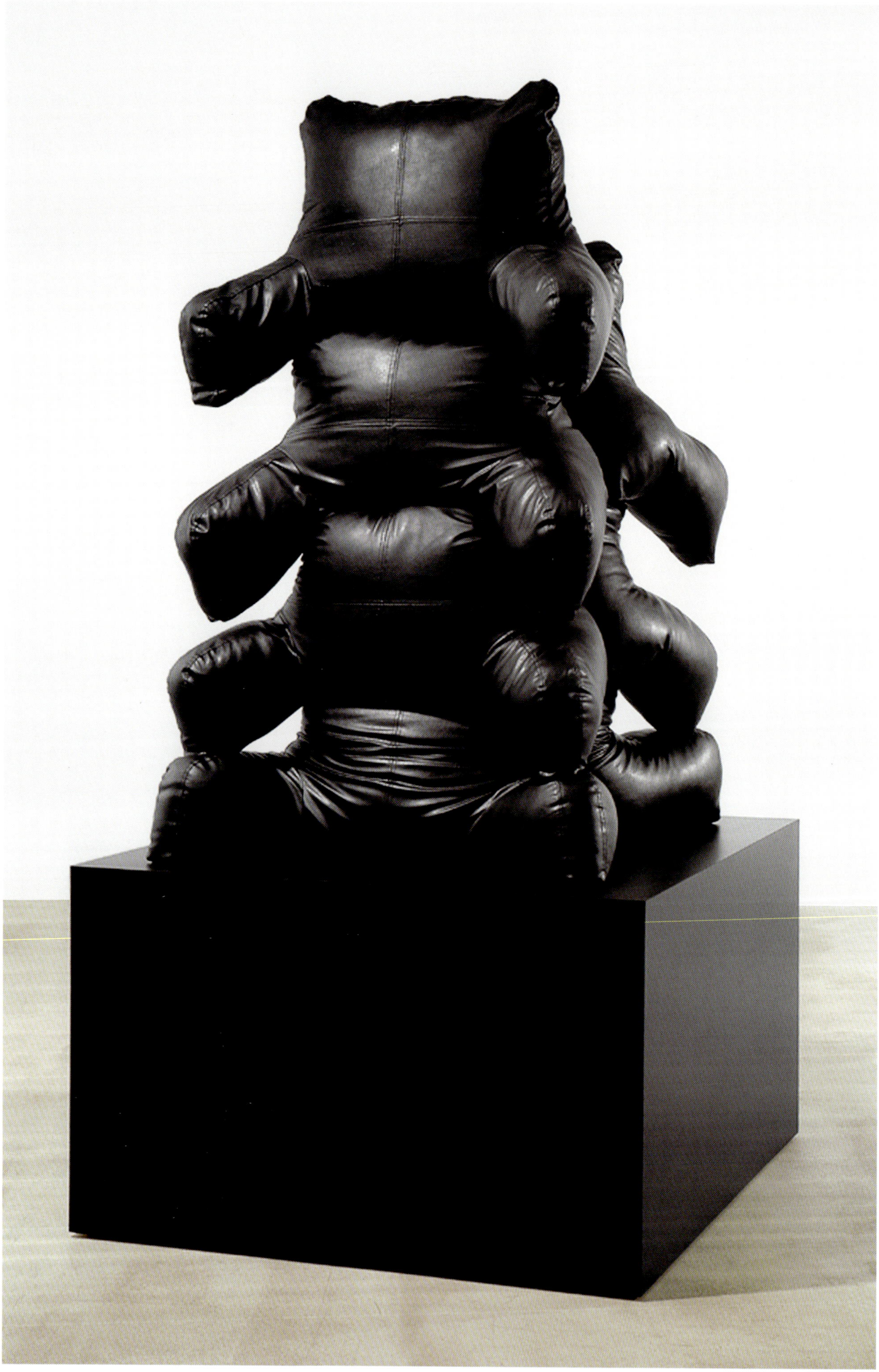

Soft Sculptures

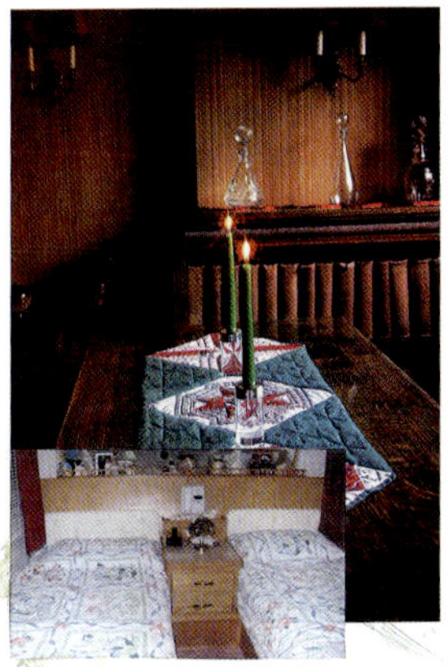

Fig. 1: *Two Candles, Two Beds*, 2004. Collage on paper

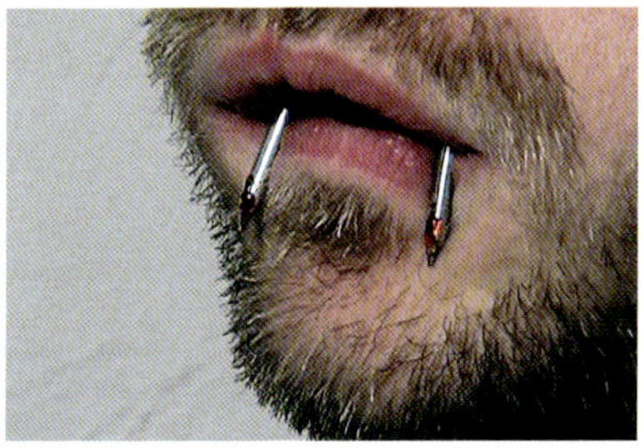

Fig. 2: *Agoraphobic* (still), 2001. Single channel video (color, sound; 11:16 minutes)

THE HUSBAND PILLOW, a common piece of quasi furniture with "arms" used for support and comfort, first appeared in Ruby's work in 2004. A year later, Ruby made his first soft sculpture, *2 Stacks of Husbands* (2005), two stacks of black leather husband pillows, each held upright with a galvanized pipe on top of a plinth covered in black laminate. In both of these works, the black leather husband pillow carries a broad range of associations. An idiosyncratic stand-in for masculinity, the pillow also suggests intimacy and domesticity, and even an interplay between the presence and absence of a supportive partner as such.

Ruby likewise repeats an inventory of motifs in his soft sculptures using various fabrics stuffed with fiberfill at monumental scales. Ruby's series of CANDLES, FIGURES, and VAMPIRES, for example, are made using textiles produced by the studio or sourced fabrics and installed in resonant, varied combinations. Like the husband pillow, the candle conjures domesticity, as in Ruby's collage *Two Candles, Two Beds* (2004) [fig. 1] complete with a Pennsylvania Dutch-style quilted table setting, but also ephemerality and the passage of time. The giant CANDLES are often presented horizontally, directly on the floor or standing upright, at times made with colorful dyed canvas or treated denim, at other times with patterned fabrics. The cartoonish FIGURES are prostrate bodies with yarn for hair connected with a shared set of arms, in pairs or in larger interconnected groupings.

The VAMPIRES are wall-mounted parted lips and fangs with drops of blood. This monstrous imagery of unbridled consumption recurs in Ruby's work, from the bloodsucker played by Ruby himself in his early video *Agoraphobic* (2001) [fig. 2], to the many images of gaping, monstrous mouths baring pointed teeth in collages such as *DRFTRS (4253)* (2013) [p. 52]. The soft VAMPIRES are made in many forms, including single mouths, doubles, or in variations such as LONG VAMPIRES, with multiple drops, or VAMPIRE FLAGS, gridded arrays of fangs and drops. The process of producing soft sculptures invariably leads to scraps of leftover textiles. Influenced by his childhood exposure to Amish quilts in rural Pennsylvania, Ruby began repurposing these scraps for a series of larger-than-life QUILTS and FLAGS constructed of various scraps that often reference the American flag, flags of countries invaded by the U.S. military, and American quilt-making traditions.

The soft sculptures—presented in a unique configuration for this exhibition—are each made using a repeating American flag patterned fabric: a giant standing DOUBLE CANDLE, a wall-mounted DOUBLE VAMPIRE, and a stacked PILE of multiple FIGURES are presented in dialogue with the monumental *QUILT (4858)* (2014). Ruby's fascination with America as a paradoxical object of compulsive examination is apparent in allusions made in this arrangement of soft sculptures and QUILT to the untenable, pathological violence and oppression that undergird American history and everyday life.

—J. D.

2 Stacks of Husbands, 2005
Wood, laminate, vinyl, fiberfill, and galvanized pipe

***DOUBLE CANDLE (6992)*, 2019**
Fabric and fiberfill

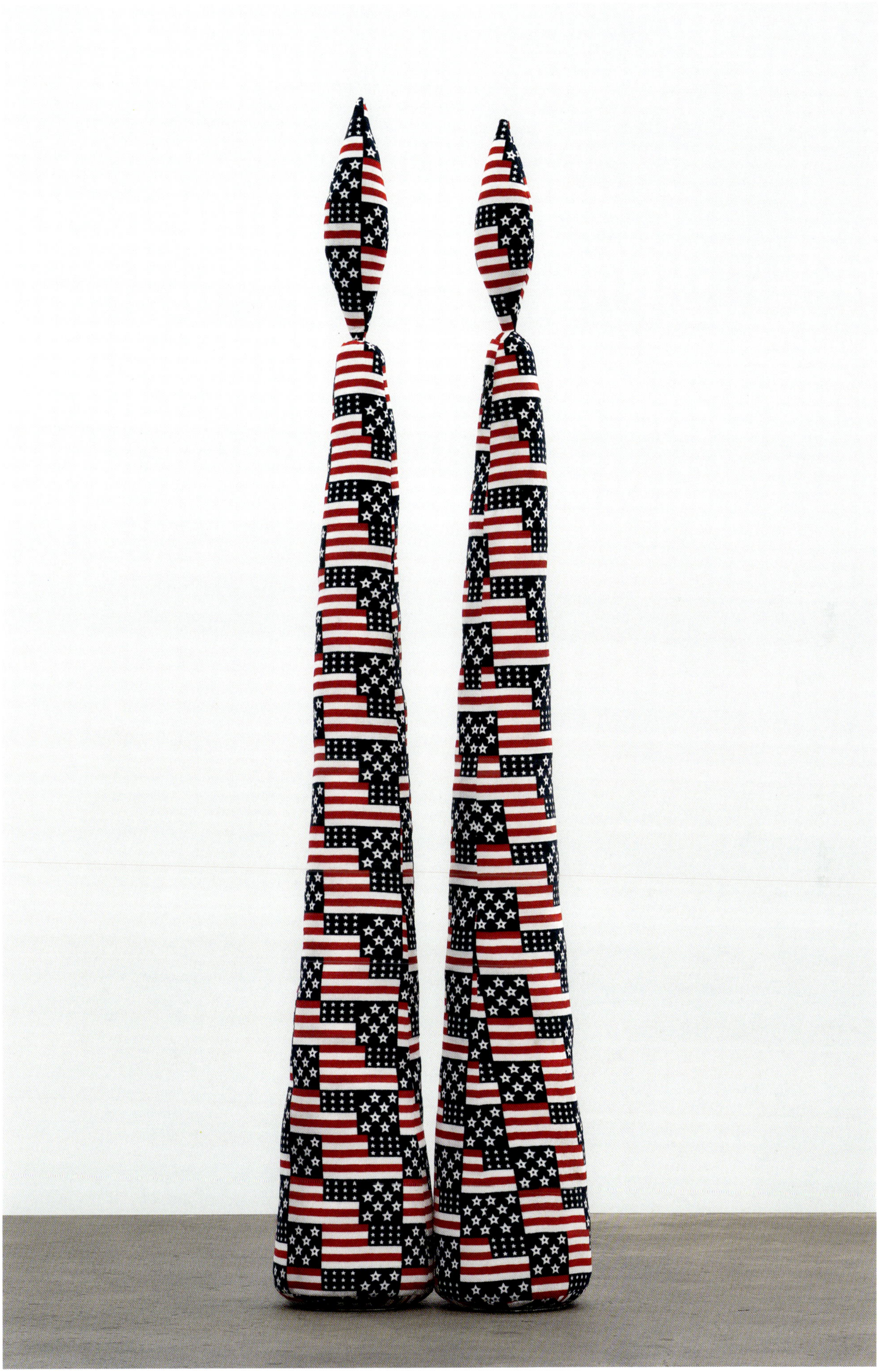

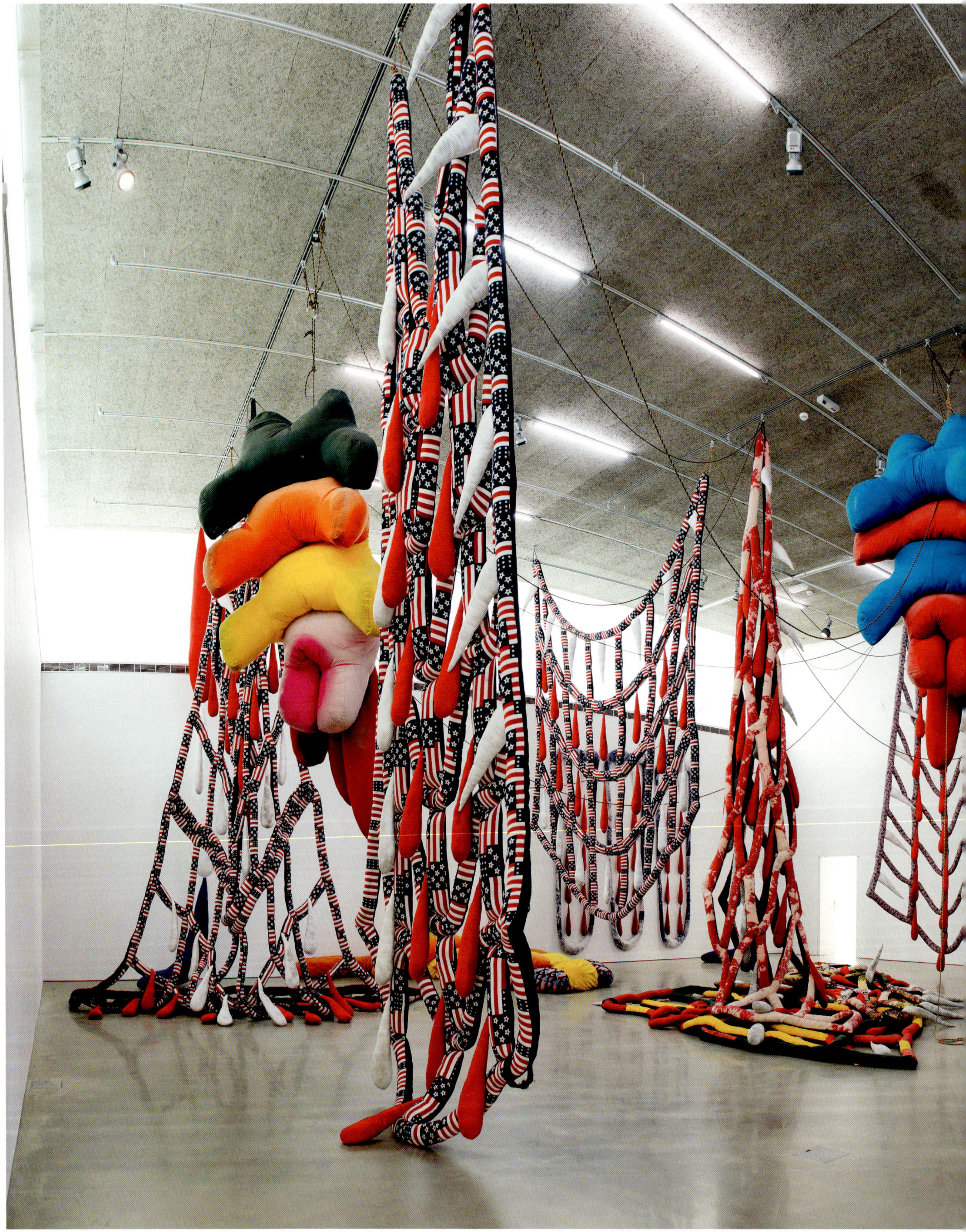

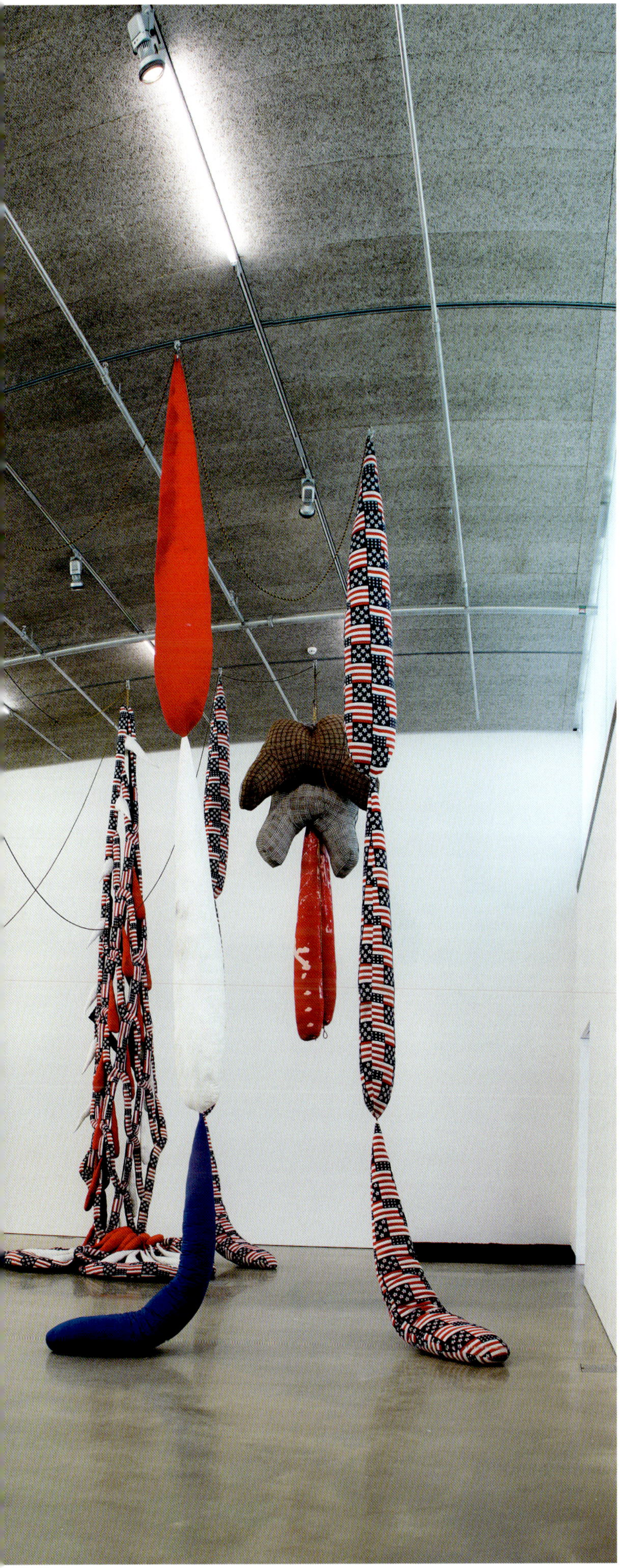

Installation view, ***STERLING RUBY: SOFT WORK*,**
Bonniers Konsthall, Stockholm, 2012–13

VAMPIRE 9, 2010
Fabric and fiberfill

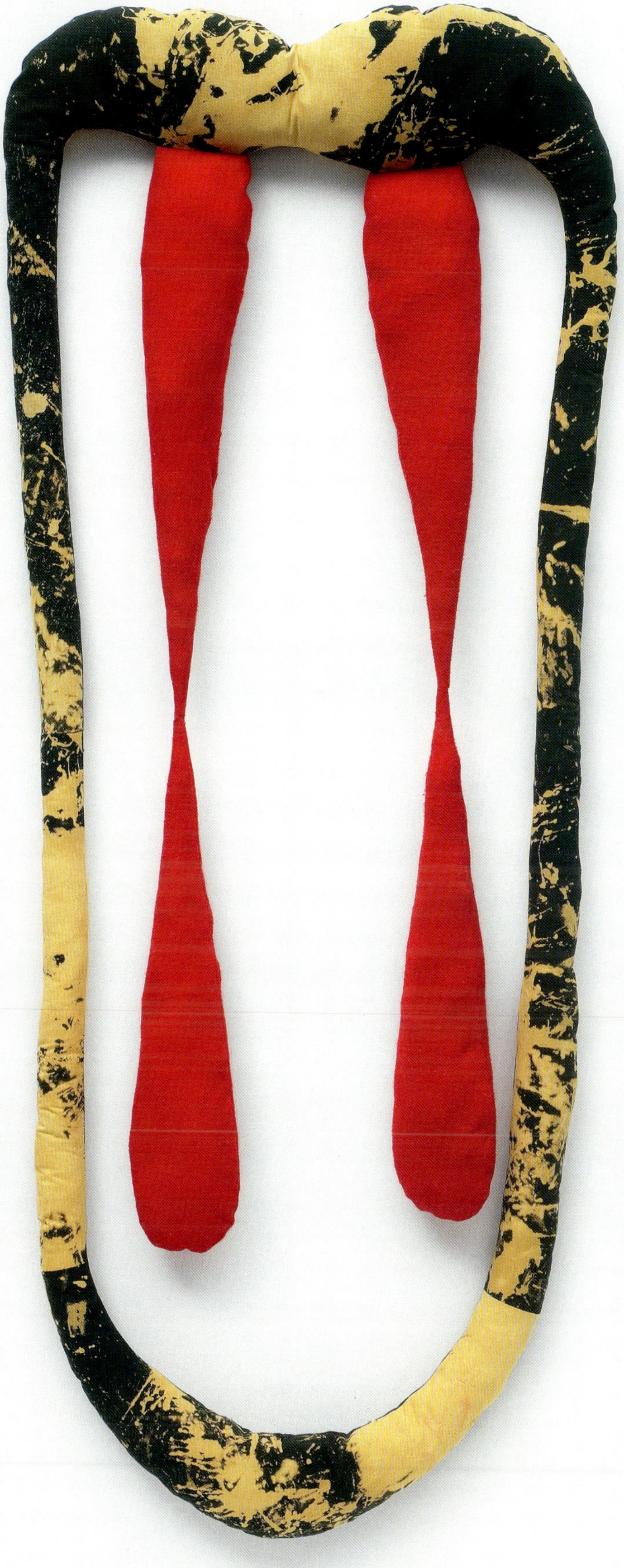

QUILT (4858), 2014
Bleached and dyed canvas and elastic

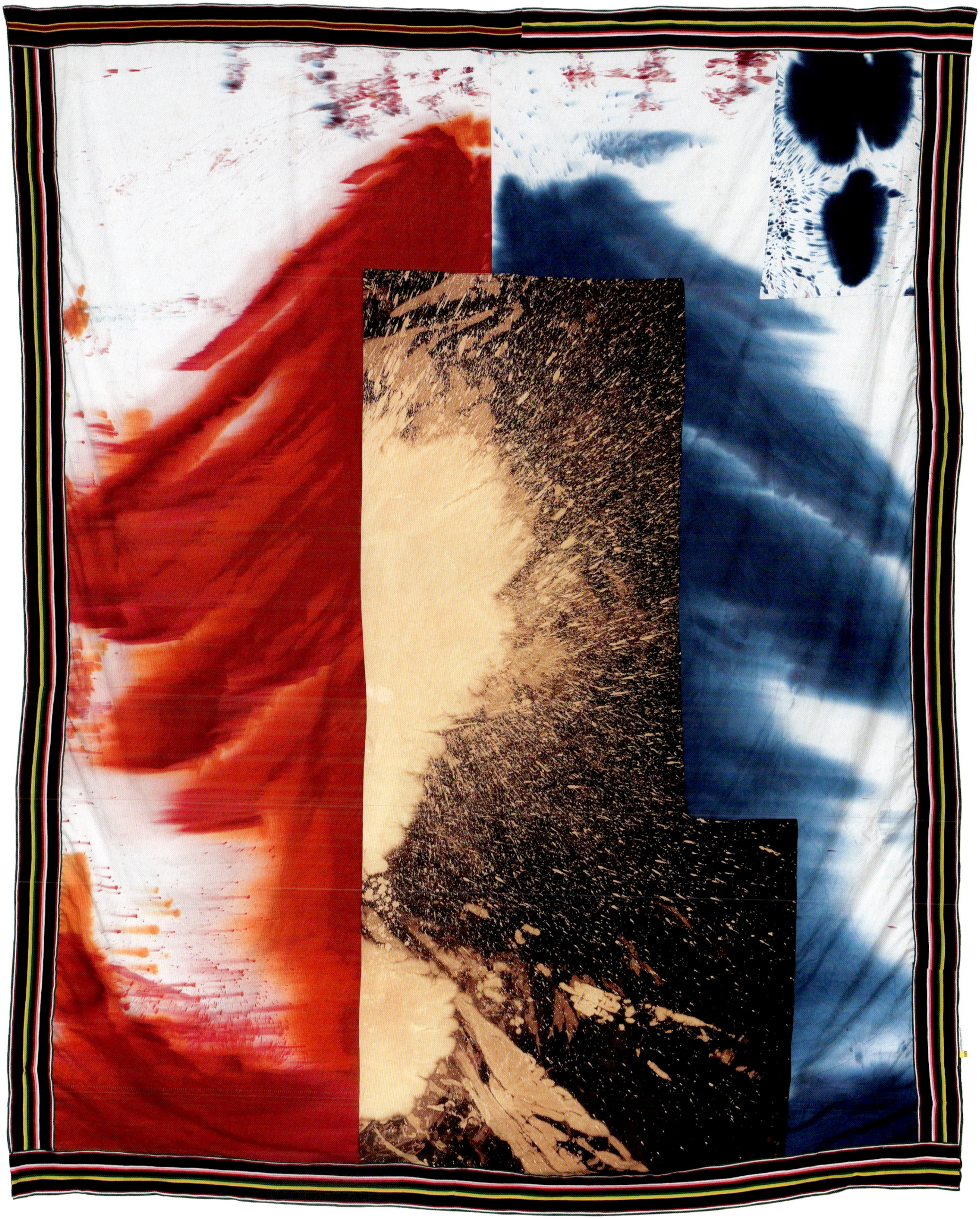

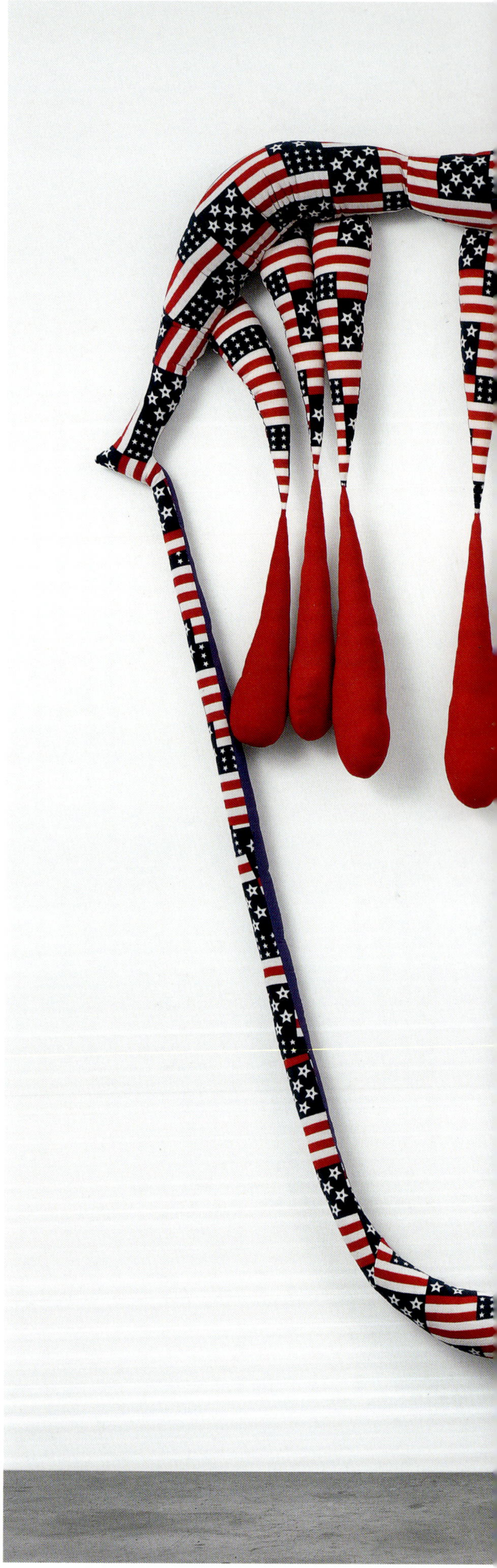

DOUBLE VAMPIRE 14, 2013
Fabric and fiberfill

Next spread:
FIGURES. PILE. (6991), 2019
Fabric, yarn, and fiberfill

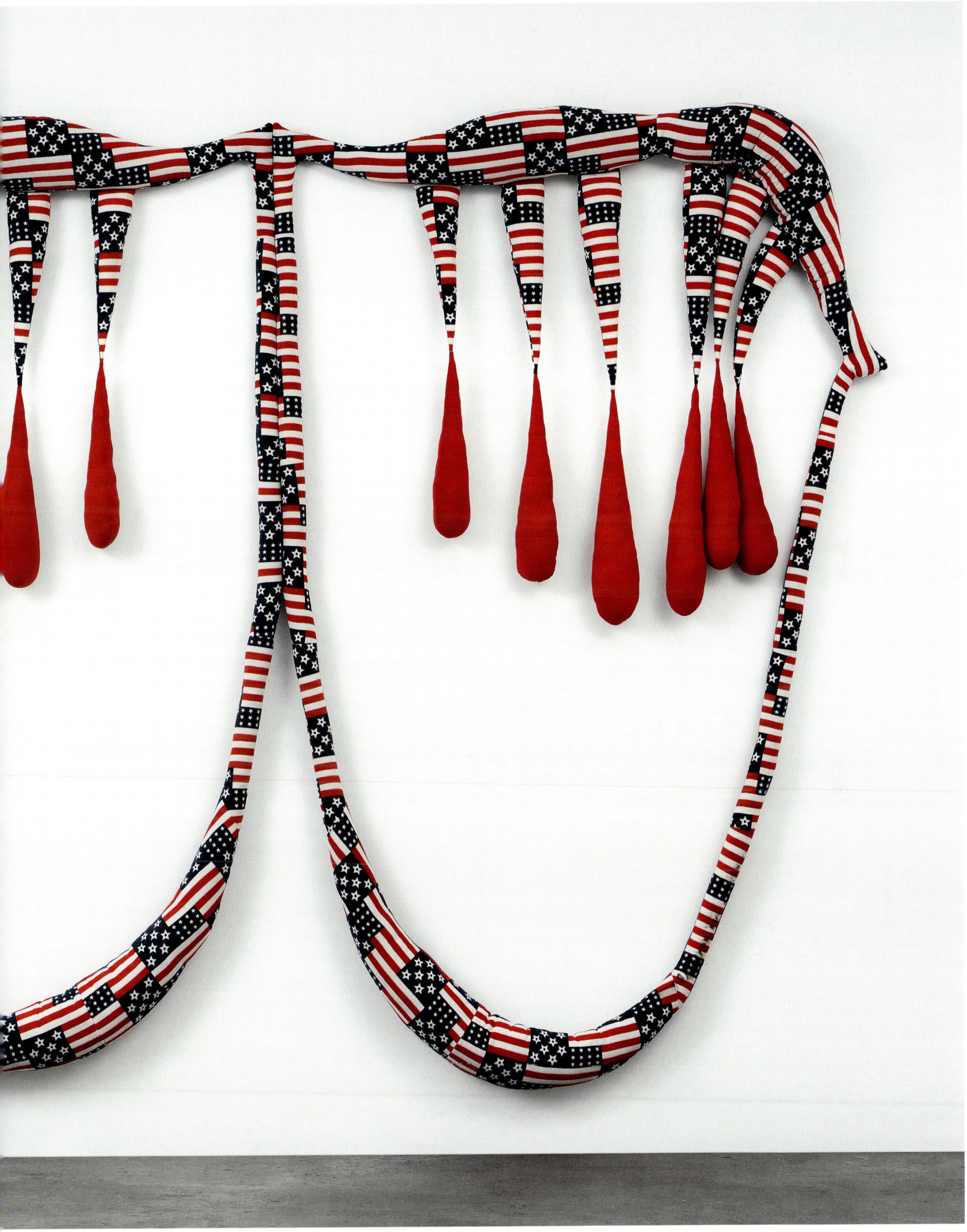

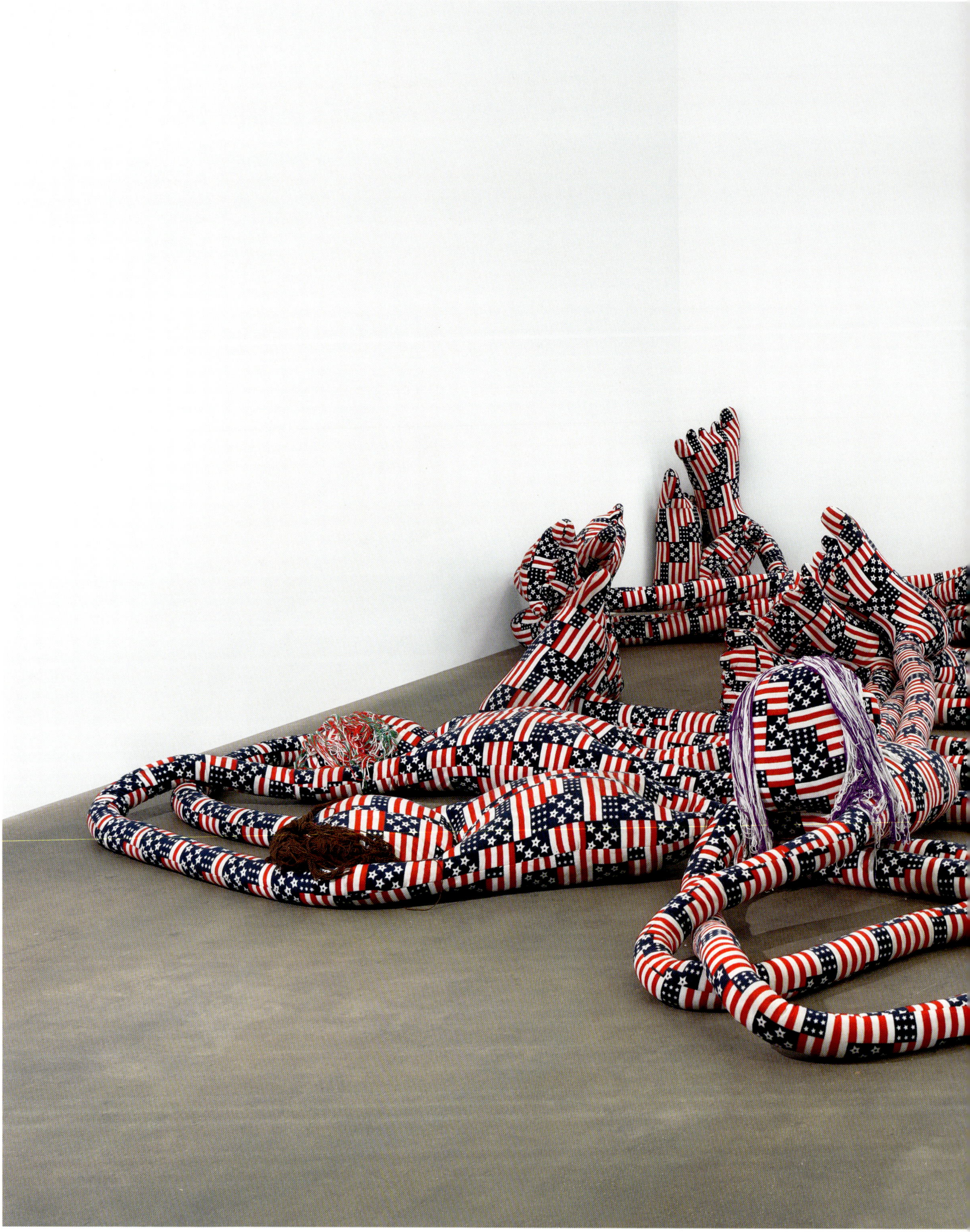

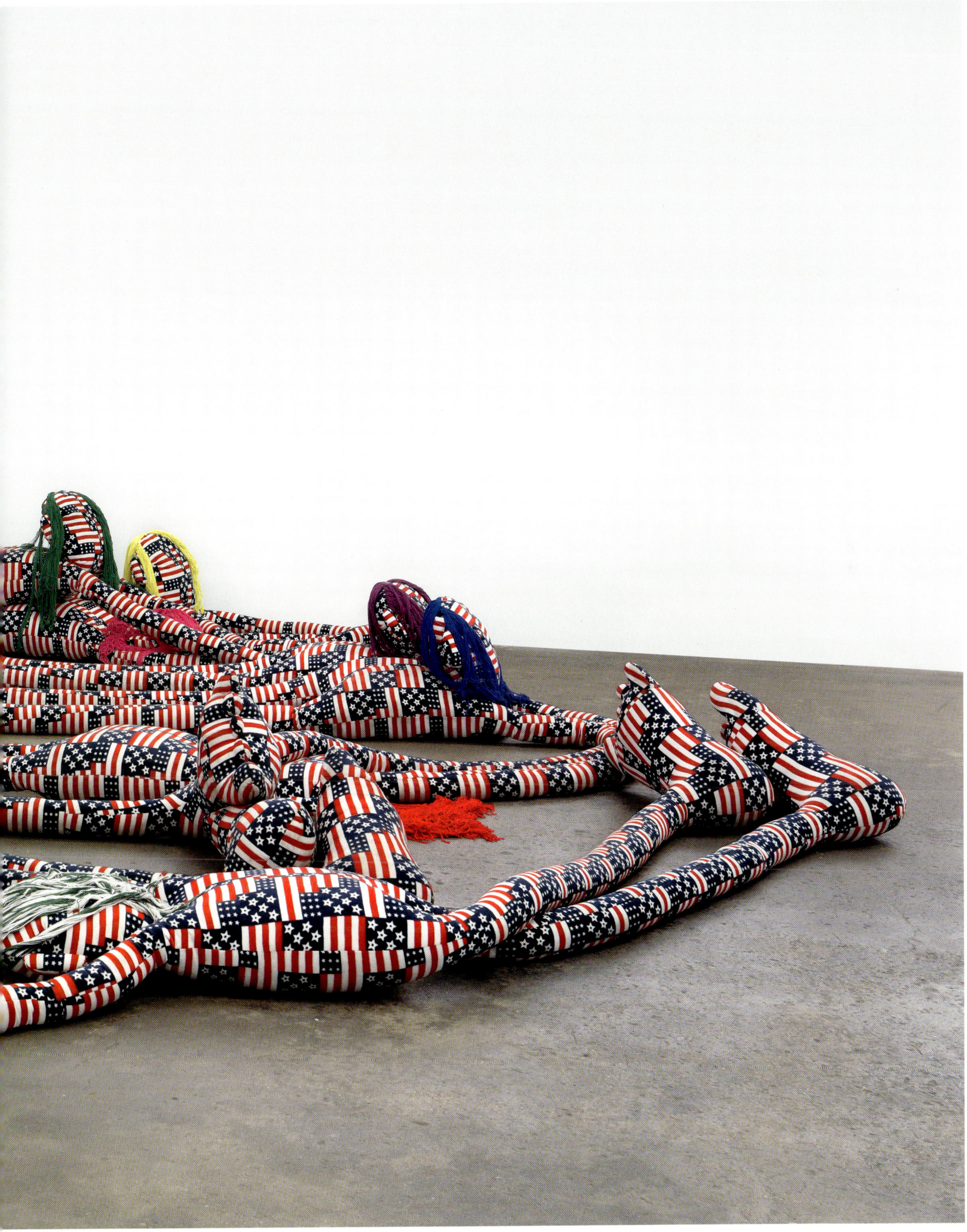

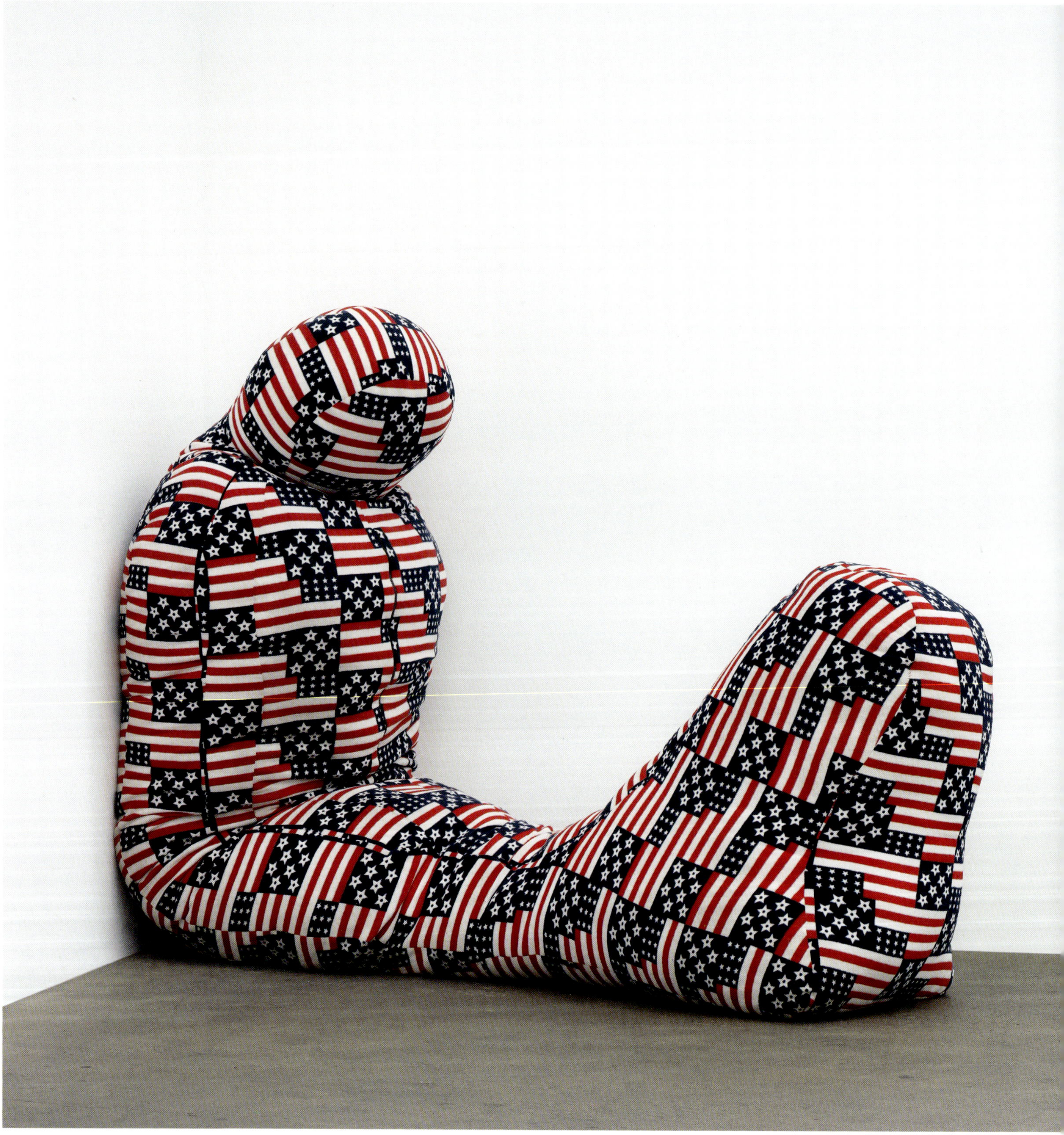

***Laying Figure*, 2013**
Fabric and fiberfill

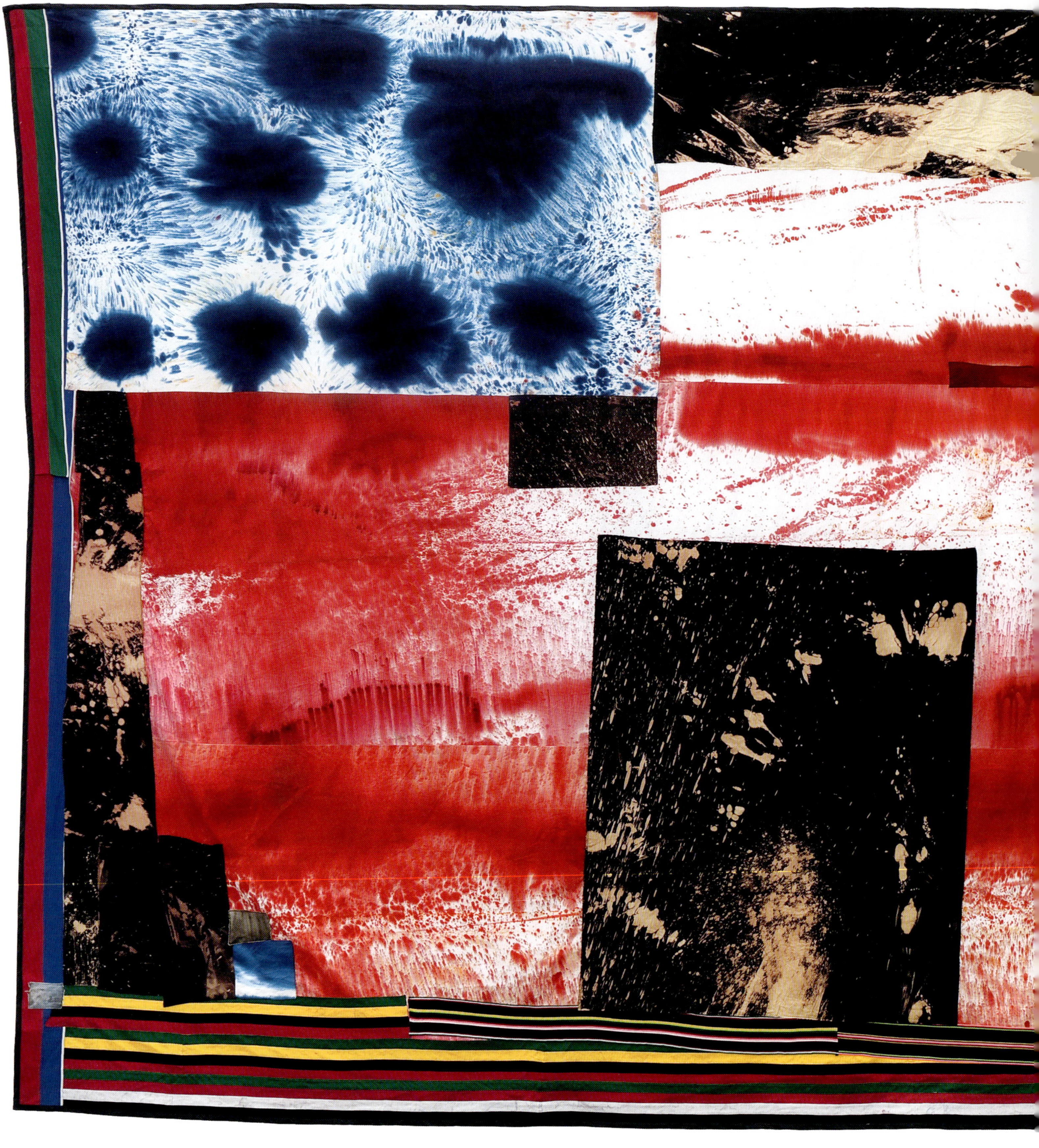

FLAG (4791), 2014
Bleached and dyed canvas, denim, and elastic

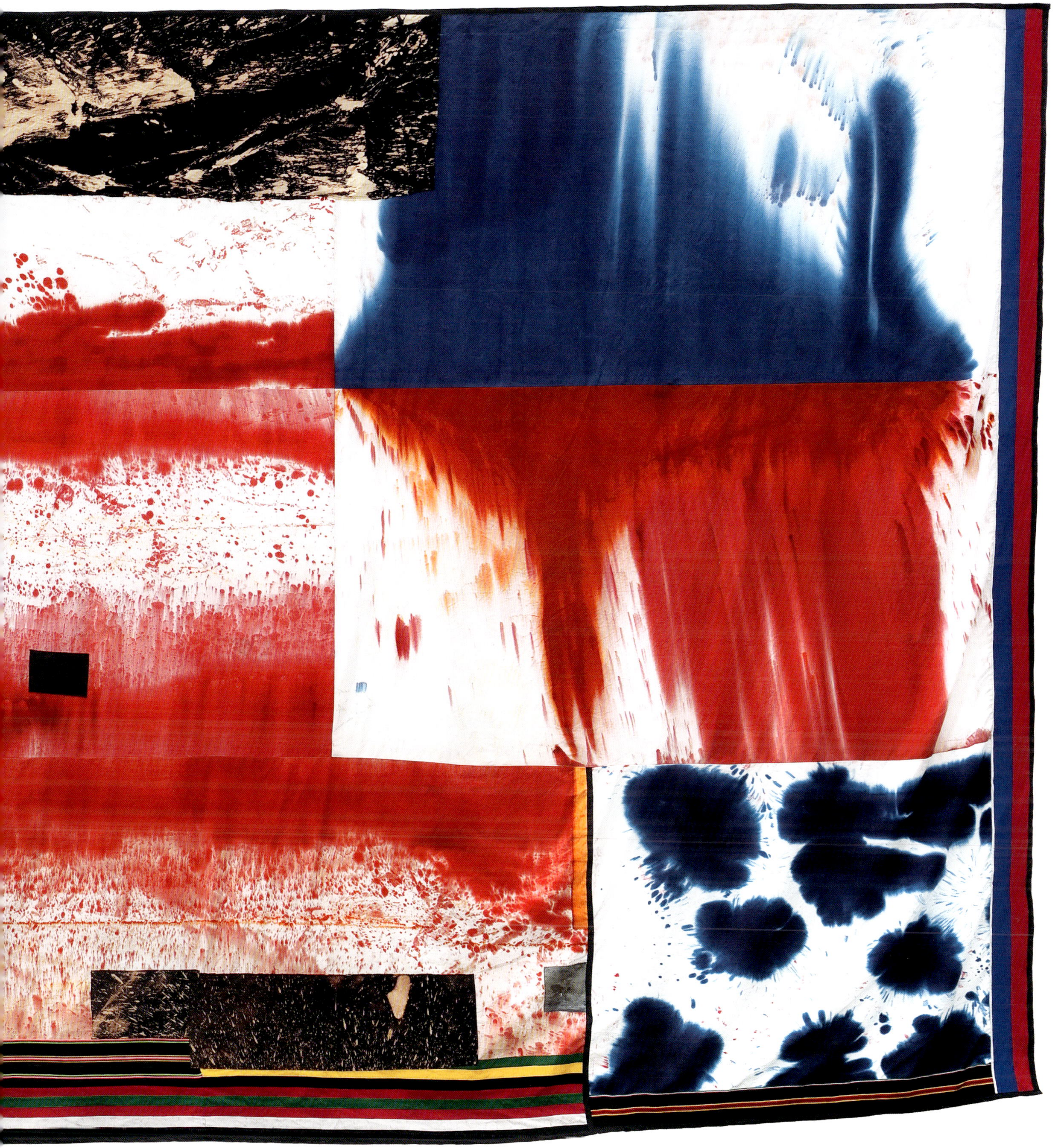

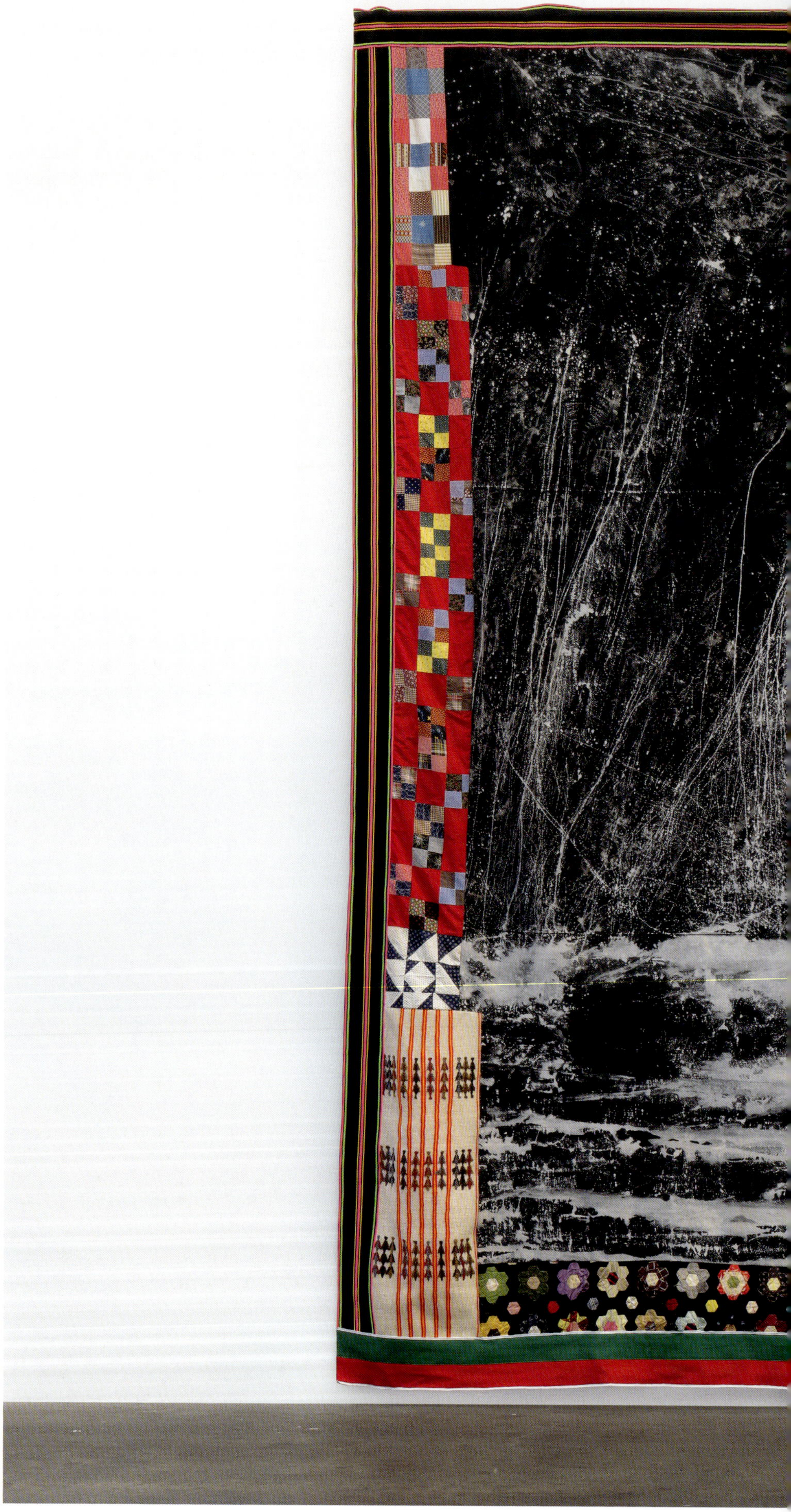

FLAG/QUILT (6625), 2018
Bleached denim, treated fabric, and elastic

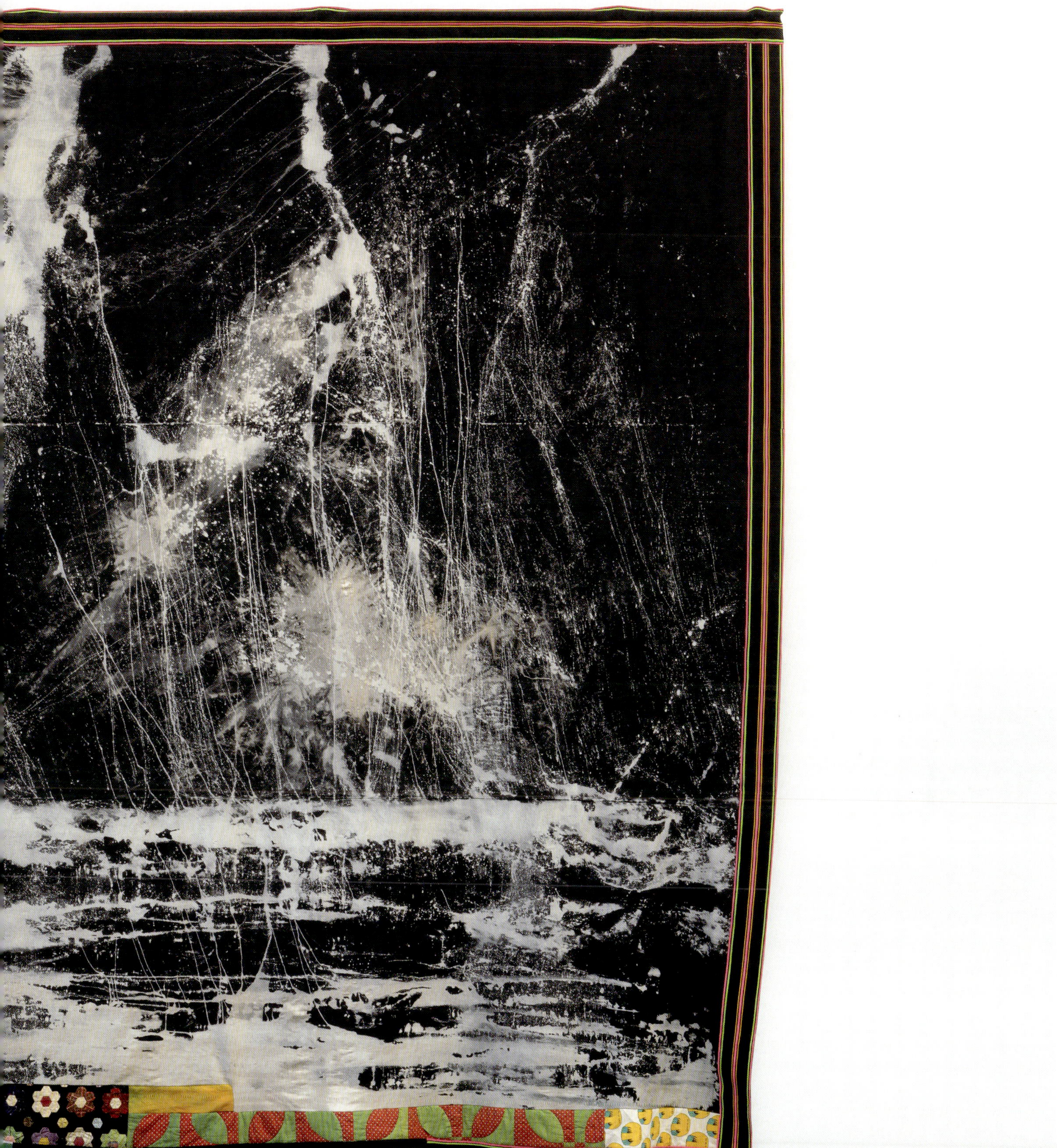

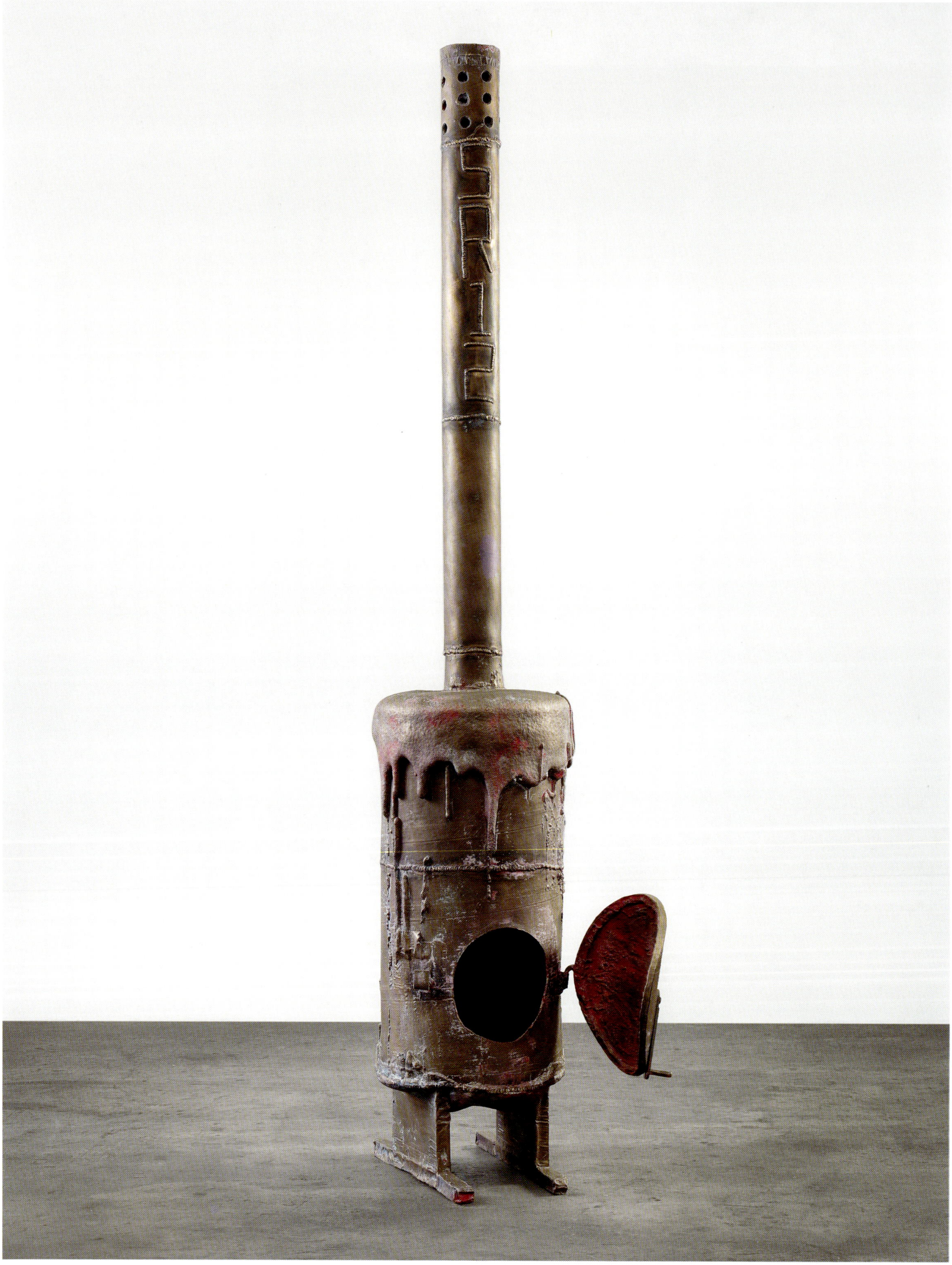
SR12

Metal Works

DURING a month-long stay in 2010 at the Chinati Foundation in Marfa, Texas near the U.S.–Mexico border, Ruby began a series of welded and cut steel sculptures he refers to as MS. Influenced as much by the social and economic conditions at the border as by the minimalist sculptures and ideas of artist and Chinati Foundation founder Donald Judd, the MS sculptures are made from widely used industrial materials, such as steel plate and rebar. The works in this series range in scale, from tabletop assemblages to large, freestanding or floor-bound sculptures. In North America and elsewhere, steel is the most recycled material—melted down as scrap in large furnaces and re-formed as raw material for new constructions. Many of the MS works are pockmarked with crude welds that lend them a makeshift aesthetic.

Like the MS sculptures, Ruby's suite of ten TABLES are similarly marked, though here aberrations in form point also to decades of industrial use. Found when he moved his studio into a former industrial warehouse in Vernon, California, the tables were employed first as welding surfaces. Like many of the found objects that enter his studio, the TABLES were made material for Ruby's sculptural investigations. As salvaged objects, the tables support dense layers of material history, interlacing manufacturing in Southern California with the legacy of artists employing industrial materials and processes. In this way, the tables are accumulations of different marks: each one bears the unique signs of industrial use and artistic utility even before being worked on by Ruby as sculptures unto themselves.

During a trip to China in 2011, Ruby observed workers in a foundry who, to provide heat during the cold winter months, were constructing an ad hoc furnace using leftover materials. Having grown up in rural Pennsylvania, in a farmhouse heated by a wood-burning stove, Ruby identified immediately—by the time he was ten, it was his responsibility to chop wood and maintain the fire at home. Inspired by the foundry workers' furnace, Ruby began to conceive of the stove as a sculptural form and, in 2012, he started to fabricate his own series. He constructed the first STOVES using cardboard and foam, creating designs that were later cast in bronze. Following the patchwork appearance of the foundry workers' furnace, these stoves are roughly welded with thickly poured patches of liquid bronze and ornate inflections of color that emphasize their status as handmade. Later, Ruby shifted to working with steel and experimenting with scale and even produced a suite that appear commercially produced, eschewing the makeshift aesthetic in favor of the slick look of industrial fabrication. In exhibitions, the STOVES appear "almost like relics," in Ruby's estimation, each with a unique sculptural presence, although in several instances STOVES were installed outdoors where they burned wood for the duration of an exhibition. Here, Ruby reenvisioned them as performative sculptures to explore how the "kinetics and the smell of burning wood"[1] influence how they are read as objects. Like all of Ruby's metal works, the STOVES foreground processes of material transformation and reuse foundational to his work, holding in dynamic tension the relationship between manufacturing and artistic production.

—J. D.

1. "Kate Fowle in Conversation with Sterling Ruby," in *Sterling Ruby* (New York: Phaidon, 2016), 21.

STOVE 3, 2012
Bronze and paint

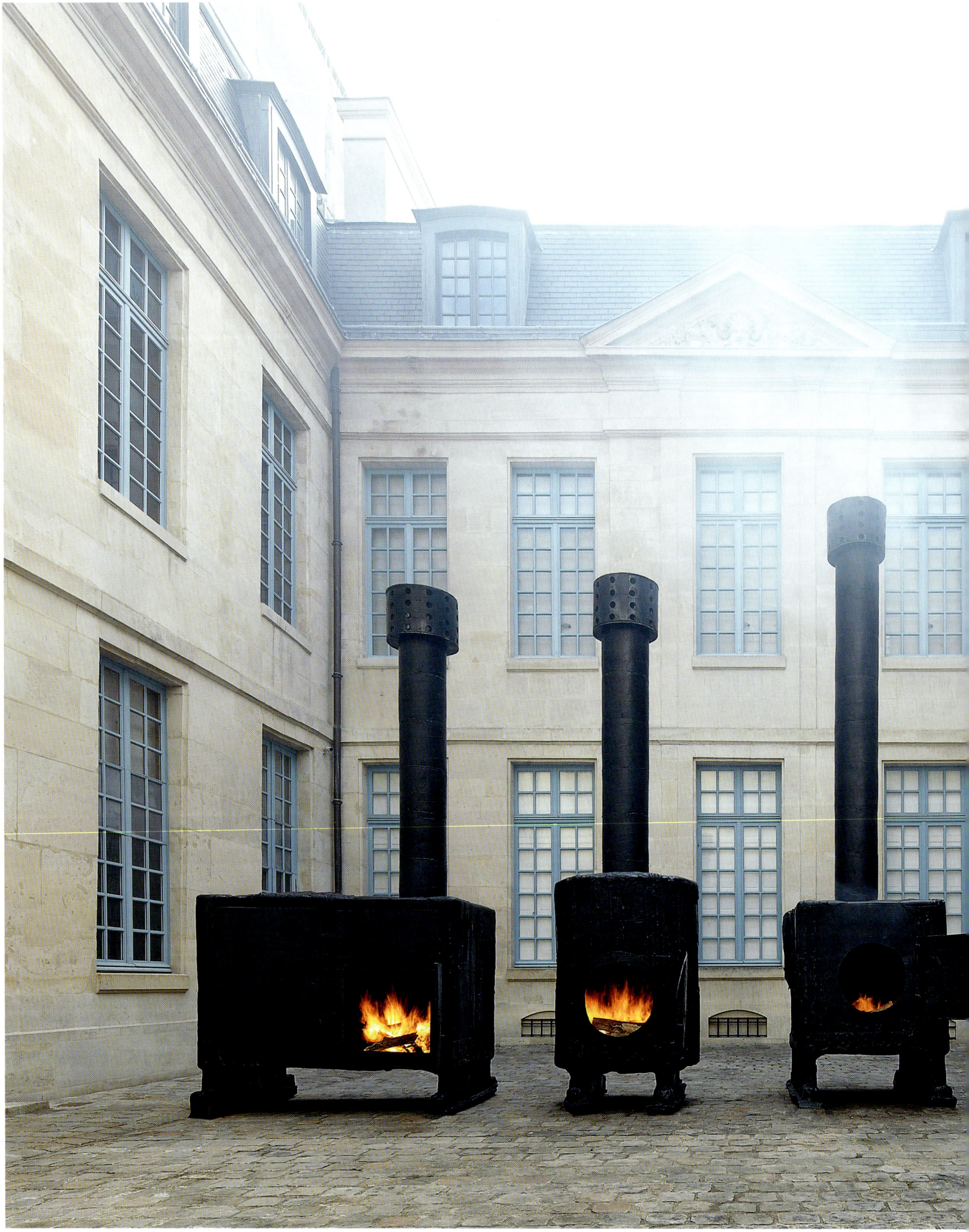

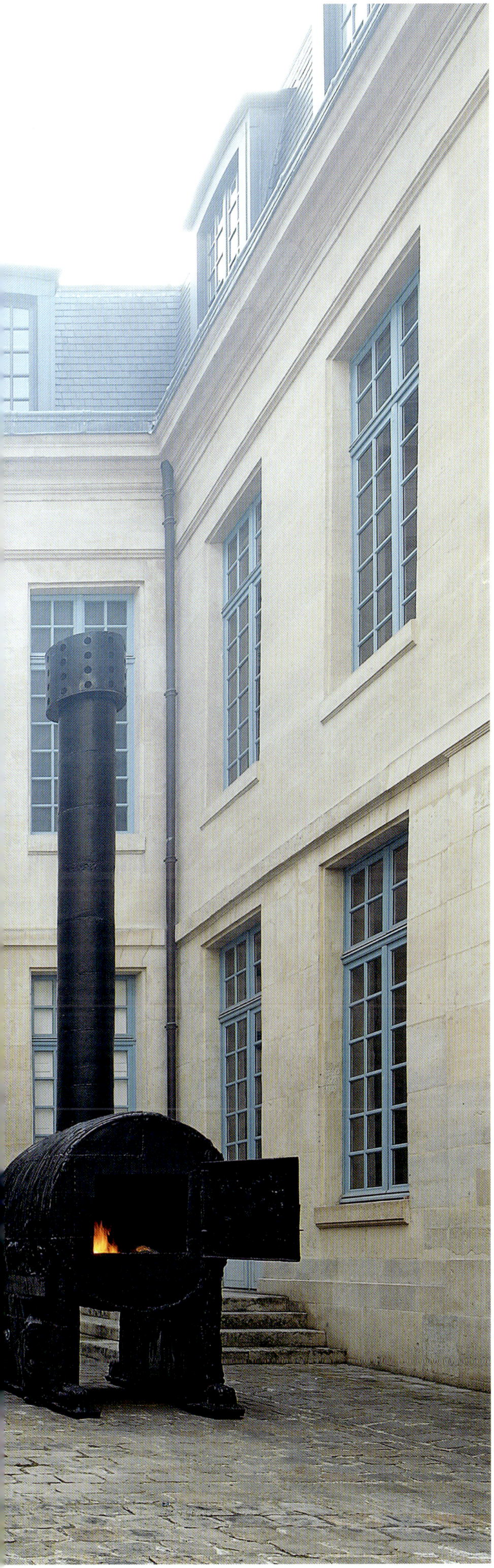

Installation view, *STOVES*,
Musée de la Chasse et de la Nature, Paris, 2015–16

Stove 4, 2013
Stainless steel

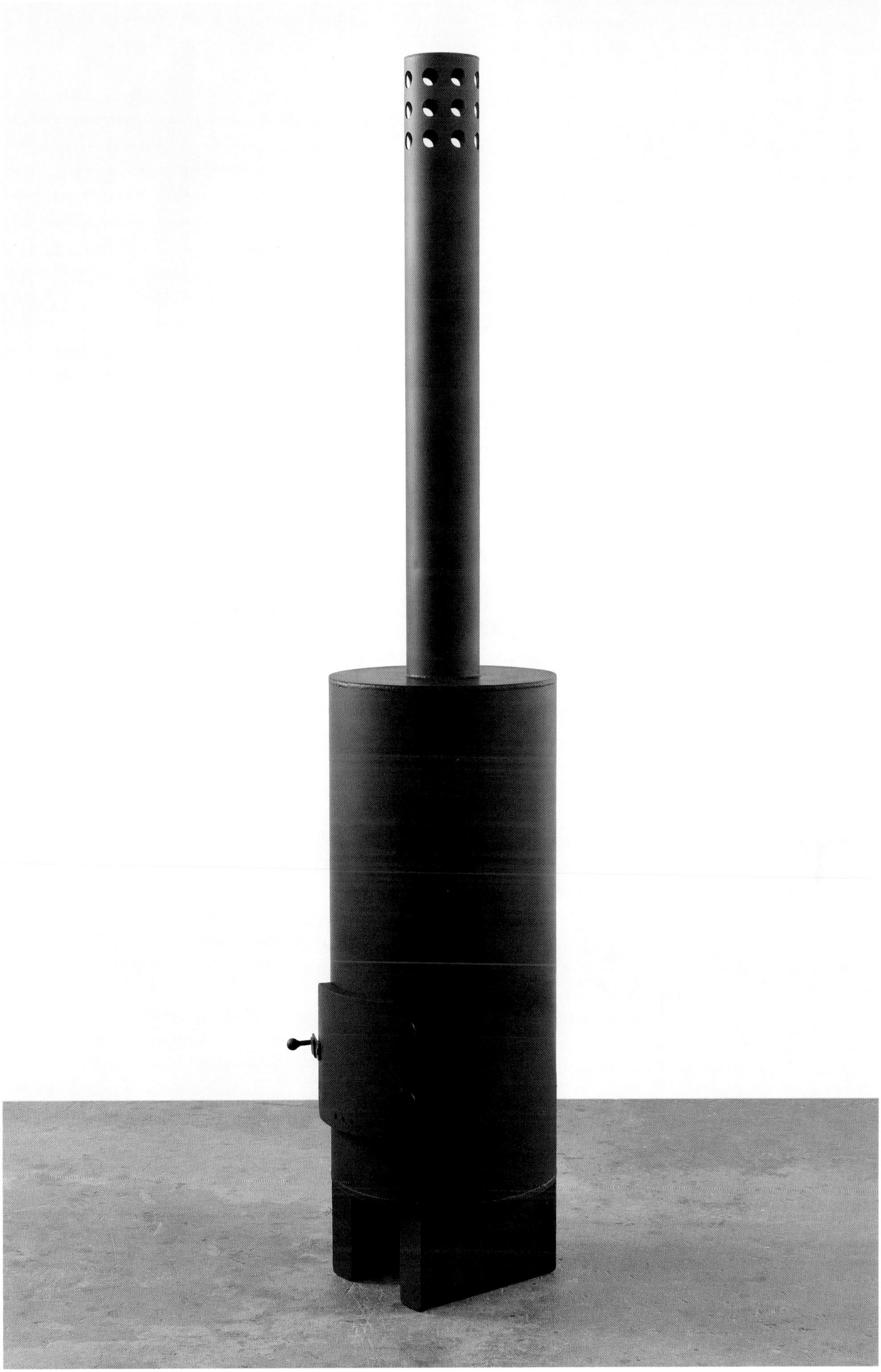

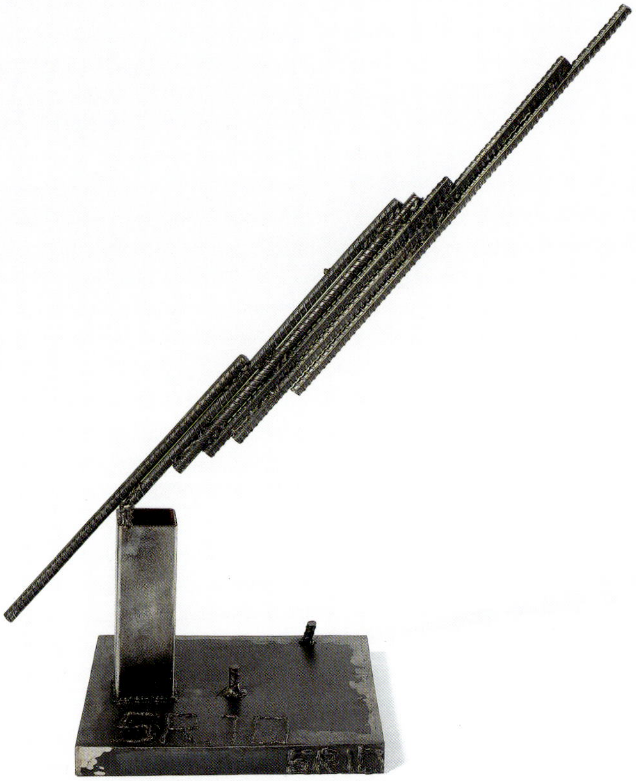

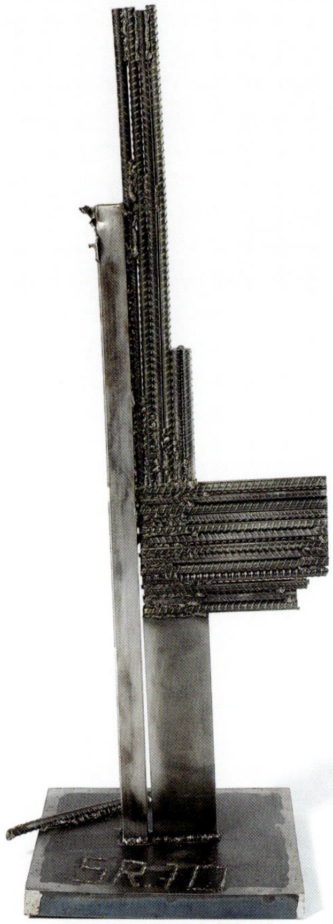

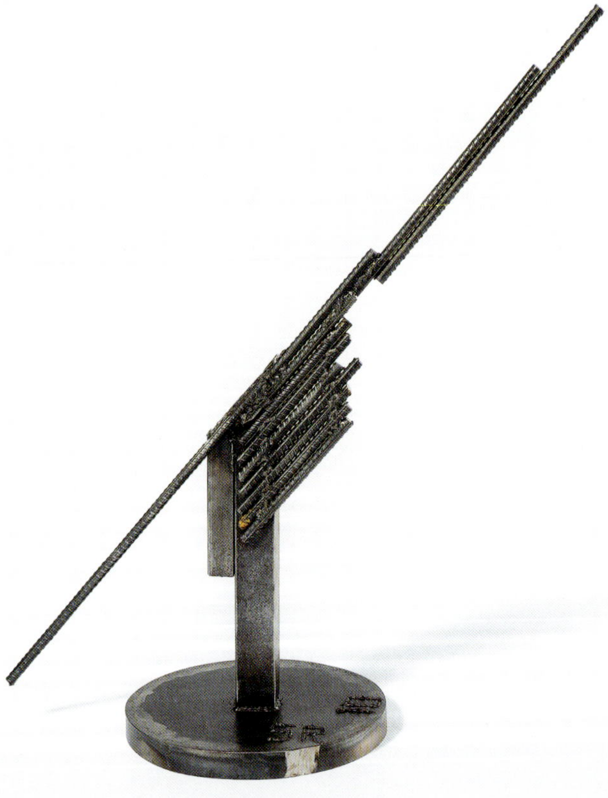

Clockwise from top left:

***MS01-2867*, 2010**
Steel

***MS07-2873*, 2010**
Steel

***MS06-2872*, 2010**
Steel

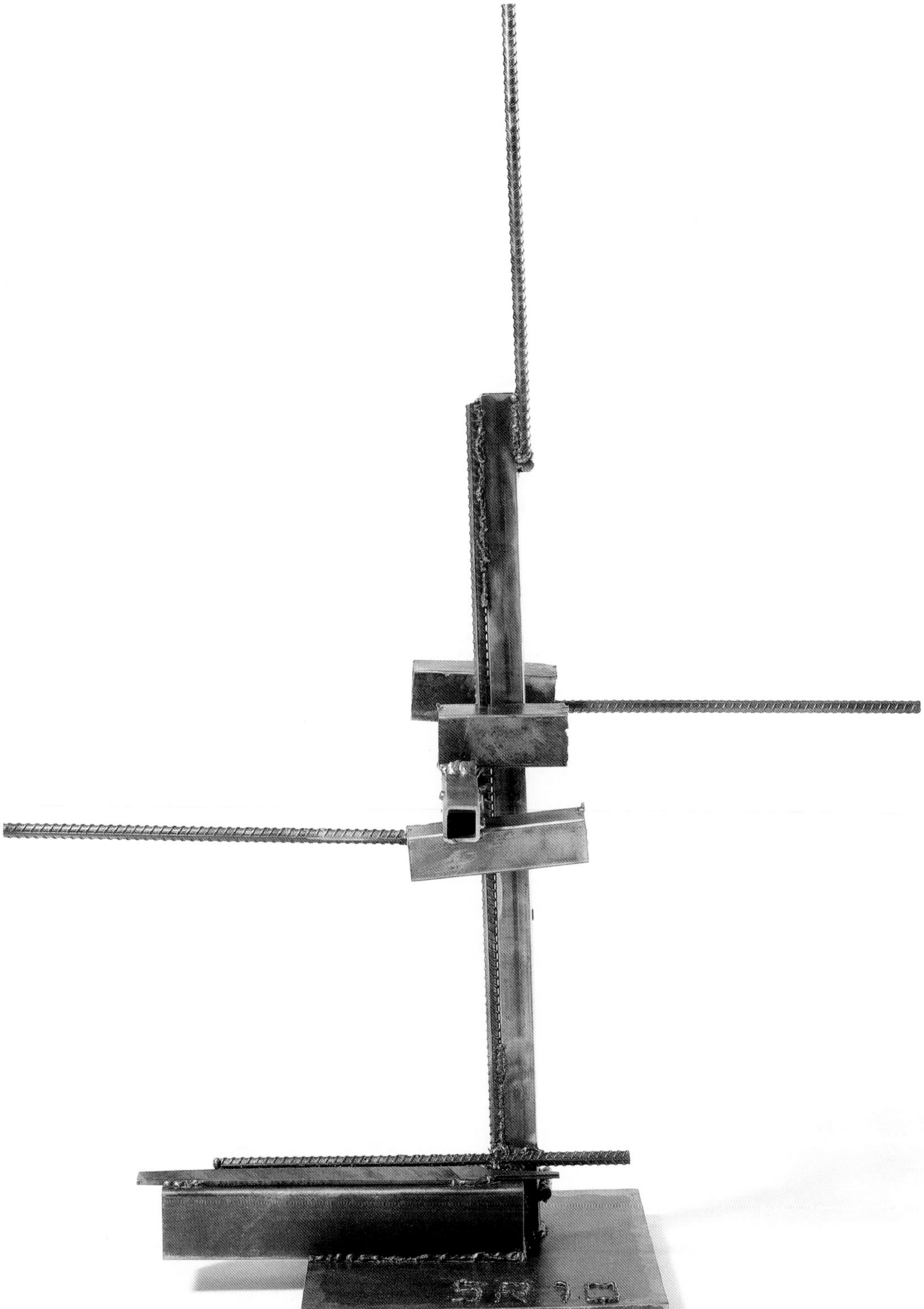

***MS13-2879*, 2010**
Steel

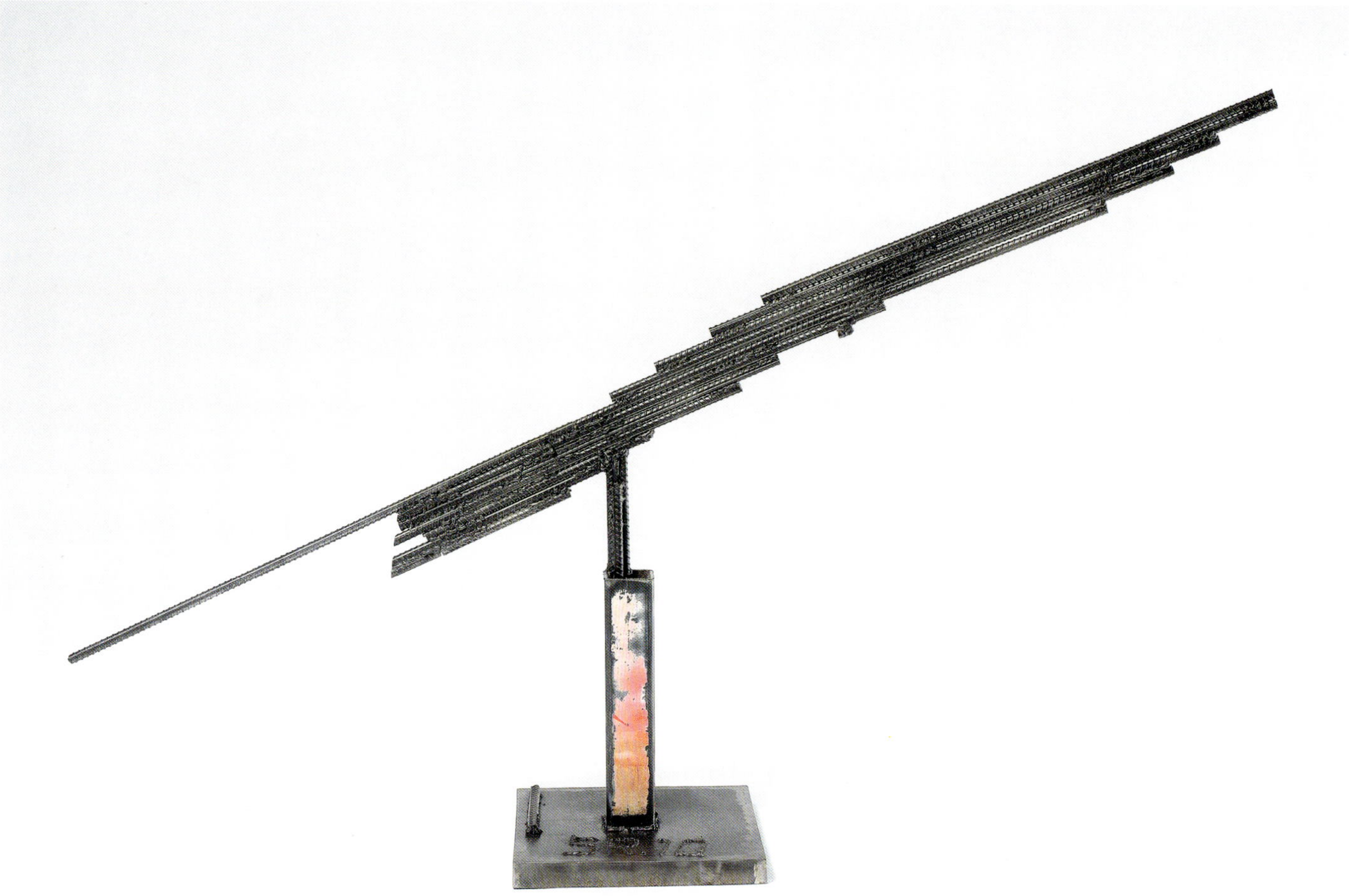

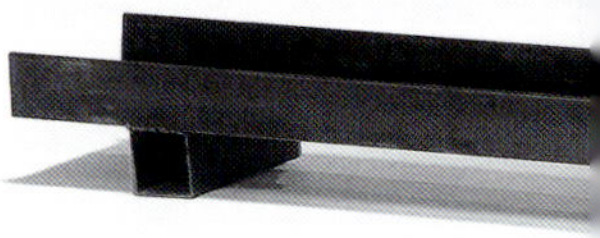

MS14-2881, 2010
Steel

Opposite:
MS16-2883, 2010
Steel

Next spread:
DRAG (LONG BLOCK 5505), 2015
Steel, engine block, and paint

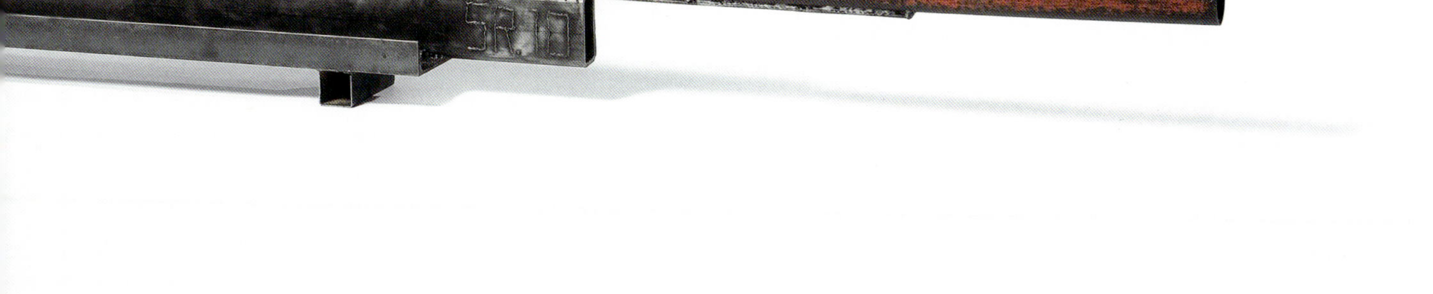
SR.10

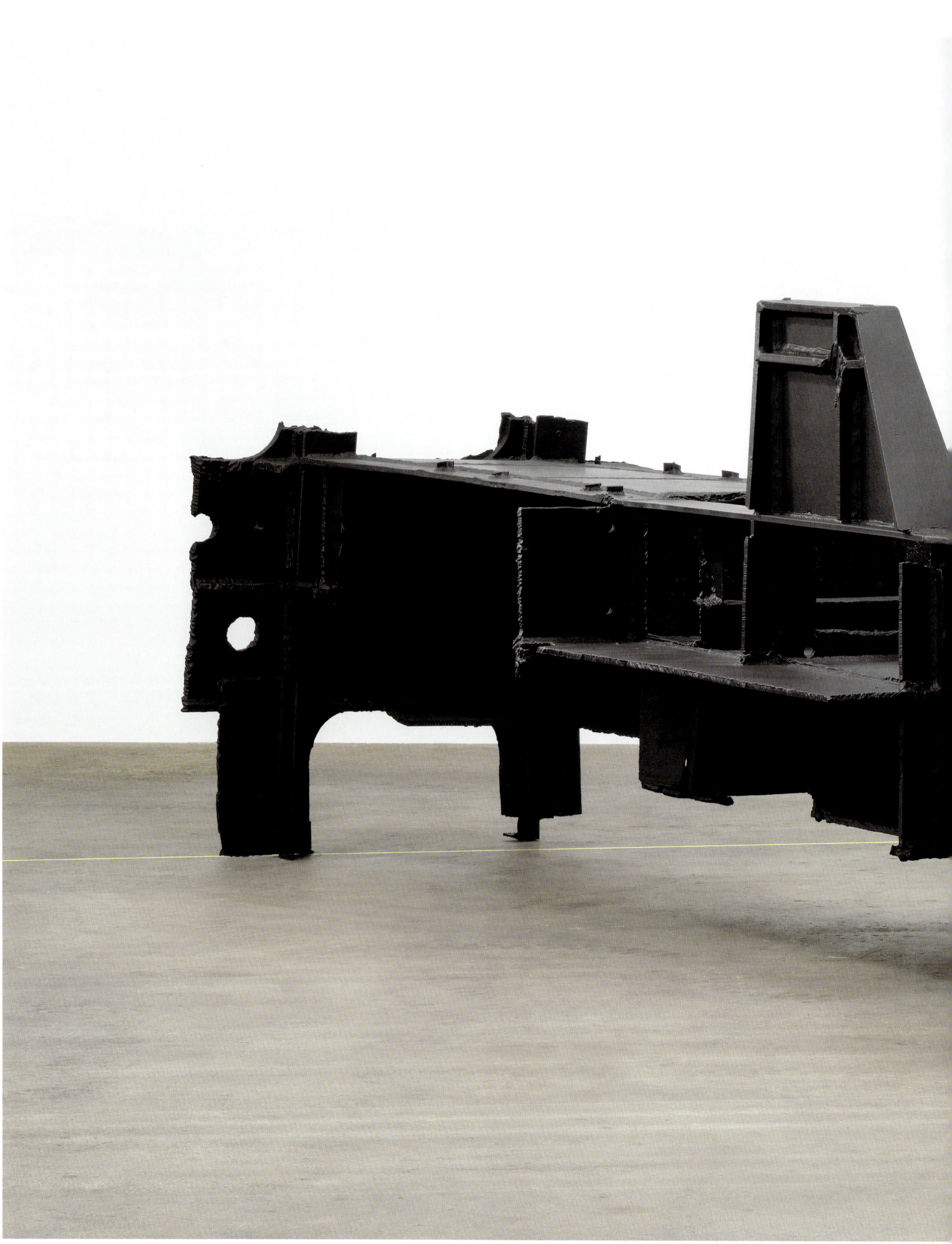

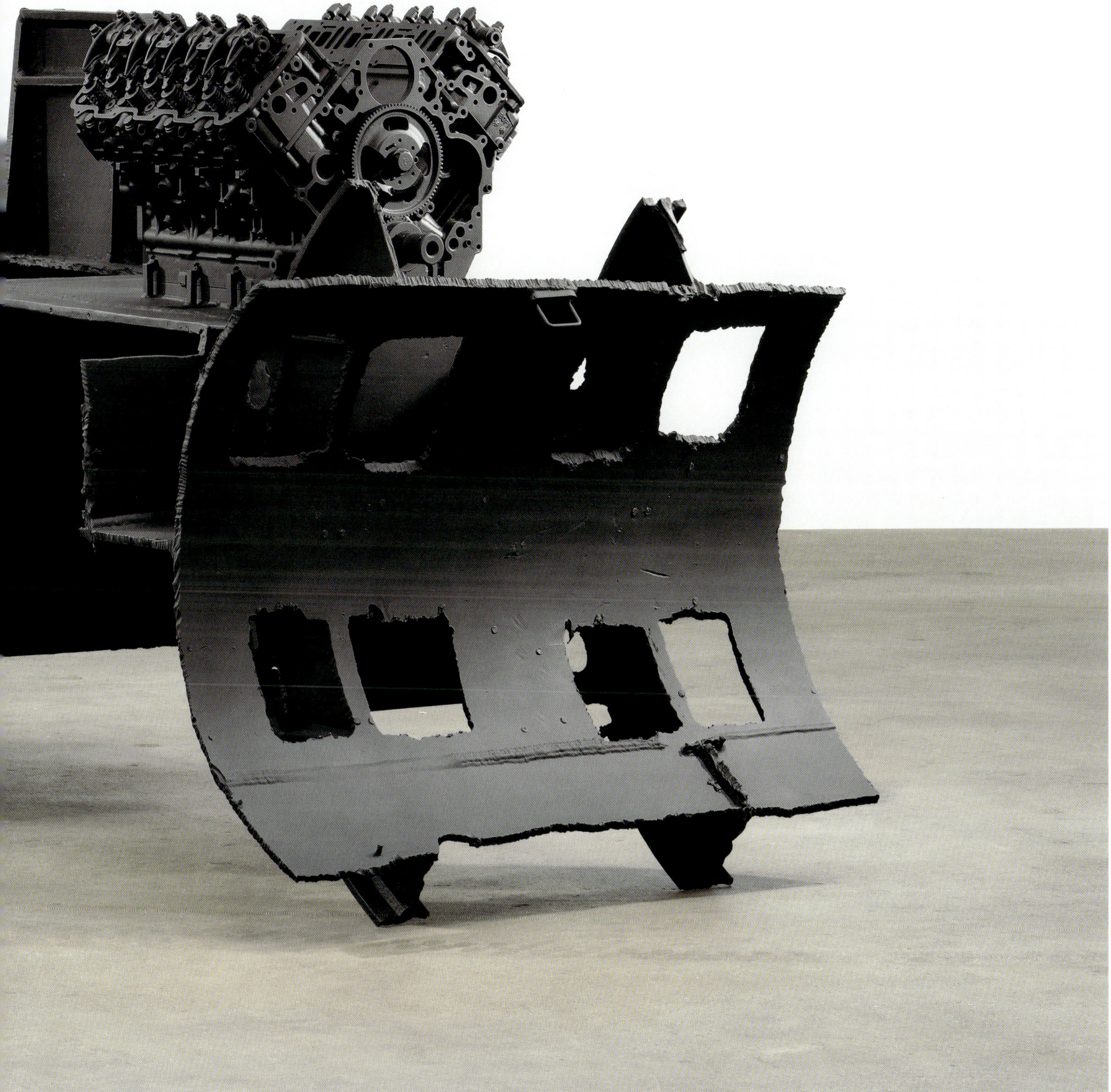

SUBHEAD (5600), 2015
Steel and paint

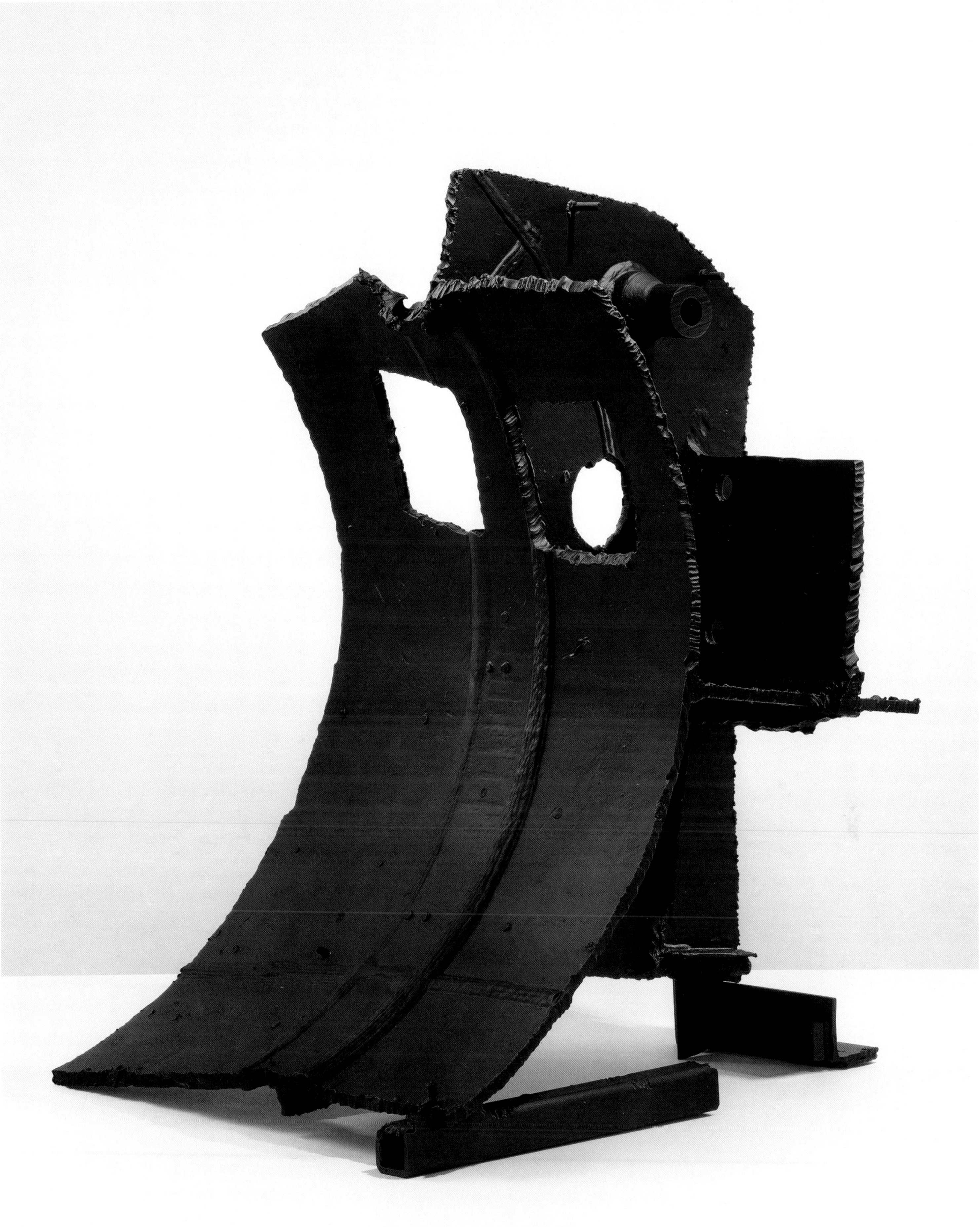

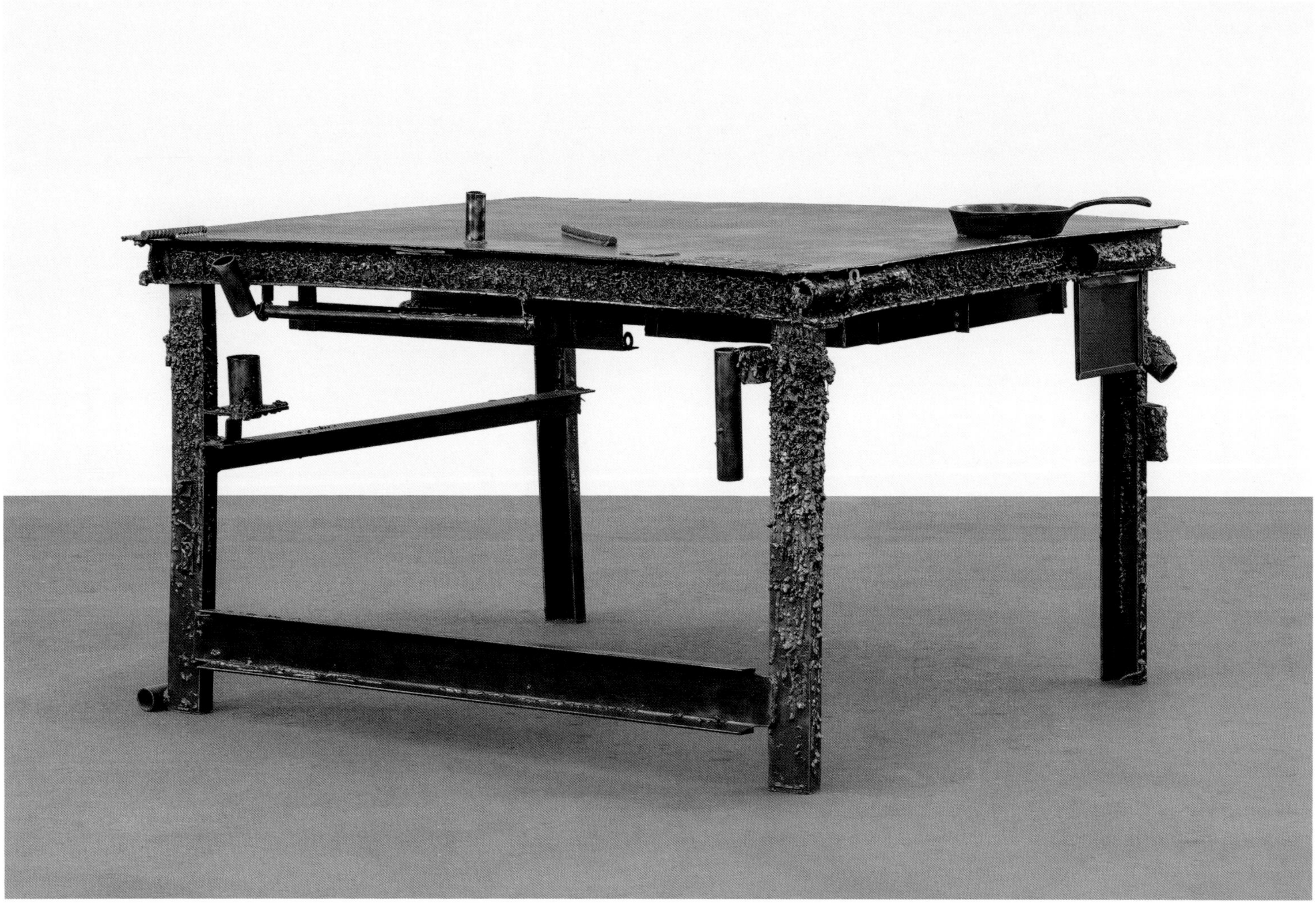

TABLE 4, 2015
Steel

Opposite:
TABLE 10, 2015
Steel

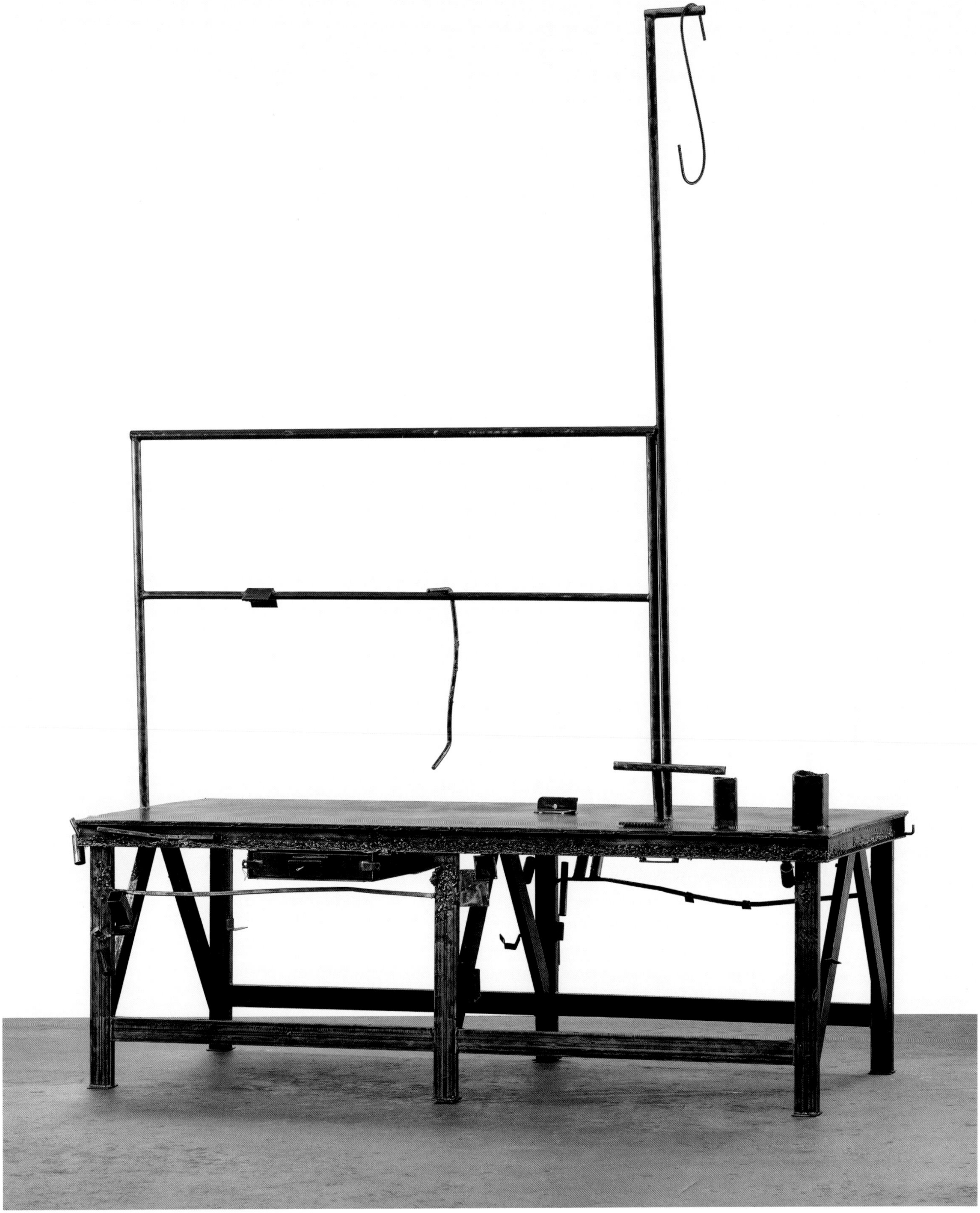

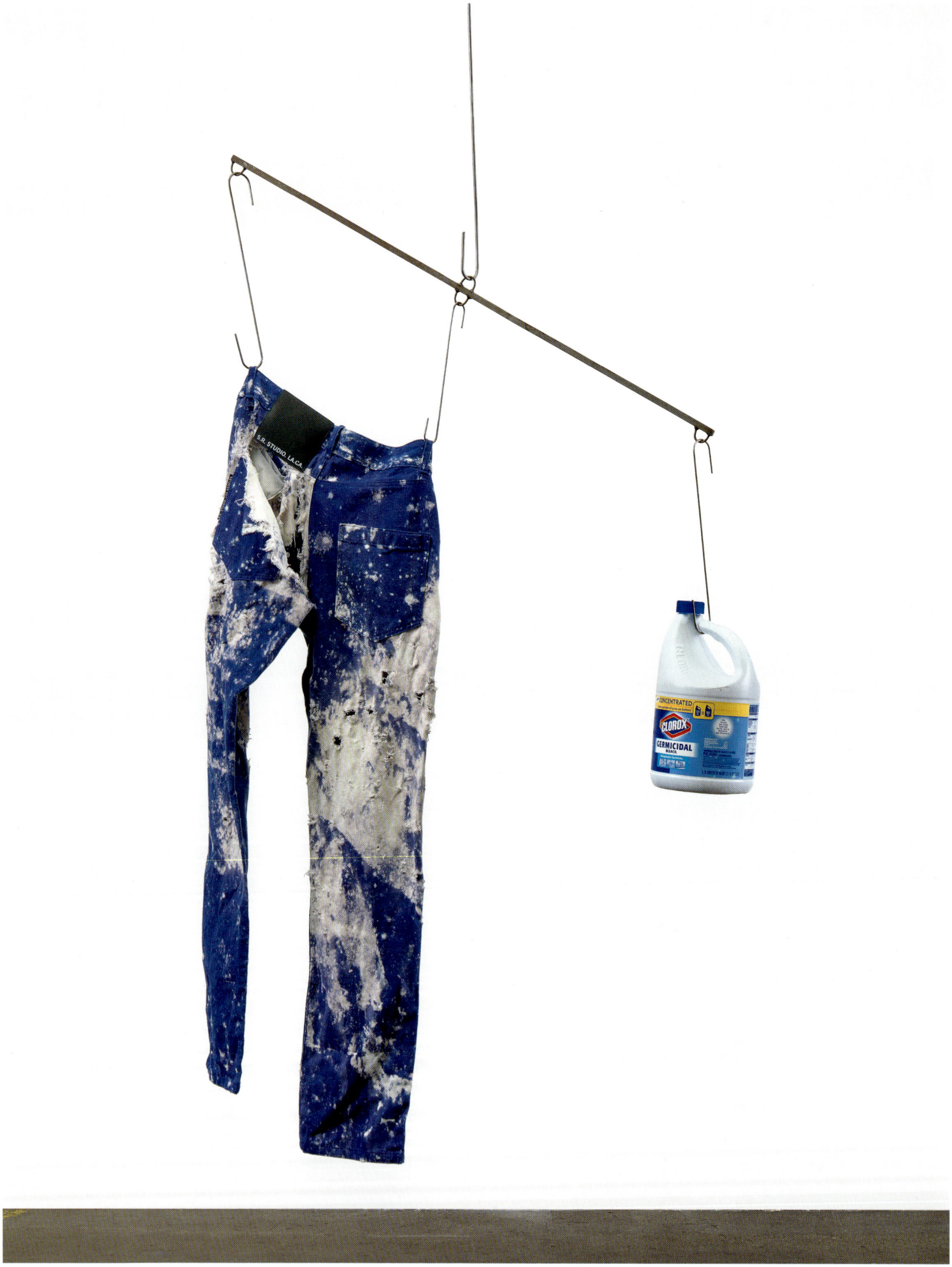
S.R. STUDIO. LA.CA
CONCENTRATED
CLOROX
GERMICIDAL
BLEACH

ECLPSE and SCALES

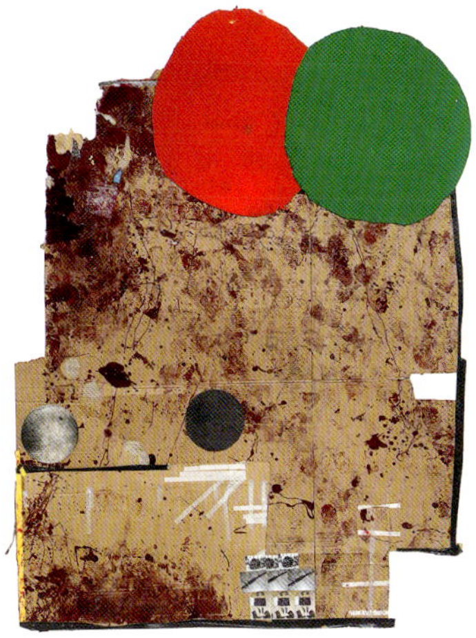

Fig. 1: *EXHM (4763)*, 2014. Collage, paint, and urethane on cardboard

IN STERLING RUBY'S STUDIO, throwaway functional materials such as cardboard are eventually incorporated into new works, carrying forward fragments of previous works into newer bodies. Ruby repurposes pieces of cardboard from his painting studio floor for a series of large-scale abstract collages called ECLPSE. The cardboard is cut into various shapes that resemble suns, moons, or other overlapping landscape elements, painted in rich, primary colors, and arrayed in various shapes and configurations. Invoking the legacy of suprematism, ECPLSE uses radically reduced means to communicate potent immediacy. In *ECLPSE (RBGBCROSS)* (2015), for example, the basic geometric shape of the cross—a recurring motif in Kazimir Malevich's suprematist paintings exploring mystical spirituality—is reinterpreted by Ruby in black and blue, roughly cut cardboard on a tarnished, overpainted, red and green cardboard support. Cardboard is a support for several of Ruby's earlier series, including EXHM, in which the artist collages elements over top of the salvaged cardboard used in the process of making his poured urethane sculptures. In *EXHM (4019)* (2012) [pp. 60–61], for example, aerial images of California prisons are placed on the urethane-stained cardboard in contrast with a suggestive agglomeration of things such as an image of Earth from space, scratch tickets, Smirnoff Ice packaging, and a flattened package of Astepro (a medication used to treat the allergic itching of the eyes). As his EXHM collages evolved, he introduced painted cardboard elements, such as the red and green overlapping circles in *EXHM (4763)* (2014) [fig. 1], which point directly to the ECLPSE series.

The persistent pattern of reuse and richly painted pieces of cut cardboard recur in Ruby's self-referential mobiles called SCALES. Monumental, three-dimensional hanging collages, the SCALES often juxtapose these monochromatically painted cardboard shapes with other recognizable elements from Ruby's creative output. Studio materials such as bottles of bleach, a fiber-filled American flag DROP sculpture, or a NIK Presumptive Drug Test package all introduce different narrative elements and function also as a compendium of Ruby's studio practice and, indeed, the studio itself. The mobile—often associated with Alexander Calder in art historical contexts—is a kinetic sculpture prone to movement, a dispersed form whose organization is dictated by chance. In *SCALE (4586)* (2013), diverse objects from various series hang in a precarious balance from a metal armature. From the painted, cut cardboard shapes of ECLPSE to the red yarn used as hair in the FIGURES, each item is a proxy for Ruby's various activities, making the mobile an assemblage rich with significance for his practice as a whole. Like the ECLPSE collages, the SCALES restage a high modernist moment using throwaway materials. In the SCALES, the studio itself is subject, expanding further on the formal and conceptual possibilities of an interlinked practice that imagines the overlapping histories of the artist's studio as a mechanism for producing new work.

—J. D.

SCALE (5415) S.R. CLOR., 2015
Steel and mixed media

ECLPSE (RBGBCROSS), 2015
Collage and paint on cardboard

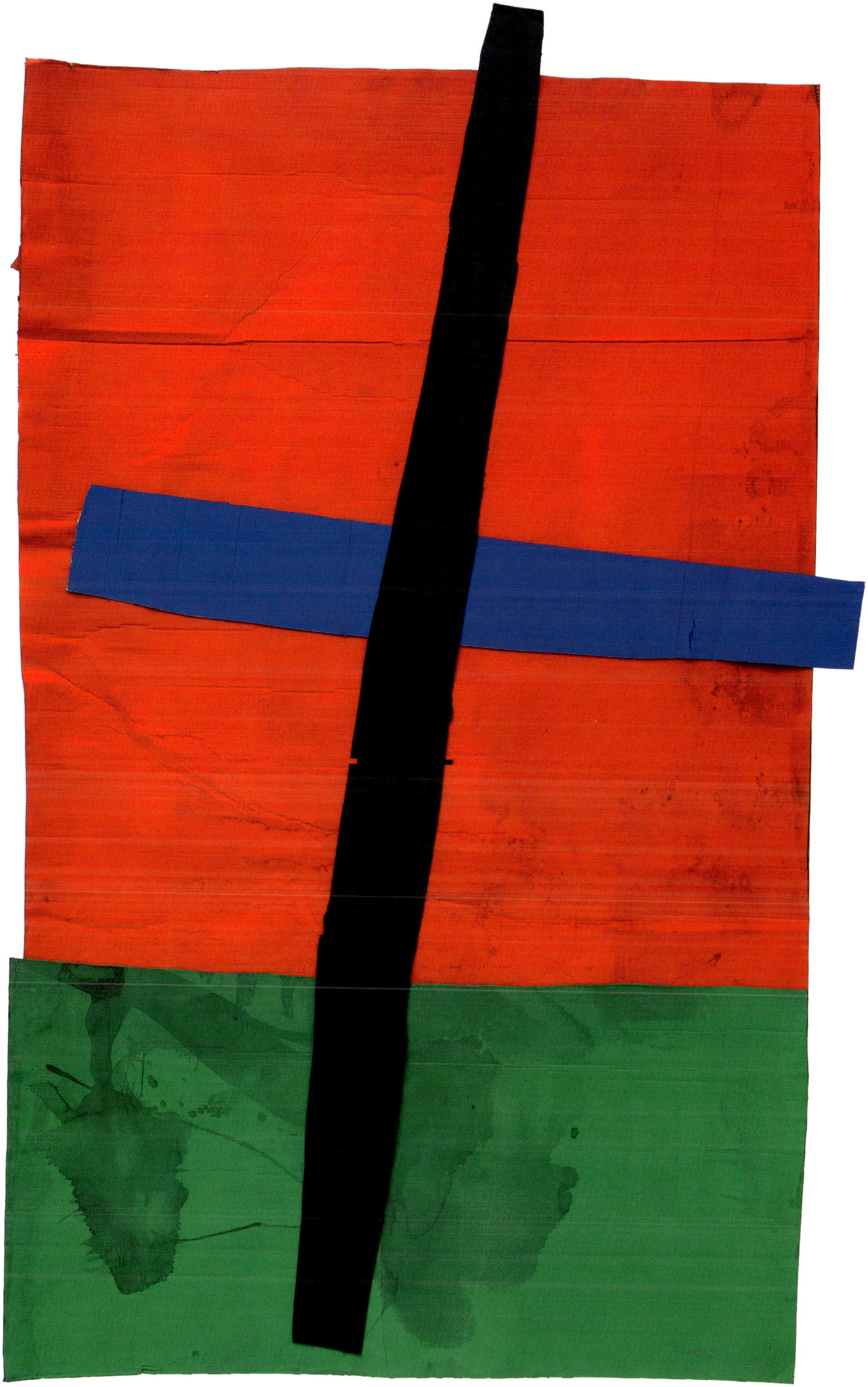

ECLPSE (GRB), 2015
Collage and paint on cardboard

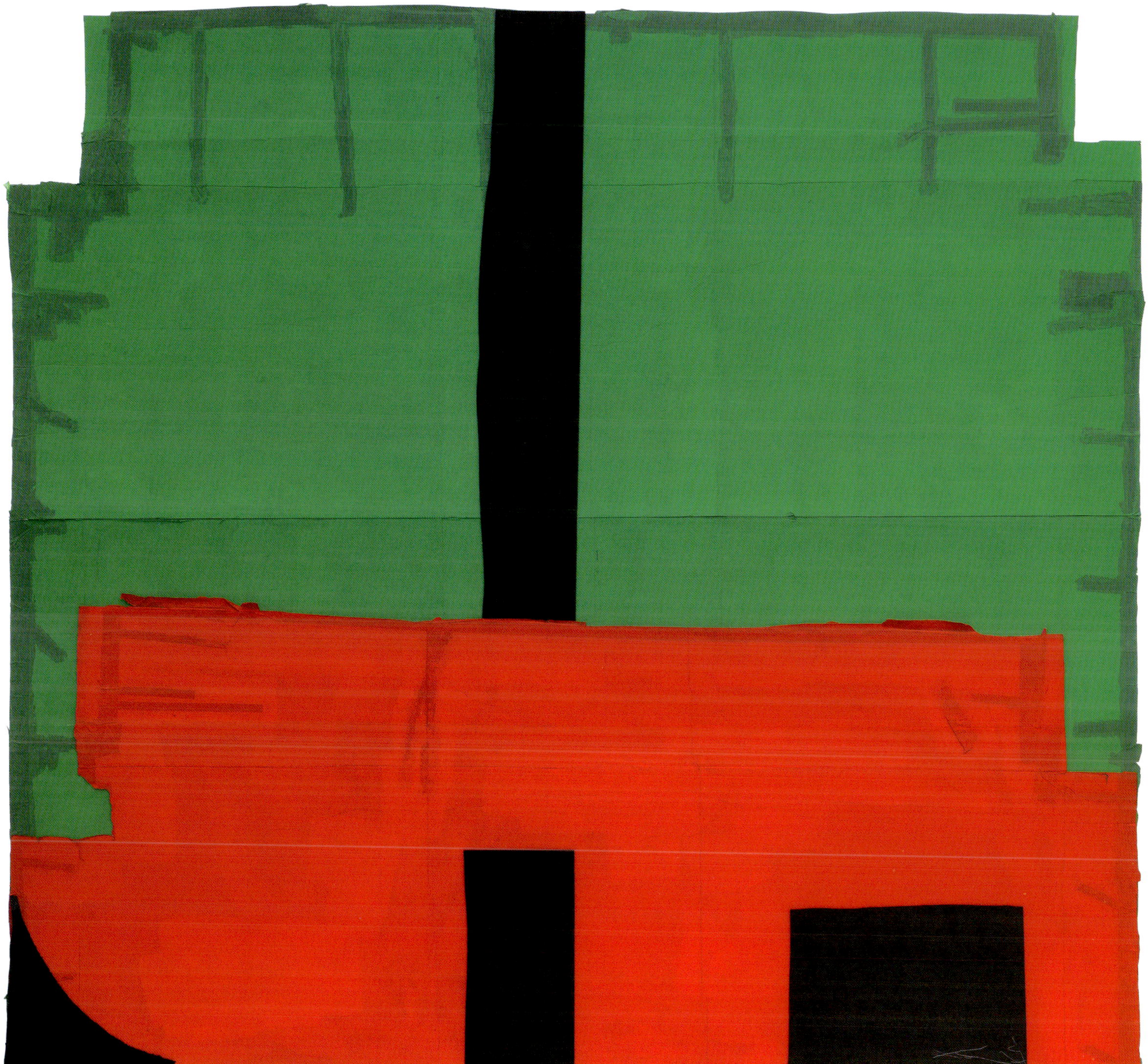

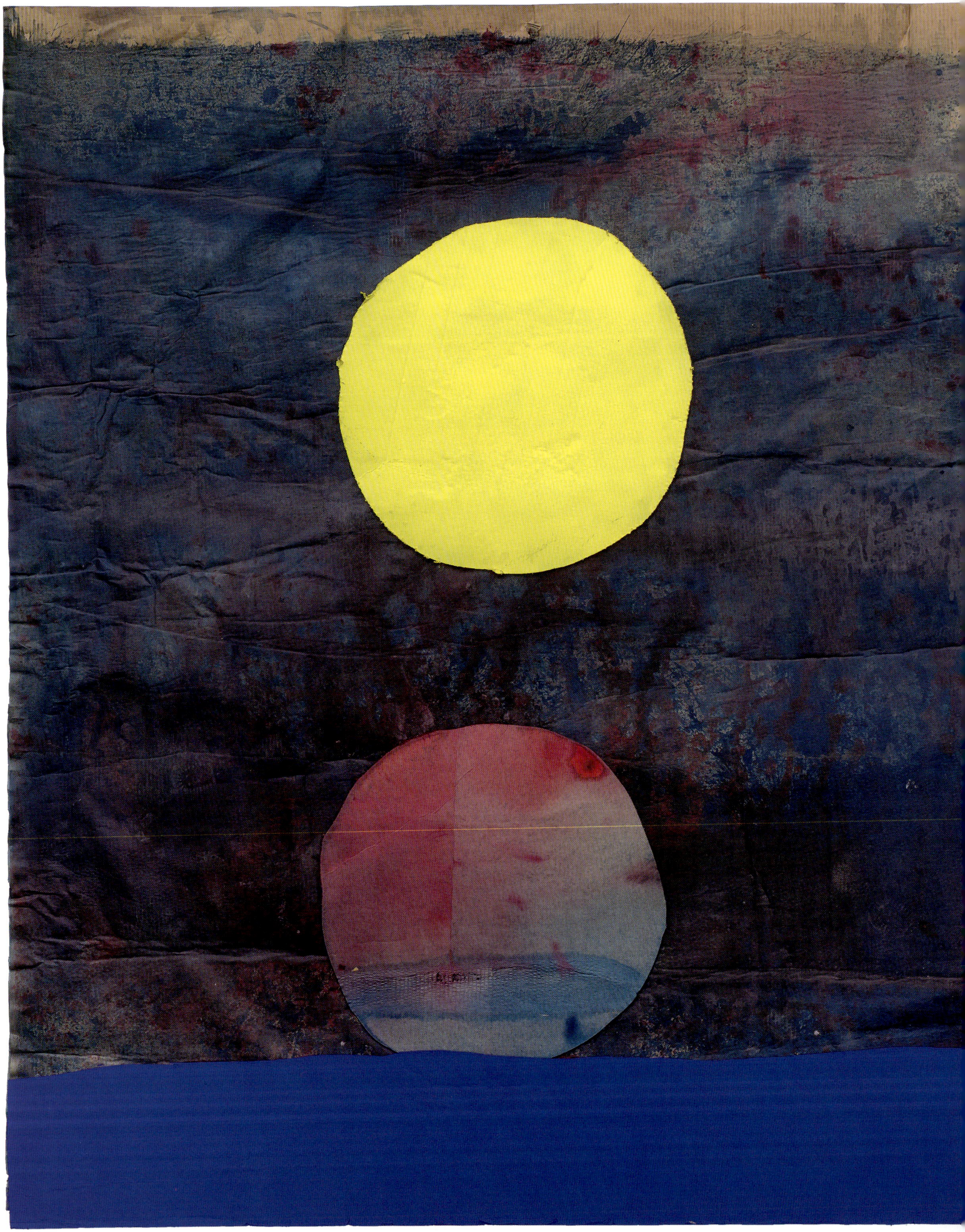

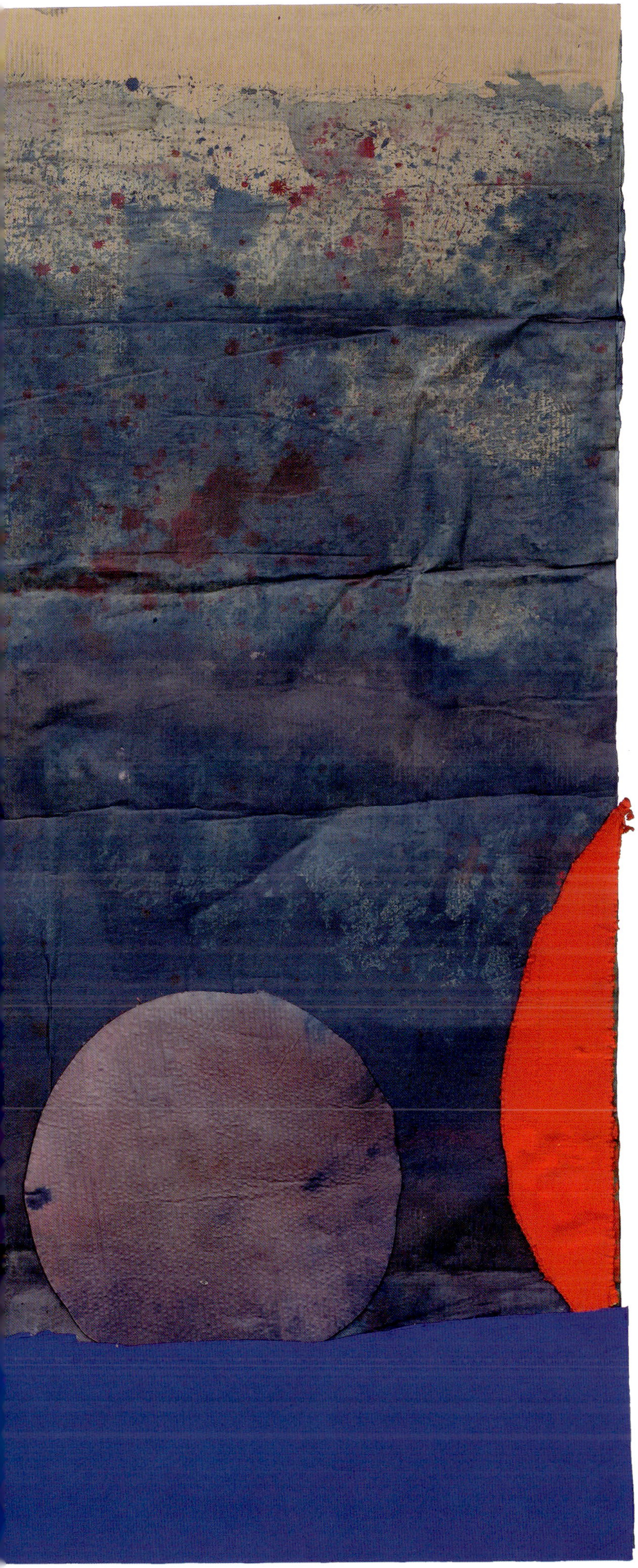

ECLPSE (Blue Horizon), 2015
Collage and paint on cardboard

SCALE (4586), 2013
Steel, paint, cardboard, yarn, and mixed media

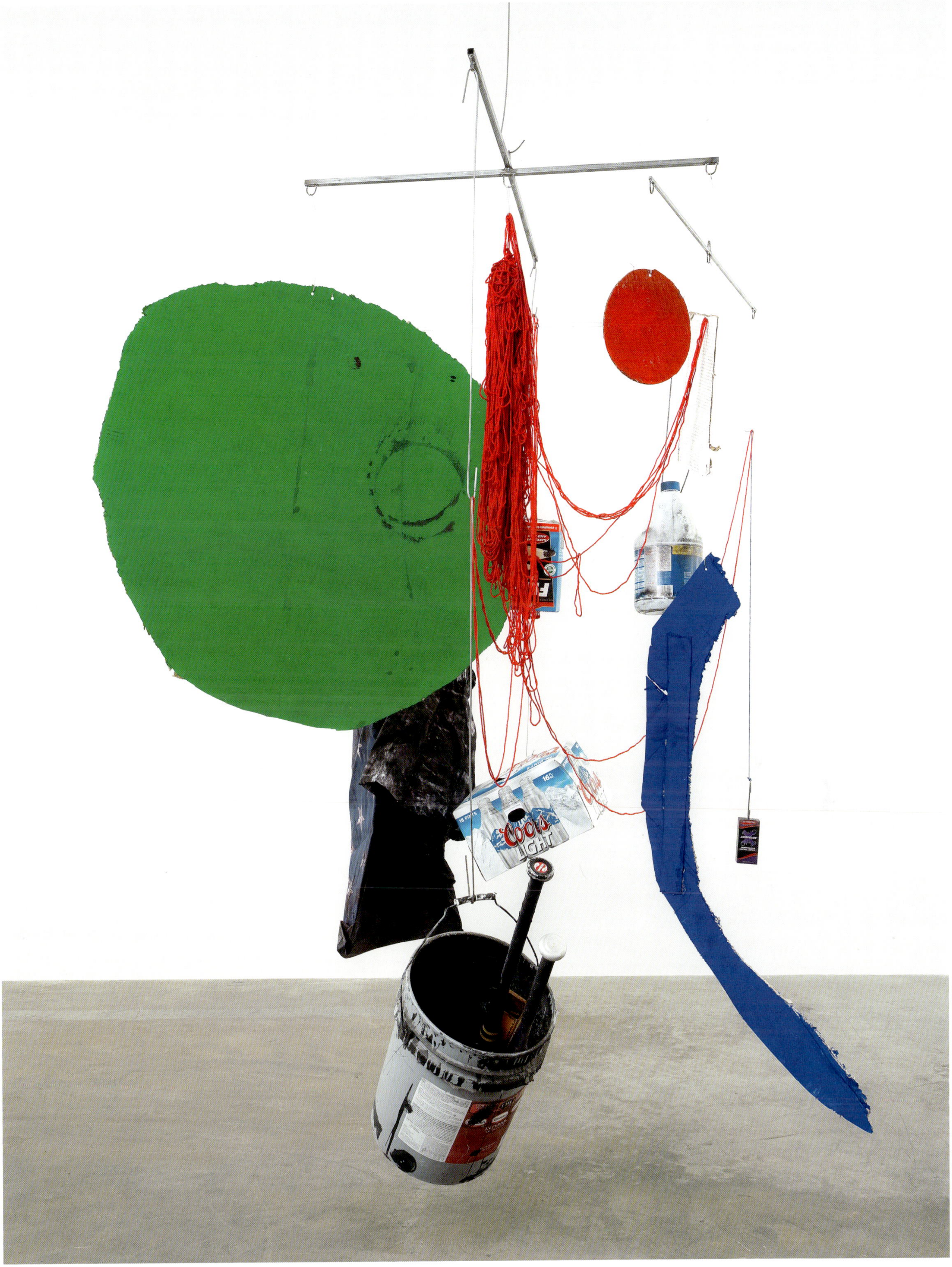
Coors
LIGHT

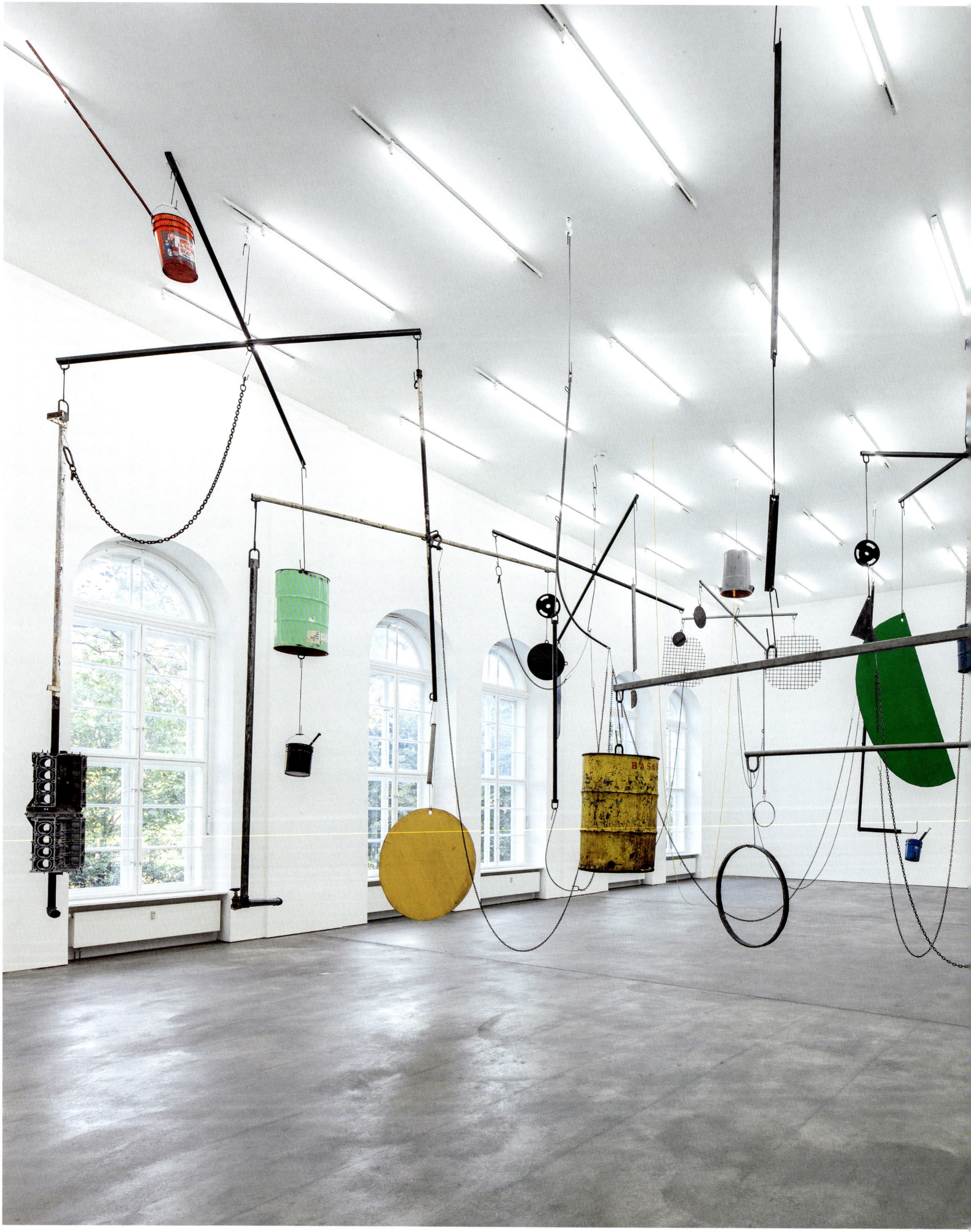

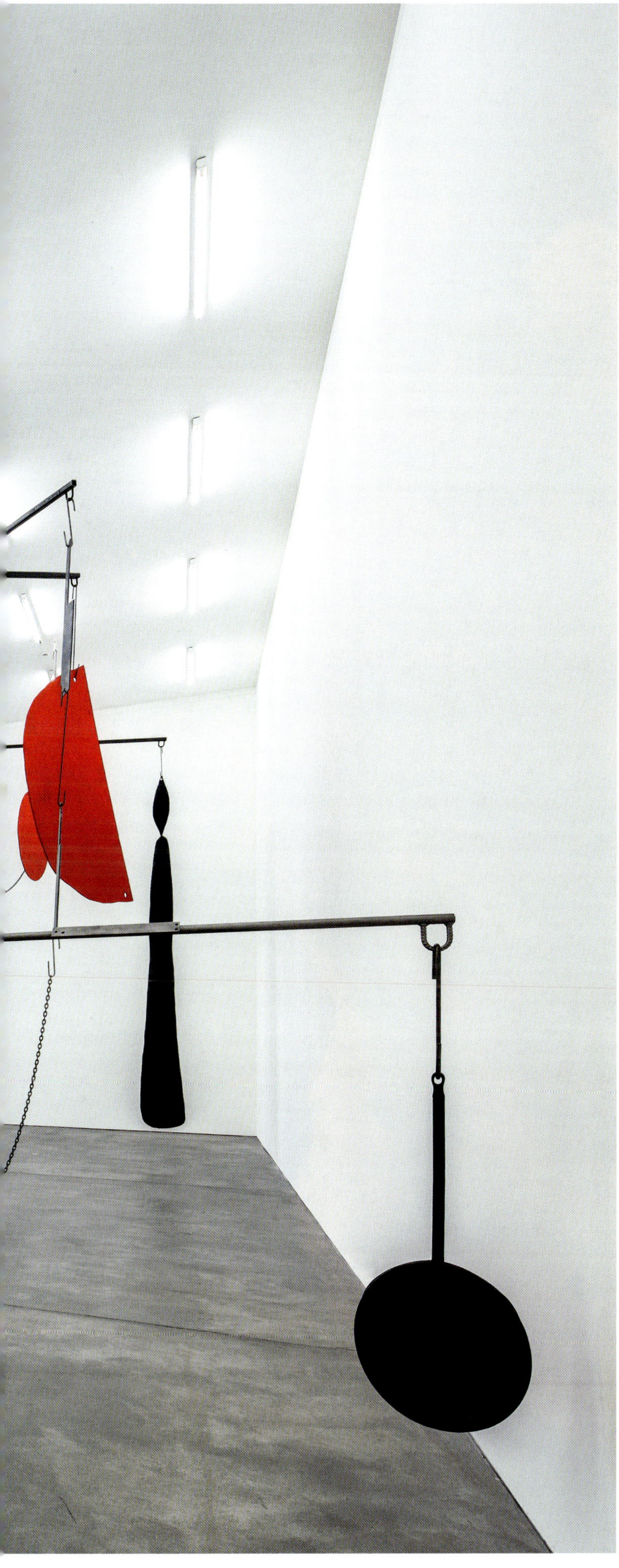

Installation view, *THE JUNGLE*, Sprüth Magers, Berlin, 2016

Works in the Exhibition

Sterling Ruby
American/Dutch, born 1972 in Bitburg, Germany
Lives and works in Los Angeles

Absolute Contempt for Total Serenity #3, 2005 *
Collage on paper
28 × 22 inches (71.1 × 55.9 cm)
Collection of José Freire

72–73 *ACTRESS 2*, 2010
Bronze with silver nitrate patina
4 1/2 × 20 1/2 × 12 1/2 inches (11.4 × 52.1 × 31.8 cm)

92–93 *ACTS/ 187 DREAMER*, 2009
Clear urethane block, dye, wood, spray paint, and formica
54 1/4 × 63 × 36 inches (137.8 × 160 × 91.4 cm)
Collection of Andre Sakhai, New York

98–99 *ACTS/WS ROLLIN*, 2011
Clear urethane block, dye, wood, spray paint, and formica
60 1/2 × 62 1/2 × 34 inches (153.7 × 158.8 × 86.4 cm)
Institute of Contemporary Art, Miami; Gift of The Hinson Family, by exchange

101 *Alabaster SR08-2*, 2008
Acrylic
45 × 92 3/4 × 2 1/2 inches (114.3 × 235.6 × 6.4 cm)

101 *Alabaster SR10-16*, 2010
Acrylic
44 1/4 × 83 1/4 × 2 1/2 inches (112.4 × 211.5 × 6.4 cm)
Collection of Javier and Monica Mora

100 *Alabaster SR11-58*, 2011
Acrylic
49 3/4 × 93 × 2 1/2 inches (126.4 × 236.2 × 6.4 cm)

100 *Alabaster SR11-63*, 2011
Acrylic
44 1/2 × 84 × 2 1/2 inches (113 × 213.4 × 6.4 cm)

81 *ANGLE OF DEPRESSION*, 2017
Ceramic
57 × 19 1/2 × 18 1/4 inches (144.8 × 49.5 × 46.4 cm)

Anti-Print Poster 1, 2, 3, 2007 *
Posters
Three parts, 23 × 16 inches (58.4 × 40.6 cm), 22 1/4 × 15 1/8 inches (56.5 × 38.4 cm), 16 1/2 × 23 1/2 inches (41.9 × 59.7 cm)

70 *ASHTRAY 141*, 2010
Ceramic
2 3/8 × 17 3/4 × 17 inches (6 × 45.1 × 43.2 cm)

Balanced Stack of Pottery and Knife, 2005 *
Collage on paper
28 × 22 1/2 inches (71.1 × 57.2 cm)
Lorinsky Collection

80 *Basin Theology/CRYPTOCRYSTALLINE*, 2016 *
Ceramic
17 × 46 × 44 inches (43.2 × 116.8 × 111.8 cm)

84–85 *Basin Theology/La Brea 2*, 2011
Ceramic
12 × 40 1/2 × 38 3/4 inches (30.5 × 102.9 × 98.4 cm)
Ovitz Family Collection, Los Angeles

82 *Basin Theology/Red Bull*, 2013
Ceramic
19 × 37 × 39 inches (48.3 × 94 × 99.1 cm)
Private collection

83 *Basin Theology/Redox*, 2013
Ceramic
38 × 41 1/2 × 41 inches (96.5 × 105.4 × 104.1 cm)
The Broad Art Foundation, Los Angeles

86–87 *Basin Theology/STYX BOAT*, 2017 *
Ceramic
26 × 46 × 74 inches (66 × 116.8 × 187.9 cm)

BASKET (6176), 2016 *
Ceramic
12 1/4 × 35 × 14 inches (31.1 × 88.9 × 35.6 cm)

62 *BC (3950)*, 2012
Fabric, paint, glue, and bleached canvas on panel
84 × 84 × 2 inches (213.4 × 213.4 × 5.1 cm)

63 *BC (5289)*, 2014
Fabric, glue, and bleached canvas on panel
84 × 84 × 2 inches (213.4 × 213.4 × 5.1 cm)

97 *Big Grid/DB Deth*, 2008
Formica, spray paint, and wood
84 × 84 × 36 inches (213.4 × 213.4 × 91.4 cm)

75 *Bishop Score 2*, 2013 *
Ceramic
19 1/2 × 19 × 9 1/2 inches (49.5 × 48.3 × 24.1 cm)
Collection of Ray Ellen and Allan Yarkin

102 *Black Star/Prostitute's Bolster*, 2007
PVC pipe, urethane, wood, aluminum, and spray paint
136 × 91 1/4 × 31 inches (345.4 × 231.8 × 78.7 cm)
La Colección Jumex, Mexico City

56–57 *Block A, Tier 3 (Spatial)*, 2008 *
Collage, spray paint, and colored pencil on paper
41 1/8 × 52 5/8 × 2 1/2 inches (104.5 × 133.7 × 6.4 cm)

68–69 *Blue Angel*, 2007
Ceramic
16 1/2 × 18 × 19 1/2 inches (41.9 × 45.7 × 49.5 cm)

51 *CDC at PDC Study*, 2008 *
Collage, paint, and colored pencil on paper
42 3/4 × 27 1/4 inches (108.6 × 69.2 cm)

Club (7005), 2019 *
Ceramic
29 1/4 × 11 × 3 inches (74.3 × 27.9 × 7.6 cm)

Cottage Drawing, 2003 *
Collage and pen on postcard
5 3/8 × 7 1/4 inches (13.7 × 18.4 cm)

65 *CRUX.YELL.*, 2016 *
Acrylic, oil, elastic, and fabric on canvas
59 × 45 1/2 × 3 1/4 inches (149.9 × 115.6 × 8.3 cm)
Collection of Pilar Crespi Robert and Stephen Robert

44 *Cry 2005*, 2005
Lambda print
62 3/4 × 46 3/4 inches (159.4 × 118.7 cm)
Private collection

36 *Crystal Cryer*, 2001
Pencil on paper
22 1/8 × 30 1/4 inches (56.2 × 76.8 cm)

The Dark Project, 2009 *
Ceramic
7 × 20 1/4 × 20 1/4 inches (17.8 × 51.4 × 51.4 cm)

45 *DEATH CULT (6148)*, 2016
Archival inkjet print
69 1/2 × 42 3/8 inches (176.5 × 107.6 cm)

45 *DEATH CULT (6150)*, 2016
Archival inkjet print
59 1/2 × 42 3/8 inches (151.1 × 107.6 cm)

Death Cult Los Angeles/Cry Me a River, 2007 *
Lambda print
59 × 47 1/2 inches (149.9 × 120.7 cm)

20 *Disintegrating Identities*, 2003–06 *
Wood, tar, latex, synthetic hair, diamonds, ceramic, and bleach
116 × 147 × 98 inches (294.6 × 373.4 × 248.9 cm)
Collection of Craig Robins and Jackie Soffer

DOG, 2012 *
Patinated bronze
3 3/8 × 8 5/8 × 18 1/8 inches (8.6 × 21.9 × 46 cm)

129 *DOUBLE CANDLE (6992)*, 2019
Fabric and fiberfill
162 × 38 × 19 inches (411.5 × 96.5 × 48.3 cm)

136–37 *DOUBLE VAMPIRE 14*, 2013
Fabric and fiberfill
163 × 205 × 7 inches (414 × 520.7 × 17.8 cm)

37 *DR (6503)*, 2017
Pen on paper
5 × 8 1/8 inches (12.7 × 20.6 cm)

52 *DRFTRS (4253)*, 2013 *
Collage, paint, and glue on paper
38 × 25 inches (96.5 × 63.5 cm)

53 *DRFTRS (4257)*, 2013
Collage, paint, and glue on paper
25 × 19 inches (63.5 × 48.3 cm)

43 *DRFTRS (6007)*, 2016
Collage, paint, and glue on paper
11 1/8 × 17 1/4 inches (28.3 × 43.8 cm)

76–77 *Drive-Thru Pewter Facial*, 2010
Ceramic
15 × 33 3/4 × 16 1/4 inches (38.1 × 85.7 × 41.3 cm)
Collection of Thomas H. Lee and Ann Tenenbaum

167 *ECLPSE (GRB)*, 2015
Collage and paint on cardboard
115 1/8 × 120 inches (292.4 × 304.8 cm)

165 *ECLPSE (RBGBCROSS)*, 2015
Collage and paint on cardboard
121 1/8 × 77 3/4 inches (307.7 × 197.5 cm)

64 *ENGULFED COROLLA*, 2017
Acrylic, oil, elastic, and cardboard on canvas
59 × 45 1/2 × 3 1/4 inches (149.9 × 115.6 × 8.3 cm)
Collection of the Witkoff Family, Miami

60–61 *EXHM (4019)*, 2012
Collage and urethane on cardboard
45 × 120 inches (114.3 × 304.8 cm)

Exorcism, 2003 *
Collage and ink on paper
11 × 8 1/2 inches (27.9 × 21.6 cm)

Facial (4466), 2013 *
Ceramic
8 × 38 × 8 1/2 inches (20.3 × 96.5 × 21.6 cm)

138–39 *FIGURES. PILE. (6991)*, 2019
Fabric, yarn, and fiberfill
Dimensions variable

144–45 *FLAG/QUILT (6625)*, 2018
Bleached denim, treated fabric, and elastic
164 × 170 inches (416.6 × 431.8 cm)

Flannel Shirt, 2008 *
Collage on paper
14 7/8 × 10 1/2 inches (37.8 × 26.7 cm)

38 *Girl in Kiln*, 2004
Lambda print
13 × 19 inches (33 × 48.3 cm)

GRID SISTER 1, 2010 *
Collage and nail polish on acrylic
32 × 49 inches (81.3 × 124.5 cm)

Header Pipes (Test 1), 2012 *
Steel
31 3/4 × 16 1/2 × 16 1/2 inches (80.6 × 41.9 × 41.9 cm)

50 *Head Trekkers 17*, 2010
Collage on paper
25 × 38 inches (63.5 × 96.5 cm)

58–59 *Head Trekkers + Gated Doors 2*, 2010 *
Collage and spray paint on paper
72 × 87 inches (182.9 × 221 cm)
Collection of Rosa and Carlos de la Cruz, Key Biscayne, FL

Head Worker Reconfigured RWB, 2009 *
Bronze and paint
9 1/4 × 20 × 17 1/2 inches (23.5 × 50.8 × 44.5 cm)

78–79 *Hiker (4949)*, 2014
Bronze with silver nitrate patina
9 × 25 5/8 × 7 inches (22.9 × 65.1 × 17.8 cm)

64 *HOT FLAT LIGHT*, 2017
Acrylic, oil, elastic, and cardboard on canvas
59 × 45 1/2 × 3 1/4 inches (149.9 × 115.6 × 8.3 cm)
Private collection

47 *HRG Suite*, 2006
Collage on paper
Nine collages, matted and framed: 57 × 58 × 2 inches
(144.8 × 147.3 × 5.1 cm)

Interior Inscriptions, 2004 *
Pen on paper
Four collages, matted and framed: 40 3/4 × 35 5/8 × 1 1/2 inches
(103.5 × 90.5 × 3.8 cm)

Inversion Marble Overlay, 2007 *
Lambda print
55 3/4 × 48 3/4 inches (141.6 × 123.8 cm)

34 *Kiln #1*, 2005
Lambda print
33 × 22 inches (83.8 × 55.9 cm)
Collection of Craig Robins and Jackie Soffer

54 *(Mapping) Jordache Nail Polish*, 2005
Nail polish on paper
31 1/2 × 39 1/2 inches (80 × 100.3 cm)
Collection of Andre Sakhai, New York

55 *Mapping (Pink)*, 2005
Nail polish on paper
39 3/4 × 31 3/4 inches (101 × 80.6 cm)

74 *Modern Brass/Ketamine User*, 2012
Ceramic
15 × 24 1/2 × 15 inches (38.1 × 62.2 × 38.1 cm)
Collection of Maurice Marciano

109 *Monument Stalagmite/Bride Jr.*, 2011
PVC pipe, foam, urethane, wood, spray paint, and formica
130 × 44 × 56 inches (330.2 × 111.8 × 142.2 cm)
Ovitz Family Collection, Los Angeles

108 *Monument Stalagmite/The Shining*, 2011
PVC pipe, foam, urethane, wood, spray paint, and formica
139 × 44 × 56 inches (353.1 × 111.8 × 142.2 cm)
Ovitz Family Collection, Los Angeles

Mortar/Fan's Mission, 2009 *
Ceramic
11 × 30 1/2 × 23 inches (27.9 × 77.5 × 58.4 cm)

152 *MS01-2867*, 2010
Steel
24 × 24 × 10 inches (61 × 61 × 25.4 cm)

152 *MS06-2872*, 2010
Steel
27 × 23 × 10 inches (68.6 × 58.4 × 25.4 cm)

152 *MS07-2873*, 2010
Steel
33 × 12 × 10 inches (83.8 × 30.5 × 25.4 cm)

153 *MS13-2879*, 2010
Steel
35 × 27 × 10 inches (88.9 × 68.6 × 25.4 cm)

154 *MS14-2881*, 2010
Steel
30 × 52 × 10 inches (76.2 × 132.1 × 25.4 cm)

154–55 *MS16-2883*, 2010
Steel
11 × 105 × 6 inches (27.9 × 266.7 × 15.2 cm)

MS42-3034, 2010 *
Steel
17 3/4 × 31 × 10 inches (45.1 × 78.7 × 25.4 cm)

43 *Nails, Mammary, Stalagmites*, 2010
Collage on paper
13 × 18 1/2 inches (33 × 47 cm)

49 *Pelican Bay Abstract*, 2009
Collage and paint on paper
Nine collages, matted and framed: 69 3/4 × 69 inches
(177.2 × 175.3 cm)
Ovitz Family Collection, Los Angeles

Physicalism/The Recombine 1-6, 2006
Lambda prints
Six prints, each 61 × 49 inches (154.9 × 124.5 cm)

37 *Prison*, 2004
Collage and colored pencil on paper
23 × 30 1/2 inches (58.4 × 77.5 cm)

50 *Pumpkin Head*, 2008
Collage on paper
28 1/4 × 44 1/2 inches (71.8 × 113 cm)

135 *QUILT (4858)*, 2014
Bleached and dyed canvas and elastic
156 × 125 inches (396.2 × 317.5 cm)

42 *Quilt/Body Snatchers*, 2004
Collage on paper
9 × 9 1/4 inches (22.9 × 23.5 cm)

Refraction Bed of John, 2005 *
Collage on paper
23 × 29 inches (58.4 × 73.7 cm)
Private collection

171 *SCALE (4586)*, 2013
Steel, paint, cardboard, yarn, and mixed media
97 × 75 × 70 inches (246.4 × 190.5 × 177.8 cm)

162 *SCALE (5415) S.R. CLOR.*, 2015
Steel and mixed media
62 × 38 × 6 inches (157.5 × 96.5 × 15.2 cm)

88 *SCXV3ST/BD*, 2012
Fiberglass, wood, spray paint, and formica
120 × 34 × 34 inches (304.8 × 86.4 × 86.4 cm)

36 *Snowball*, 2001
Pencil on paper
22 3/8 × 30 inches (56.8 × 76.2 cm)

112 *SP04*, 2007
Spray paint on canvas
96 × 84 × 2 inches (243.8 × 213.4 × 5.1 cm)

115 *SP49*, 2008
Spray paint on canvas
96 × 84 × 2 inches (243.8 × 213.4 × 5.1 cm)
Private collection, New York

123 *SP131*, 2010
Spray paint on canvas
96 × 84 × 2 inches (243.8 × 213.4 × 5.1 cm)

125 *SP242*, 2013
Spray paint on canvas
96 × 84 × 2 inches (243.8 × 213.4 × 5.1 cm)
Whitney Museum of American Art, New York;
Gift of Guy Starkman

43 *STAR SKY*, 2014
Collage, paint, and glue on paper
9 1/2 × 15 5/8 inches (24.1 × 39.7 cm)

146 *STOVE 3*, 2012
Bronze and paint
74 3/4 × 14 1/4 × 18 inches (189.9 × 36.2 × 45.7 cm)
Collection of Isabel and Ricardo Ernst

151 *Stove 4*, 2013
Painted stainless steel
72 1/4 × 14 × 14 3/4 inches (183.5 × 35.6 × 37.5 cm)

159 *SUBHEAD (5600)*, 2015 *
Steel and paint
41 × 28 × 33 1/2 inches (104.1 × 71.1 × 85.1 cm)

160 *TABLE 4*, 2015
Steel
35 5/8 × 64 1/2 × 51 1/4 inches (90.5 × 163.8 × 130.2 cm)

This Range 1-7, 2005 *
Lambda prints
Seven prints, each 22 1/2 × 30 inches (57.2 × 76.2 cm)

40–41 *Transient Bed of John*, 2003
Lambda print
14 5/8 × 20 1/4 inches (37.1 × 51.4 cm)

86 *TROOPER*, 2017
Ceramic
41 × 14 1/2 × 14 inches (104.1 × 36.8 × 35.6 cm)
Private collection

VAMPIRE 129, 2014
Fabric and fiberfill
85 × 34 × 5 inches (215.9 × 86.4 × 12.7 cm)

VAMPIRE 170, 2016 *
Treated fabric and fiberfill
86 × 37 × 7 inches (218.4 × 94 × 17.8 cm)

90–91 *ZEN RIPPER*, 2008
Formica, spray paint, and wood
88 × 132 × 48 inches (223.5 × 335.3 × 121.9 cm)

All works courtesy Sterling Ruby Studio, Los Angeles, unless otherwise indicated.

* Included in the ICA Miami presentation only.

Works in the Exhibition as of July 8, 2019.

Works illustrated that are not in the exhibition are listed on page 187.

Acknowledgements

STERLING RUBY (the exhibition and book) is the result of the collective efforts of many talented people. This endeavor—a collaboration between ICA/Boston and ICA Miami—requires a spirit of open collaboration and coordination across two institutions. We extend our heartfelt appreciation to both of our institutions' fearless boards of trustees for their continuous support, and to Jill Medvedow, Ellen Matilda Poss Director of ICA/Boston, for championing the project from its inception.

We are grateful to the exhibition's major supporters: Sprüth Magers, Gagosian, and Xavier Hufkens. Exhibitions at ICA Miami are generously supported by the Knight Contemporary Art Fund at The Miami Foundation. We are grateful for major support of the ICA Miami presentation provided by Carlo Bronzini Vender, Andre Sakhai, and Inigo Philbrick. Additional support at ICA Miami is provided by Michelle Simkins and Jason Rubell. We are also grateful for the additional support for the Boston presentation generously provided by Stephanie Formica Connaughton and John Connaughton, Jean-François and Nathalie Ducrest, Bridgitt and Bruce Evans, James and Audrey Foster, Ted Pappendick and Erica Gervais Pappendick, David and Leslie Puth, and Charlotte and Herbert S. Wagner III. We would also like to express our deep appreciation to our exhibition lenders, who graciously shared Sterling Ruby's works from their collections (they can be found on page 186).

This project would not have been possible without the support of the artist and his invaluable studio team. We salute Tyler Britt, Director, Sterling Ruby Studio, for his tireless and kind assistance throughout the project. Other individuals in Sterling Ruby Studio who were crucial to the success of this project are: Sarah Conaway, Publications Assistant; Julia Holladay, Head of Staff; Jennifer Kishi, Archivist; Reid Ulrich, Assistant Director; and Celeste Voce, Registrar. In addition, we thank those who represent and work closely with the artist at Gagosian, Xavier Hufkens, Taka Ishii Gallery, and Sprüth Magers.

This publication intends to be an important resource for many years to come. We are proud of it, and we wish to express our sincere thanks to our contributors for their insightful texts: Isabelle Graw, Professor for Art Theory and Art History at Staatliche Hochschule für Bildende Künste (Städelschule), Frankfurt am Main, Germany, and Jeffrey De Blois, Assistant Curator and Publications Manager, ICA/Boston. We are greatly appreciative of Alex Scrimgeour, Text Editor, for his keen editorial eye, and Matthew Christensen, Managing Editor, for making this a fluid book. Our praise and thanks go to Eric Wrenn, for his elegant design of this publication.

Our heartfelt thanks go to Jeffrey De Blois for his superb management of the book and coordination of the project in Boston. We also sincerely thank Amanda Morgan, Curatorial Assistant, Exhibitions and Publications, for her efficient coordination of countless details of the project in Miami.

The exhibition was realized with the help of many within our two organizations.

At the ICA/Boston, our sincere thanks go to: Liz Adrian, Director of Retail; John Andress, Bill T. Jones Director/Curator of Performing Arts; Jack Arbaugh, Associate Registrar; Karin France, Director of Institutional Giving; Zelana Davis, Exhibition Coordinator; Monica Garza, Charlotte Wagner Director of Education; Kelly Gifford, Deputy Director of Public Engagement and Planning; Fabienne Keck, Curatorial Department Coordinator; Whitney Leese, Director of Development Operations; Tsugumi Maki, Chief Operating Officer; Katie Mayshak, Director of Development; Toru Nakanishi, Preparator; Abigail Newbold, Director of Exhibitions; Tim Obetz, Chief Preparator; Colette Randall, Director of Audience Development and Communications; Natasa Vucetic, Chief Financial Officer; Kris Wilton, Director of Creative Content and Digital Engagement; and the ICA's installation crew.

At the ICA Miami, our sincere thanks go to: Courtney Casci, Director of Development; Marvin Hernandez, Chief Preparator and Director of Building Operations; Kerri Kneer, Director of Exhibitions and Collections; Juan Ledesma, Executive Assistant; Nicholas Mandrus, Director of Finance; Amanda Morgan, Curatorial Assistant; Tommy Ralph Pace, Deputy Director; and Inigo Philbrick and Sarah Watson for their research and enthusiasm.

Our foremost and final thanks go to Sterling Ruby. His prolific and daring experimentations with materials, methods, and ideas inspire us. He makes truly compelling artworks that resist simplistic reductions or easy categorizations, and he encouraged us to think creatively and expansively about his work. We are thankful for the gift of his art and for the privilege of working with him to present it to our audiences.

Alex Gartenfeld
Artistic Director, Institute of Contemporary Art, Miami

Eva Respini
Barbara Lee Chief Curator, the Institute of Contemporary Art/Boston

Contributors

JEFFREY DE BLOIS is Assistant Curator and Publications Manager at the Institute of Contemporary Art/Boston. He has supported major exhibitions and publications including *Art in the Age of the Internet, 1989 to Today* (2018) and *The Artist's Museum* (2016–17), and organized *Caitlin Keogh: Blank Melody* (2018), and *The Freedom of Information* (2016–17), in conjunction with *First Light: A Decade of Collecting at the ICA*, among others. De Blois previously served as curatorial fellow at MIT List Visual Arts Center.

ALEX GARTENFELD is Artistic Director at the Institute of Contemporary Art, Miami. His recent exhibitions include *Ettore Sottsass and the Social Factory* (with Gean Moreno, 2019), *Judy Chicago: A Reckoning* (2018–19), *Terry Adkins: Infinity Is Always Less Than One* (2018), and *The Everywhere Studio* (with Gean Moreno and Stephanie Seidel, 2017–18). Gartenfeld organized *Songs for Sabotage*, the 2018 New Museum Triennial in New York with Gary Carrion-Murayari. Previously he served as senior editor of *Art in America* and *Interview* online. His writing has appeared in many museum publications and journals on contemporary art.

ISABELLE GRAW is Professor of Art Theory and Art History at Staatliche Hochschule für Bildende Künste (Städelschule), Frankfurt am Main, where she cofounded the Institute of Art Criticism. She is an art critic and cofounder of *Texte zur Kunst* magazine. She has published numerous books, including *The Love of Painting: Genealogy of a Success Medium* (Sternberg Press, 2018), *Painting beyond Itself: The Medium in the Post-Medium Condition* (coedited with Ewa Lajer-Burcharth, Sternberg Press, 2016), and *High Price: Art between the Market and Celebrity Culture* (Sternberg Press, 2010), among others.

EVA RESPINI is Barbara Lee Chief Curator at the Institute of Contemporary Art/Boston. Her recent exhibitions include *When Home Won't Let You Stay: Migration through Contemporary Art* (2019–20), *John Akomfrah: Purple* (2019), *Huma Bhabha: They Live* (2019), *William Forsythe: Choreographic Objects* (2018–19), and *Art in the Age of the Internet, 1989 to Today* (2018). Respini previously served as Curator at the Museum of Modern Art, New York, where she organized numerous exhibitions, including the retrospectives *Walid Raad* (2015–16), *Robert Heinecken: Object Matter* (2014), and *Cindy Sherman* (2012). She has published numerous books and her writing has appeared in many museum publications and journals on contemporary art and photography.

Lenders to the Exhibition

The Broad Art Foundation, Los Angeles
La Colección Jumex, Mexico City
Rosa and Carlos de la Cruz, Key Biscayne, FL
Isabel and Ricardo Ernst
José Freire
Lorinsky Collection
Maurice Marciano
Javier and Monica Mora
Ovitz Family Collection, Los Angeles
Private collection, New York
Private collections
Pilar Crespi Robert and Stephen Robert
Craig Robins and Jackie Soffer
Andre Sakhai, New York
Sterling Ruby Studio, Los Angeles
Thomas H. Lee and Ann Tenenbaum
Whitney Museum of American Art, New York
Ray Ellen and Allan Yarkin

Reproduction Credits

All images courtesy Sterling Ruby Studio, Los Angeles, and photos by Robert Wedemeyer, unless otherwise indicated. © Sterling Ruby

Page 14 [fig. 2]: Digital image © The Museum of Modern Art, New York/Licensed by SCALA/Art Resource, NY. © VAGA at ARS, NY
Page 14 [fig. 3]: Photo by Charles Mayer Photography. © Françoise Grossen
Page 14 [fig. 4]: Image courtesy Smithsonian American Art Museum, Washington DC/Art Resource, NY. © Voulkos Family Trust.
Page 14 [fig. 5]: Photo by Charles Mayer Photography. © Cady Noland
Page 16 [fig. 6]: Courtesy Christian Dior
Page 16 [fig. 8]: Photographed at Rubell Museum, Miami. © Willy Vanderperre
Page 22 [fig. 4]: Photo by Mark Woods
Page 22 [fig. 5]: Courtesy Museum of Contemporary Art, Los Angeles. Photo by Brian Forrest
Page 22 [fig. 6]: *SUICIDE (LG)*, 2015. Acrylic, elastic, and treated fabric on canvas. 126 × 96 × 2 inches (320 × 243.8 × 5.1 cm)
Page 26 [fig. 1]: © 2017 Elizabeth Felicella/Esto Photographics
Page 26 [fig. 2]: *The Cup*, 2013. Foam, urethane, wood, and spray paint. 92 × 115 1/2 × 88 inches (233.7 × 293.4 × 233.5 cm)
Page 39: *Kiln #2*, 2005. Lambda print. 33 × 22 inches (83.8 × 55.9 cm)
Page 51: *Scratch/Chanel La Vernis*, 2008. Collage, nail polish, and glue on paper. 44 × 28 inches (111.8 × 71.1 cm)
Page 66: *Basin Theology/The Pipe*, 2013. Ceramic. 39 3/4 × 43 1/2 × 44 inches (101 × 110.5 × 111.8 cm). Whitney Museum of American Art, New York. Purchase, with funds from Gaurav Kapadia. Licensed by SCALA/Art Resource, NY
Page 71: *ASHTRAY 465*, 2018. Ceramic. 4 7/8 × 19 1/4 × 14 1/8 inches (12.4 × 48.9 × 35.9 cm)
Page 89 [fig. 1]: *(4C) Study for Cubes, Codes, Crypts and Cosmetic*, 2006. Collage and paint on paper. 50 × 38 1/2 inches (127 × 97.8 cm)
Page 89 [fig. 2]: *Absolute Contempt for Total Serenity #2*, 2005. Collage on paper. 28 × 22 inches (71.1 × 55.9 cm)
Pages 94–95: Photo by Mark Woods
Pages 104–105: *BASIN CDCR*, 2011. PVC pipe, foam, urethane, wood, spray paint, and formica. 91 1/2 × 160 × 108 inches (232.4 × 406.4 × 274.3 cm)
Page 107: *American Risk*, 2009. PVC pipe, foam, urethane, wood, spray paint, and formica. 166 × 90 × 72 inches (421.6 × 228.6 × 182.9 cm)
Page 111: *Monument Stalagmite/Baseline*, 2008. PVC pipe, foam, urethane, wood, spray paint, and formica. 198 × 40 × 48 inches (502.9 × 101.6 × 121.9 cm). Private collection, New York
Pages 116–17: *SP21*, 2008. Spray paint on canvas. 100 × 144 × 2 inches (254 × 365.8 × 5.1 cm). Private collection, New York
Pages 118–19: *SP250*, 2013. Spray paint on canvas. 160 × 235 × 2 inches (406.4 × 596.9 × 5.1 cm)
Page 121: *SP302*, 2014. Spray paint on synthetic canvas. 96 × 84 × 2 inches (234.8 × 213.4 × 5.1 cm). Private collection, New York
Page 126: *2 Stacks of Husbands*, 2005. Wood, laminate, vinyl, fiberfill, and galvanized pipe. 76 1/2 × 40 × 45 inches (194 × 101.6 × 114.3 cm)
Page 127 [fig. 1]: *Two Candles, Two Beds*, 2004. Collage on paper. 11 × 8 inches (27.9 × 20.3 cm)
Pages 130–31: Photo by Olle Kirchmeier/Rockfoto
Page 133: *VAMPIRE 9*, 2010. Fabric and fiberfill. 84 × 45 × 4 inches (213.4 × 114.3 × 10.2 cm)
Pages 140–41: *Laying Figure*, 2013. Fabric and fiberfill. 78 × 98 × 70 inches (198.1 × 248.9 × 177.8 cm)
Pages 142–43: *FLAG (4791)*, 2014. Bleached and dyed canvas, denim, and elastic. 174 1/2 × 343 inches (443.2 × 871.2 cm). Rubell Museum, Miami
Pages 148–49: Photo by Thomas Lannes
Pages 156–57: *DRAG (LONG BLOCK 5505)*, 2015. Steel, engine block, and paint. 54 × 181 1/2 × 47 1/2 inches (137.2 × 461 × 120.7 cm)
Page 161: *TABLE 10*, 2015. Steel. 135 3/4 × 102 3/4 × 50 inches (344.8 × 261 × 12.7 cm)
Page 163 [fig. 1]: *EXHM (4763)*, 2014. Collage, paint, and urethane on cardboard. 121 × 94 inches (307.3 × 238.8 cm)
Pages 168–69: *ECLPSE (Blue Horizon)*, 2015. Collage and paint on cardboard. 95 1/2 × 120 inches (242.6 × 304.8 cm)
Pages 172–73: Courtesy Sprüth Magers. Photo by Timo Ohler

This book was published on the occasion of the exhibition

Sterling Ruby

Organized by Alex Gartenfeld, Artistic Director, Institute of Contemporary Art, Miami and Eva Respini, Barbara Lee Chief Curator, the Institute of Contemporary Art/Boston.

Institute of Contemporary Art, Miami
November 7, 2019–February 2, 2020

The Institute of Contemporary Art/Boston
February 26–May 26, 2020

Major support for *Sterling Ruby* is provided by Sprüth Magers, Gagosian, and Xavier Hufkens

Sprüth Magers GAGOSIAN Xavier Hufkens

Exhibitions at ICA Miami are generously supported by the Knight Contemporary Art Fund at The Miami Foundation.

KNIGHT FOUNDATION

Major support at ICA Miami is provided by Carlo Bronzini Vender, Andre Sakhai, and Inigo Philbrick. Additional support at ICA Miami is provided by Michelle Simkins and Jason Rubell.

Additional support for the Boston presentation is generously provided by Stephanie Formica Connaughton and John Connaughton, Jean-François and Nathalie Ducrest, Bridgitt and Bruce Evans, James and Audrey Foster, Ted Pappendick and Erica Gervais Pappendick, David and Leslie Puth, and Charlotte and Herbert S. Wagner III.

Published in 2019 by the Institute of Contemporary Art/Boston, Institute of Contemporary Art, Miami, and DelMonico Books · Prestel

Institute of Contemporary Art/Boston
25 Harbor Shore Drive
Boston, MA 02210
www.icaboston.org

Institute of Contemporary Art, Miami
61 NE 41st Street
Miami, FL 33137
www.icamiami.org

DelMonico Books, an imprint of Prestel Publishing, a member of Verlagsgruppe Random House GmbH

Prestel Verlag
Neumarkter Strasse 28
81673 Munich

Prestel Publishing Ltd.
14-17 Wells Street
London W1T 3PD

Prestel Publishing
900 Broadway, Suite 603
New York, NY 10003

www.prestel.com

Library of Congress Control Number: 2019909061
ISBN: 978-3-7913-5879-6
A CIP catalogue record for this book is available from the British Library.

Editors: Alex Gartenfeld and Eva Respini
Text Editor: Alex Scrimgeour
Managing Editor: Matthew Christensen
Publication Coordinator: Jeffrey De Blois
Proofreader: Anni Pullagura
Design: Eric Wrenn Office Inc, New York
Typeset in Times New Roman and Helvetica
Color separations: Echelon, Santa Monica, California
Printed in China